TJ Publishers
Advantage Business Centre
132-134 Great Ancoats Street
Manchester
M4 6DE

Tel: 0141 880 6839

Fax: 0870 124 9189

e-mail: teejaypublishers@btinternet.com

web page: www.teejaypublishers.co.uk

Printed by :-

Elanders Ltd
Merlin Way
New York Business Park
North Tyneside NE27 0QG
Registered in England number 3788582
   http://www.elanders.com/uk

Year 6 Textbook

Book 6

Produced by members of the TeeJay Writing Group.

T Strang, J Geddes and J Cairns.

Front and Back Cover designed by *Fraser McKie*.
(http://www.frasermckie.com)

TEXTBOOK
6

National Curriculum Textbook 6

- This book covers every outcome of the Year 6 course, as laid out in the National Curriculum England Framework Document, (September 2013).

- There are no A and B exercises. The book covers the entire Year 6 course without the teacher having to pick and choose which questions to leave out and which exercises are important. They all are !

- The book follows on directly from TeeJay's Year 5 Book and includes revision and consolidation of the work covered in the Year 5 course.

- The Year 6 Book contains an 8 page "Chapter Zero" which primarily revises every topic from the Year 5 course and can be used as a diagnostic tool. This could be followed by TeeJay's diagnostic assessments* of the work covered in our Year 5 book.

- It also contains a Chapter 21, which revises every topic from the Year 6 course, prior to an end of year assessment.

- Non-calculator skills are emphasised and encouraged throughout the book.

- Each chapter has a "Revisit - Review - Revise" exercise as a summary.

- Homework*, mirroring exercise by exercise, the topics in this book, is available as a photocopiable pack.

- TeeJay's Assessment Pack* for Year 6 work, is also available as a photocopiable pack, and can be used topic by topic or combined to form a series of Year 6 Cumulative Tests. It also contains a series of longer assessments covering the Outcomes as laid out in the National Curriculum England Framework Document (Sept 2013).

We make no apologies for the multiplicity of colours used throughout the book, both for text and in diagrams - we feel it helps brighten up the pages !!

T Strang, J Geddes, J Cairns

(August 2014)

* Available for purchase separately.

Contents

CH	TOPIC	EX	CONTENT	PAGES
0	Revision		Revision of all Year 5 book	1-8
1	Whole No's 1	1	Place value up to 10 000 000	9-10
		2	Rounding to any degree of accuracy	11
		3	Multiplication by a single digit	12-13
		4	Multiplication by 2 digits	14-15
		5	Multiplication/Division by multiples of 10, 100, 1000	16-17
			Revisit-Revise-Review	18
2	Negative Numbers	1	Negative numbers in context	19-22
		2	Adding integers (Extension)	23
			Revisit-Revise-Review	24
3	2-D Shapes	1	Drawing triangles (2 sides and included angle)	25-26
		2	Drawing triangles (2 angles and a side)	27-28
		3	Drawing triangles (3 sides)	29-30
		4	Drawing quadrilaterals and regular polygons	31-33
		5	The Circle	34-35
			Revisit-Revise-Review	36
4	Whole No's 2	1	Division by a single digit (Revision)	37
		2	Division by 2 digits (no remainder)	38-39
		3	Division by 2 digits (with a remainder)	40-41
		4	Addition, subtraction, multiplication and division	42-44
		5	Add, subtract, multiply and divide mentally	45-46
		6	Rounding and estimating	47
		7	BOMDAS	48
			Revisit-Revise-Review	49
5	Algebra 1	1	Evaluating expressions and formulae	50-51
		2	Constructing and evaluating formulae	52-53
		3	Sequences	54-55
			Revisit-Revise-Review	56-57
6	Multiples and Factors	1	Multiples and lowest common multiple	58-59
		2	Factors and highest common factor	60-61
		3	Prime Numbers	62
		4	Prime Decomposition (Extension)	63
			Revisit-Revise-Review	64

CH	TOPIC	EX	CONTENT	PAGES
7	Fractions 1	1	Equivalent fractions (Revision)	65
		2	Improper fractions and mixed numbers	66
		3	Comparing fractions (Revision)	67
		4	Adding and subtracting any fractions	68-70
			Revisit-Revise-Review	71
8	Coordinates	1	Coordinates in all 4 quadrants	72-74
		2	Translation and reflection	75-78
			Revisit-Revise-Review	79
9	Ratio & Proportion	1	Understanding ratio	80-81
		2	Simplifying ratios	82-83
		3	Ratio calculations	84-86
		4	Proportion	87
		5	Direct proportion	88-89
			Revisit-Revise-Review	90-91
10	Percentages	1	Percentages without a calculator	92-93
		2	Finding a percentage using a calculator (optional)	94-96
			Revisit-Revise-Review	97
11	Algebra 2	1	Simple linear patterns	98-101
		2	More difficult linear patterns	102-105
			Revisit-Revise-Review	106
12	Area and Perimeter	1	Area of a right angled triangle	107-108
		2	Area of any triangle	109-110
		3	Perimeter/Area of square, rectangle and triangle	111-112
		4	Area of a parallelogram	113-114
		5	Mixed exercise	115
			Revisit-Revise-Review	116
13	Decimals	1	Multiplying/dividing decimals by 10, 100, 1000	117
		2	Multiplication by a single digit	118
		3	Division by a single digit	119
		4	Mixed problems	120-121
		5	Changing a fraction to a decimal	122
			Revisit-Revise-Review	123

CH	TOPIC	EX	CONTENT	PAGES
14	Algebra 3	1	Solving basic equations	124
		2	Harder equations	125-126
		3	Solving equations with 2 variables	127-128
			Revisit-Revise-Review	129
15	Angles	1	Angles (Revision)	130
		2	Angles round a point	131
		3	Vertically opposite angles	132
		4	Angles in triangles and polygons	133-137
		5	Mixed exercise	138
			Revisit-Revise-Review	139
16	Fractions 2	1	Multiplying fractions	140
		2	Dividing a fraction by a whole number	141
		3	Mixed Exercise	142
			Revisit-Revise-Review	143
17	Measure	1	Converting units of metric measure	144
		2	Metric and Imperial units	145
		3	Approximate and exact conversions	145-146
		4	Mixed problems	147-148
			Revisit-Revise-Review	149
18	Similar Shapes	1	Similar figures	150-153
			Revisit-Revise-Review	154
19	Statistics	1	Bar graphs and line graphs	155-157
		2	Interpreting and drawing pie charts	158-159
		3	Drawing pie charts using a protractor	160-161
		4	The mean and the range	162-163
			Revisit-Revise-Review	164-165
20	3-D and Volume	1	3-D shapes (Revision)	166-167
		2	Volumes by counting cubes	168-170
		3	Volume of a cuboid - a formula	171-173
		4	Volumes - the cubic millimetre and cubic metre	174
			Revisit-Revise-Review	175
21	Revision		Revision of all Year 6 work	176-184
	Answers		Answers	185-195

Chapter 0

1. Write the following numbers out fully in words :- a 19 070   b 108 940.

2. A satellite flew a total of two hundred and sixty thousand, seven hundred and five kilometres in one orbit round the earth.

    Write this number using digits.

3. Write down the number that is :-

    a   2000 less than 19 500   b   20 000 more than 780 000.

4. Find the missing numbers :-

    a   23 200,   23 700,   24 200, ...   b   850 000,   ...,   750 000   ... .

5. a   Round to the nearest 1000 :-   (i)   8491   (ii)   26 705
    b   Round to the nearest 10 000 :-   (i)   37 299   (ii)   305 500
    c   Round to the nearest 100 000 :-   (i)   748 000   (ii)   499 999.

6. Round both numbers to the nearest 1000, then estimate :-   26 830 – 6147.

7. What Roman Numerals are used to write the number :-

    a   140   b   455   c   779   d   880 ?

8. What numbers do these Roman symbols represent :-

    a CXLI   b CCCLXXXV   c CDLVII   d CMXL ?

9. Try these mentally. Write down the answers to :-

    a   260 + 540   b   8000 – 5700   c   47 000 + 33 000
    d   78 900 – 26 900   e   263 124 + 412 815   f   1 000 000 – 599 000.

10. Copy each example and work out the answer :-

    a   58 726   b   427 635   c   574 946
         – 17 493   + 45 394   – 247 097

11. When Mr Brown retired, he had £327 000 in his savings account.

    He used £195 000 to buy a bungalow.

    How much did Mr Brown then have in his account ?

12. Name each of the angles below using **3 letters** and the "∠" sign, and state what **type** of angle each is :-

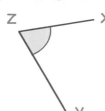 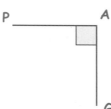 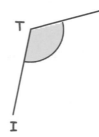 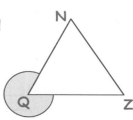

a   Z ———— X   b   P ———————— A   c   T ... F   d   N ... Q ... Z

13. Use a protractor to measure each of these angles :-

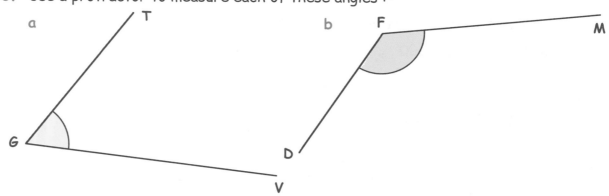

a   G ... T ... V   b   F ... M ... D

14. Draw and label these two angles :-   a   ∠PQR = 47°   b   ∠FHG = 135°.

15. How many degrees will I turn through if I rotate clockwise from **NW** to **SW** ?

16. Copy the following and work out the answers :-

   a   82   b   356   c   7 x 2054   d   3804 x 9.
       x 6   x 8
   _____   _____

   _____   _____

17. Set down and work out :-

   a   6 5   b   3 4 7   c   2 1 0 6
       x 2 4   x 8 2   x 6 3
      ....
     0   ....
      ....

????

18. Write down the answer to each of these :-

   a   10 x 2050   b   127 x 100   c   58 030 ÷ 10   d   370 000 ÷ 1000.

19. Set down the following, show your working and complete each calculation :-

   a   4368 ÷ 7   b   26 048 ÷ 8   c $\dfrac{3258}{6}$ d $\dfrac{64 800}{9}$.

20. a Do these, expressing the remainder as a fraction :- (i) 173 ÷ 2 (ii) 1535 ÷ 6.
    b Do these, expressing the remainder as a decimal :- (i) 255 ÷ 4 (ii) 1874 ÷ 5.

21. State what temperature is represented on this thermometer :-

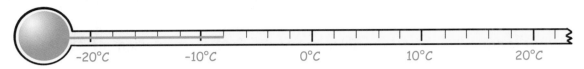

22. Write down the missing numbers :-
    a 15, 11, 7, ..., ..., –5, ..., –13   b –31, –21, -11, ..., ..., 19, ...

23. What is :-
    a 7°C down from 2°C   b 10°C up from –11°C
    c 6°C down from –8°C   d 22°C up from –45°C ?

24. Write down the area in cm²
    of this shape :-

= 1 cm²

25. Calculate the areas of these
    shapes in cm² or in m² :-

a
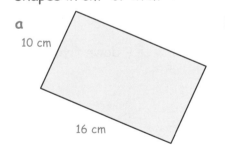
10 cm
16 cm

b
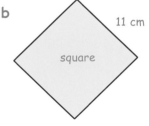
square
11 cm

c
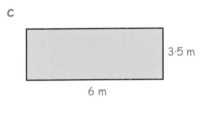
3·5 m
6 m

26. Write down the first six multiples of :-   a 4   b 12.

27. Write down all the factors of :-   a 15   b 40.

28. Write down all the common factors of :-   a 24 and 30   b 60 and 90.

29. List all the prime numbers between :-   a 10 and 20   b 80 and 90.

30. Find :-

   a 6^2 b 12^2 c 3^3 d 20^3.

31. Of the 5 angles, 95°, 297°, 180°, 89° and 90°, one is a right angle, one an acute angle, one an obtuse angle, one a reflex angle and one a straight angle. Which is which ?

32. What is the :-   a   complement of 45°   b   supplement of 45° ?

33. Copy and complete each diagram below, filling in **all** missing angles :-

a
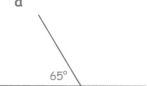

b
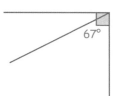

c

d
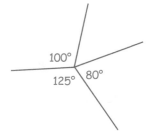

e
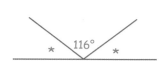

f
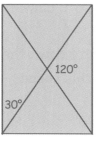

34. What does the 9 represent in :-   a   0·209   b   16·902 ?

35. What number is :-

   a $\frac{7}{10}$ down from 9·9   b $\frac{3}{100}$ up from 0·89   c $\frac{5}{1000}$ down from 3·888 ?

36. Set down and work out :-

   a   384·86   b   100 – 19·99   c   32·285   d   0·625 + 0·375.
        + 69·77   – 8·369

37. Write as a fraction in its simplest form :-   a   0·6   b   1·25.

38. Round to the nearest whole number :-   a   38·501   b   49·488.

39. Round to 1 decimal place :-   a   6·837   b   0·976.

40. Write down the answers to :-

   a   20·07 x 10   b   0·055 x 100   c   214·5 ÷ 10   d   930 ÷ 1000.

41. List all the mathematical shapes that make up this figure :-

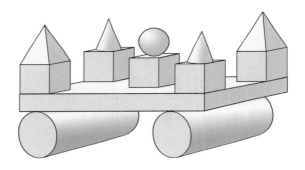

42.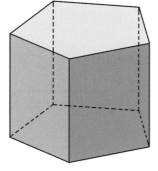

This shape is called a PENTAGONAL based PRISM.

  a   How many faces does it have ?

  b   How many edges does it have ?

  c   How many vertices does it have ?

43. Which 3-D figures do you get when you cut out these two shapes and fold them ?

  a 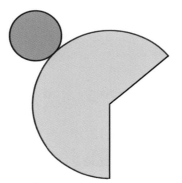   b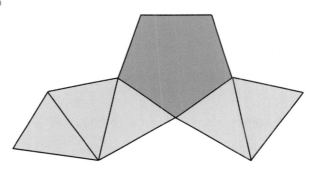

44. Make a neat sketch of a regular hexagon.

45. Simplify these fractions as far as possible :-

  a $\frac{10}{16}$ b $\frac{12}{30}$ c $\frac{15}{45}$ d $\frac{17}{51}$.

46. Write these fractions in order (*smallest first*) :- $\frac{1}{4}$, $\frac{5}{16}$, $\frac{3}{8}$, $\frac{1}{2}$, $\frac{9}{32}$.

47. Change to an improper fraction :-   a $4\frac{2}{5}$ b $10\frac{1}{10}$.

48. Change to a mixed number :-   a $\frac{19}{3}$ b $\frac{27}{4}$.

49. Draw a coordinate diagram and plot the point A(6, 3).

     Plot and write down the coordinates of point A', when A is translated 4 left and 2 up.

50. a Copy the diagram shown.

     b Plot these 4 points on your diagram :-
        P(2, 0), Q(4, 4), R(2, 8) and S(0, 4).

     c What shape is PQRS ?

     d Plot and write down the coordinates of
        P', Q', R' and S' after P, Q, R and S are
        reflected over the blue dotted line.

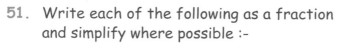

51. Write each of the following as a fraction
     and simplify where possible :-

     a 27%   b 60%   c 36%   d 4%.

52. Change each of these fractions to a percentage :-

     a $\frac{1}{4}$ b $\frac{9}{10}$ c $\frac{23}{25}$ d $\frac{3}{20}$.

53. Work out :-

     a 50% of 70 kg   b 20% of £35   c 10% of 650 g   d 5% of 80 cm.

54. A summer sale offer was **25% off** all items. This bike was £120.

     a How much would Dave save if he bought the bike in the sale ?

     b How much would the bike actually cost him ?

55. Write down the volume of each shape, in cm^3.

     a

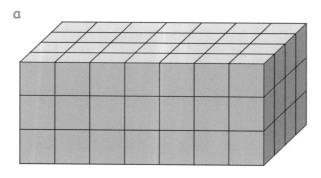

     b

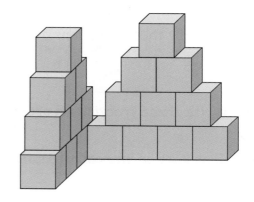

56. Change :-

     a 10·3 centimetres to millimetres   b 98·5 millimetres to centimetres

     c 0·85 kilometres to metres   d 16 050 metres to kilometres

     e 11·005 litres to millilitres   f 13 200 grams to kilograms.

57. Tom had his reaction rate measured four times.

He had to press a buzzer when a light flashed.

| 1st shot - 0·786 secs | 2nd shot - 0·877 secs |
| 3rd shot - 0·805 secs | 4th shot - 0·768 secs |

a   What was Tom's fastest reaction time ?

b   How much **slower** was his slowest reaction time than his fastest ?

58. Find the value of # in each of the following :-

a   3 + # = 15   b   # - 5 = 4   c   12 - # = 7

d   5 × # = 45   e   11 × # = 132   f   24 ÷ # = 3.

59. In each of the following, ⬡ stands for +, -, × or ÷.

Decide which symbol is needed each time here :-

a   12 ⬡ 4 = 8   b   12 ⬡ 4 = 16   c   12 ⬡ 4 = 48

d   12 ⬡ 4 = 3   e   15 ⬡ 15 = 1   f   20 ⬡ 20 = 0.

60. Copy each **equation** and solve it to find the value of x each time :-

a $x + 8 = 11$ b $9 + x = 18$ c $x - 5 = 6$

d $20 - x = 2$ e $6 × x = 42$ f $x × 8 = 96$

g $4·5 + x = 6$ h $\dfrac{x}{4} = 8$ i $\dfrac{x}{11} = 9$

j $x ÷ 5 = 6$ k $x - 37 = 63$ l $21 ÷ x = 3.$

61. Find and **simplify** where possible :-

a $\dfrac{5}{6} - \dfrac{1}{6}$ b $\dfrac{7}{8} - \dfrac{3}{8}$ c $\dfrac{3}{5} + \dfrac{1}{5}$ d $\dfrac{3}{4} - \dfrac{1}{8}$

e $\dfrac{7}{10} + \dfrac{1}{5}$ f $1 - \dfrac{3}{5}$ g $\dfrac{9}{10} - \dfrac{3}{5}$ h $\dfrac{3}{4} - \dfrac{1}{2} + \dfrac{5}{8}.$

62. Find each of the following, leaving your answer as a **mixed number** :-

a $2\dfrac{2}{5} + 3\dfrac{1}{5}$ b $5\dfrac{3}{8} + 1\dfrac{1}{8}$ c $7\dfrac{3}{4} - 2\dfrac{1}{4}$ d $3\dfrac{5}{6} + 3\dfrac{1}{6}$

e $4\dfrac{1}{10} + 2\dfrac{3}{10}$ f $5\dfrac{5}{8} - 2\dfrac{3}{8}$ g $18 - 3\dfrac{3}{5}$ h $3\dfrac{7}{8} + 4\dfrac{5}{8}.$

63. Find :-

a $8 × \dfrac{1}{3}$ b $6 × \dfrac{3}{4}$ c $2 × 3\dfrac{2}{5}$ d $3 × 1\dfrac{3}{4}.$

64. Write these times as **24 hour times** :-　　　a　2:50 am　　　b　7:35 pm.

65. Write these times using **am** and **pm** :-　　　a　2155　　　b　0310.

66. Change the following into **mins** and **secs** :-　　　a　160 secs　　　b　400 secs.

67. Change these to **minutes** :-　　　a　2 hr 15 mins　　　b　$1\frac{3}{4}$ hours.

68. I caught the 1530 plane from Glasgow, arriving in Stanstead at 1645.

    a　How long did my flight take ?

    An hour and a half later, I caught a plane for Rome.

    The flight to Rome took 2 hours and 35 minutes.

    b　At what time (British time) did I touch down in Rome Airport ?

69. Ben had a device on his bike that showed the height above sea level every 10 mins.

    The graph shows this height on a journey.

    a　What was his height after :-

    　　(i)　0 minutes　(ii)　30 minutes

    　　(iii)　60 minutes　(iv)　20 minutes ?

    b　There was a steep **descent** on part of his cycle route.

    　　Between what times was this ?

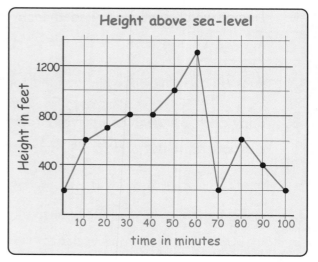

70. Corsvale School pupils were asked to name their favourite fruit.

    The pie chart shows the distribution of fruit.

    a　Write down and simplify the fraction $(\frac{?}{10})$ of the children who chose :-

    　　(i)　Bananas　　　(ii)　Apples

    　　(iii)　Grapes　　　(iv)　Oranges.

    b　There are 250 children attending Corsvale School.

    　　How many of the 250 chose :-

    　　(i)　Banana　　　(ii)　Apple　　　(iii)　Grapes or Oranges ?

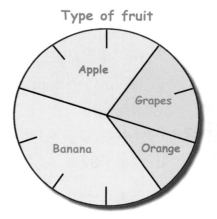

Type of fruit

Chapter 1

Place Values

Understand place value for numbers up to 10 000 000.

Example :-

In the number 6 234 598,

1000000	100000	10000	1000	100	10	1
6	2	3	4	5	9	8

the 6 stands for six million   6 000 000
the 2 stands for two hundred thousand   200 000
the 3 stands for thirty thousand   30 000
the 4 stands for four thousand   4 000
the 5 stands for five hundred   500
the 9 stands for nine tens   90
the 8 stands for eight units (ones)   8
                              6 234 598

Six million, two hundred and thirty four thousand, five hundred and ninety eight.
6 234 598 ✓

Exercise 1

1. What do the following **digits** stand for in the number 3 859 716 :-

    a   3   b   9   c   8   d   5 ?

2. What does the **8** stand for in each of these numbers :-

    a   1 840 632   b   2 748 201   c   8 123 900   d   5 580 609 ?

3. Write the following numbers out fully **in words** :-

    a   9006   b   64 205   c   89 898   d   675 020

    e   3 501 000   f   4 000 603   g   7 789 987   h   9 999 999.

4. Write the following numbers **using digits** :-   ????

    a   five thousand, six hundred and twenty nine

    b   twenty thousand and twelve

    c   seven hundred and eighty thousand three hundred and one

    d   six million, two hundred and forty thousand and seven

    e   four million, four hundred and seven thousand and three

    f   nine million, ninety thousand and nine.

5. Put the following sets of numbers in order, **largest first** :-

    a   64 205,   52 450,   65 420,   54 206,   52 540,   62 405,   65 204.

    b   5 768 000,   6 875 000,   7 568 000,   5 678 000,   6 587 000.

6. Write down the number that is :-

    a   500 more than 320   b   700 less than 2500

    c   6000 more than 7200   d   8000 less than 113 300

    e   40 000 more than 90 000   f   20 000 less than 140 200

    g   300 000 more than 610 000   h   500 000 less than 1 400 000

    i   4 000 000 more than 2 250 000   j   9 500 000 less than 10 000 000.

7. Look at these scales. What numbers are represented by the letters A, B, C, ... ?

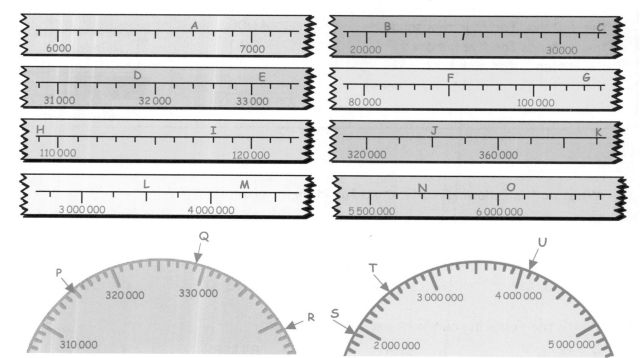

8. What number lies halfway between :-

    a   5200 and 6000   b   72 000 and 72 700

    c   680 000 and 760 000   d   320 000 and 480 000

    e   1 200 000 and 1 800 000   f   9 200 000 and 10 000 000 ?

9. Write out in figures :-

    a   7 million   b $4\frac{1}{2}$ million   c $8\frac{1}{4}$ million   d $9\frac{3}{4}$ million.

10. Cornwall Rovers paid out £4·95 million for an international goalkeeper.

    That was the largest transfer fee they had ever paid.

    a   Write out this amount of money in full, in figures.

    b   Now write it out fully, using words.

Rounding a Whole Number to a Required Degree of Accuracy

You already know how to round a whole number to the nearest :-

> 10, 100, 1000, 10000 and 100000.

The rule was to look at the **next digit** from the left, then round it **up** or **down** depending on whether it is **less than 5** or **5 and over**.

In the same way :-

To round to the nearest 1000000 (million)

Look at the **hundred thousands** digit :-
- if it is a 0, 1, 2, 3 or 4 - leave the million's digit as it is.
- if it is a 5, 6, 7, 8 or 9 - round the million's digit **up** by one.

7 2̲91 645 —> 7 000 000

3 8̲41 290 —> 4 000 000

Be able to round a whole number to the nearest ten, through to the nearest million.

Exercise 2

1. Round to the nearest 10 :-

   a 74   b 83   c 127   d 6244
   e 75 505   f 372 989   g 1 285 641   h 5 298 785.

2. Round to the nearest 100 :-

   a 86   b 237   c 8334   d 9495
   e 25 550   f 562 821   g 2 475 397   h 9 885 985.

3. Round to the nearest 1000 :-

   a 841   b 4628   c 46 280   d 72 500
   e 541 100   f 387 449   g 3 864 876   h 4 845 485.

4. Round to the nearest 10 000 :-

   a 9760   b 62 000   c 76 200   d 99 950
   e 110 910   f 220 550   g 1 625 300   h 6 284 001.

5. Round to the nearest 100 000 :-

   a 75 000   b 120 000   c 385 000   d 799 995
   e 849 900   f 2 643 000   g 7 859 000   h 1 949 900.

6. Round to the nearest 1 000 000 :-

   a 721 621   b 1 003 003   c 1 675 000   d 3 856 397
   e 6 499 999   f 5 500 980   g 8 092 304   h 9 750 000.

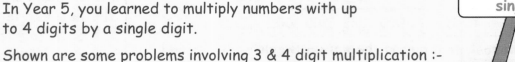

Multiplication by a Single Digit - Problems

Be able to work out problems, multiplying up to 4 digits by a single digit.

In Year 5, you learned to multiply numbers with up to 4 digits by a single digit.

Shown are some problems involving 3 & 4 digit multiplication :-

Example 1 :- 5286 × 4

```
   5 2 8 6
   1 3× 2 4
   2 1 1 4 4 ✓
```

Example 2 :-

Zara bought 3 jigsaw puzzles, each puzzle having 598 pieces.

How many pieces was that altogether ?

```
   5 9 8
   2× 2 3
   1 7 9 4 ✓
```

1794 jigsaw pieces altogether

Exercise 3

1. Copy the following and complete the calculation :-

| a | 16 × 7 | b | 53 × 5 | c | 89 × 6 | d | 34 × 8 |

| e | 136 × 4 | f | 248 × 9 | g | 608 × 3 | h | 789 × 6 |

| i | 2134 × 5 | j | 3073 × 6 | k | 4650 × 8 | l | 8719 × 7 |

2. Write each of these in the form of Question 1 and find :-

   a 37 × 7   b 96 × 4   c 78 × 6   d 89 × 8

   e 9 × 126   f 4 × 307   g 268 × 8   h 2 × 999

   i 2545 × 5   j 3195 × 6   k 1867 × 9   l 3107 × 7

   m 6 × 9578   n 4 × 2087   o 1856 × 8   p 5 × 8560.

3. Check your answers to Question 2 by dividing.

   For example, if your calculation shows that 37 × 7 = 329, then to check this, try dividing 329 by 7 to see if you get back to 37.

4. There are 245 Jersey potatoes in a sack.

    If a greengrocer has 6 identical sacks, how many potatoes does he have ?

5.  382 trains pass through Potters Station each day during the working week.

    How many trains is that over the 5 days ?

6. A bag of lawn seed contains 529 grams.

    Anton buys 8 bags.

    What weight of seed has he bought ?

7.  Odeano own 9 cinemas.

    There are 426 seats in each of the cinemas.

    How many people are in these cinemas when they are all full ?

8. Joleen earns £2387 per month.

    How much will she earn over 6 months ?

9.   A day consists of 1440 minutes.

    How many minutes are there in a week ?

10. A crate holds 2847 bananas.

    How many bananas on a lorry with 9 crates ?

11.  There are 4 football stands in Elderbury Park.

    Each stand is built to hold a maximum of 3288 people.

    When the stands are full, how many will be at the match ?

12. A restaurant bought in 1889 ketchup packets.

    How much did it cost at 8 pence a packet ?

13.  You will find out later that the area of a rectangle can be found by multiplying its length by its breadth.

    Calculate (in square metres), the area of a rectangular piece of land with length 2386 metres and width 7 metres.

14. By remembering that (48 = 6 x 8), try to find 48 x 125, using two steps.

Multiplication by Two Digits - Problems

Be able to work out problems, multiplying up to 4 digits by a two digit number.

You already know how to do long multiplication.

Here, we highlight multiplying by 2 digits in context.

Example 1 :- 247 × 56

```
      2 4 7
    ×  5 6
    ───────
    1 4 8 2
  1 2 3 5 0
  ─────────
  1 3 8 3 2  ✓
```

Example 2 :-

23 students are hired by an advertising company to carry out a survey.

If they are paid £348 each for the task how much does the company have to pay out to them in total ?

```
      3 4 8
    ×  2 3
    ───────
    1 0 4 4
    6 9 6 0
    ───────
    8 0 0 4  ✓
```

The company has to pay out **£8004.**

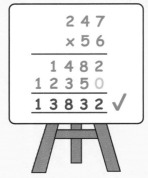

Exercise 4

1. Set down and work out :-

a
```
        2 4
      × 1 8
      ──────
      ........
      ......0
      ──────
      ........
```

b
```
        6 3
      × 2 5
      ──────
      ........
      ......0
      ──────
      ........
```

c
```
      9 0 2
      × 3 4
      ──────
      ........
      ......0
      ──────
      ........
```

d
```
      3 6 8
      × 5 7
      ──────
      ........
      ......0
      ──────
      ........
```

e
```
      4 5 9
      × 8 7
      ──────
      ........
      ........
      ──────
      ........
```

f
```
    1 0 7 5
      × 6 4
      ──────
      ........
      ........
      ──────
      ........
```

g
```
    2 9 0 3
      × 9 3
      ──────
      ........
      ........
      ──────
      ........
```

h
```
    6 1 8 2
      × 7 5
      ──────
      ........
      ........
      ──────
      ........
```

Set down the following as long multiplications and solve each problem.

2. There are 64 small squares on a chess board (*32 white and 32 black*).

   How many small squares are there on 15 chess boards ?

3.  Apples arrive in a supermarket in barrels of 48.

   The supermarket took delivery of 36 barrels.

   How many apples was that in total ?

4.   Miss Thom has 34 boxes of coloured pencils with 20 pencils in each box.

How many coloured pencils does she have ?

5.      When Maggie goes to the gym she is on the exercise bike for 25 minutes at a time.

How long does she spend on the bike when she goes to the gym every day for a fortnight ?

6.   There are 125 metres of line on a fishing rod.

A shop stocks 16 of these rods.

How many metres of line do the rods in the shop have altogether ?

7.      Fishermen buy maggots, 260 in a tin.

38 fishermen are fishing from the pier, each with one tin of maggots.

What's the total number of maggots ?

8.   a   Sally earns £68 for every day she works.

She worked for 319 days last year.

How much did Sally earn ?

b   Trish earns £1235 per month.

How much did she earn last year ?

9.      Tamsley United got an average crowd of 3064 at each of their 15 home games.

How many people altogether attended these games ?

10. There are 49 cars in a large car showroom.

Each car is valued at £8888.

Work out the total value of all the cars.

11.   A box of board pins contains 99 pins.

A company is preparing to ship 5750 boxes to a foreign customer.

If all these boxes were to burst open, how many board pins would be scattered around the ship ?

Multiplication/Division by Multiples of 10, 100 and 1000

Be able to multiply and divide by 30, 200, 4000 etc.

To multiply a number by 30, 200 or 4000, etc., use 2 steps :-

| **Step 1** | => | multiply by the 10, (100 or 1000) first, |
| **Step 2** | => | then multiply by the 3, (2, 4) etc. |

Example 1 :-

To multiply 382 × 30

Step 1   Find 382 × 10 = 3820

Step 2   Find 3820 × 3 ...

```
      3820
      ×  3
    11 460
```

Example 2 :-

To multiply 218 × 400

Step 1   Find 218 × 100 = 21 800

Step 2   Find 21 800 × 4 ...

```
     21 800
      ×   4
     87 200
```

Exercise 5

1. Try to do the following **mentally** :-   (*Use the 2-step approach.*)

    a 17 × 20   b 42 × 30   c 19 × 60

    d 33 × 50   e 40 × 223   f 70 × 204

    g 61 × 200   h 400 × 34   i 115 × 600

    j 800 × 212   k 2000 × 24   l 130 × 9000.

2. Calculate each of the following (*not necessarily mentally*) :-

    a 436 × 30   (*Find 436 × 10 first = 436<u>0</u> and then find 4360 × 3*)

    b 617 × 40   c 209 × 50   d 3218 × 60

    e 70 × 980   f 1231 × 80   g 6507 × 90

    h 2184 × 30   i 90 × 3046   j 12 345 × 20.

3. Work out each of the following using the same 2 steps :-

    a 108 × 400   (*Find 108 × 100 first = 10 8<u>00</u> and then find 10 800 × 4*)

    b 352 × 300   c 456 × 500   d 179 × 700

    e 758 × 200   f 600 × 305   g 975 × 300

    h 407 × 800   i 900 × 821   j 2000 × 732

    k 706 × 6000   l 452 × 4000   m 734 × 3000

    n 8000 × 119   o 7000 × 2043   p 9000 × 5320.

There is a quick way of doing the following multiplications mentally :-

Example :- 4000 x 800

> => simply find 4 x 8 (= 32) and then add on 5 zeros*   =>   3 200 000

Can you explain why, in this case, you add on 5 zeros ?

4.   Do the following mentally :-

a   60 x 20   b   80 x 90   c   700 x 40

d   500 x 90   e   50 x 7000   f   80 x 600

g   200 x 900   h   500 x 900   i   3000 x 700

j   600 x 9000   k   4000 x 7000   l   6000 x 8000.

Similarly, there is a quick way of doing the following divisions mentally :-

Example :- 420 000 ÷ 6000

> => simply cancel out equal numbers of zeros*   420 0̸0̸0̸ ÷ 60̸0̸0̸
>
> => then do the simpler division   420 ÷ 6 = 70.

Can you explain why you do this "cancelling out" ?

5.   Do the following mentally :-

a   2100 ÷ 30   b   2800 ÷ 40   c   49 000 ÷ 70

d   24 000 ÷ 400   e   180 000 ÷ 3000   f   600 000 ÷ 200

g   5 600 000 ÷ 800   h   25 500 000 ÷ 500   i   4 200 000 ÷ 600

j   4 160 000 ÷ 8000   k   21 700 000 ÷ 7000 l   5 670 000 ÷ 9000.

6.   a   20 cars in a garage forecourt had each travelled 38 000 miles.

What is the combined number of miles these cars have travelled ?

b    A machine automatically puts chewy sweets into jars.
7500 chews are placed equally among 60 jars.

How many are in each jar ?

c   300 workers in a telesales company are in a lottery syndicate.
They win the second prize of £417 000.

How much should each person receive ?

d    There are 1440 minutes in 1 day.

How many minutes are there in 50 days ?

Revisit - Review - Revise

1. What does the **4** stand for in each of these numbers :-

   a   1 481 067   b   3 864 201   c   4 123 700   d   6 640 970 ?

2. Write the following numbers out fully **in words** :-

   a   4007   b   56 807   c   891 898   d   2 523 720.

3. Write the following numbers **using digits** :-

   a   three hundred and fourteen thousand and one

   b   six million, two hundred and five thousand and seventy nine

   c   ten and a quarter million.

4. Write down the number that is :-

   a   700 000 more than 1 320 000   b   400 000 less than 4 200 000.

5. Round :-

   a   86 763 to the nearest 10   b   548 759 to the nearest 100

   c   3 745 218 to the nearest 1000   d   335 000 to the nearest 10 000

   e   7 564 374 to the nearest 100 000   f   8 491 889 to the nearest 1 000 000.

6. Find :-

   a   145 x 30   b   74 x 200   c   125 x 500   d   123 x 8000

   e   540 ÷ 60   f   23 800 ÷ 700   g   8 108 100 ÷ 900   h   7 160 000 ÷ 4000.

7. Martin can process 4975 forms in a day.

   How many can he process in a five day week ?

8. A truck driver noted that he travels 1225 km each week.

   How far will he travel over 8 weeks at this rate ?

9. An electrical store has 46 freezers for sale at £382 each.

   How much will the store take in if all are sold ?

10. Use short or long multiplication to do these :-

   a   237 x 12   b   85 x 15   c   314 x 26   d   4053 x 62.

 # Chapter 2

Negative Numbers

Negative Numbers in Context

The set of Positive and Negative Whole numbers, along with Zero are called the set of Integers.

Examples of Integers :- -8, -25, 17, 76, 0, -14, 4003, -3067.

* Note 2·5, $\frac{1}{3}$, $-5\frac{1}{4}$, -3·25, -213·8 etc. are **not** integers.

Exercise 1

1. What temperatures are shown on these thermometers ?

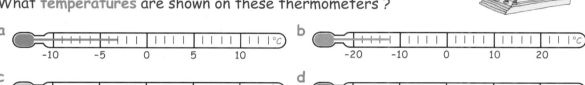

a [-10 -5 0 5 10 °C]

b [-20 -10 0 10 20 °C]

c [-40 -20 0 20 40 °C]

d [-100 -50 0 50 100 °C]

2. Banks deal with positive and negative values of money.

   Discuss :-
   (i) what being "in the red" or being "in the **black**" means.
   (ii) what an "overdraft" is.

3. Gerry has £100 in his bank account. The bank computer will show this as £100·00.
   Mary has overdrawn by £50. The computer will show this as - £50·00.

   a Sammi's account shows £375·00. What does this balance mean ?

   b George's account shows - £400·00. What does this balance mean ?

   c Henry had **£45·00** in his account. He then withdrew £12·00.
   What will his balance now show on the bank computer ?

   d Brenda's balance last week was – £20, but she paid in £15.
   What's her new balance and how much more will she
   need to pay in to clear her overdraft ?

   e Len's bank balance showed **£70**.
   He bought a lawnmower for £100 and a rake for £20, using his debit card.
   How will his new balance show up on the bank computer ?

Negative numbers can be used in the context of time.

The London Olympics were held in the year 2012 A.D. (*Anno Domini*).

This means 2012 years since the birth of Christ.

We can think of this as a positive time, or +2012.

The Roman Emperor Claudius was born in the year 10 B.C. (*before Christ*).

This means 10 years before the birth of Christ.

We can think of this as a negative time, or –10.

4. a Use "+" or "–" signs to describe the following dates :–

(i) 1966 A.D. (ii) 312 A.D. (iii) 21 B.C. (iv) 729 B.C.

b Bugatis Lavius was born in 100 B.C. and died in 44 B.C.

How old was Bugatis when he died ?

c Augustus Caesar was born in 63 B.C. and died in 19 A.D.

What age was Augustus when he died ?

d Minimus was born in 42 B.C. and lived to the age of 77.

In which year did Minimus die ?

e Maximus died aged 63 in 54 A.D.

In which year was Maximus born ?

f Annoyus Irritus died in 74 A.D. at the age of 97.

When was he born ?

5.  A famous Greek Mathematician named Pythagoras of Samos was born in 570 B.C. He died in 495 B.C.

How old was Pythagoras when he died ?

6. a Write a list of famous people who were born thousands of years ago.

b Find their dates of birth and dates they died.

c Investigate what made them famous.

d Create a poster of your findings.

7. Positive and negative numbers are used to describe heights above or below sea-level.

Heights above sea level are *positive* (+).

Heights below sea level are *negative* (-).

a Use "+" or "-" to describe the heights (depths) of the following :-

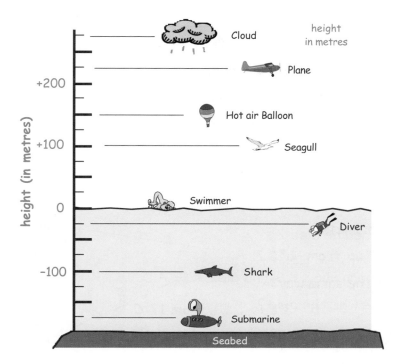

(i)   the seagull

(ii)   the shark

(iii) the swimmer

(iv)   the hot air balloon

(v)   the seabed

(vi)   the plane

(vii) the diver

(viii) the submarine

(ix)   the cloud.

b How far is :-

(i)   the seagull above the swimmer

(ii)   the diver below the swimmer

(iii) the balloon above the seagull

(iv)   the submarine below the shark

(v)   the plane below the cloud

(vi)   the plane above the diver

(vii) the shark below the seagull

(viii) the seagull below the plane

(ix)   the cloud above the diver

(x)   the submarine below the cloud ?

8. A mountaineer is 260 metres above sea level on a mountain.

A miner directly below the mountaineer is 340 metres below sea level under the mountain.

How far apart are the two people ?

9.  A lift on a mineshaft at ground level 0, can go down to level -9.

Each level is 25 metres down.

At what depth is level -9 ?

10. We previously learned how helpful the drawing of a thermometer could be in carrying out integer calculations.

Copy the thermometer shown opposite into your exercise book and use it to help you do the following :-

Find the temperature that is :-

a   5°C up from 9°C
b   23°C up from 0°C
c   14°C up from 18°C
d   9°C down from 21°C
e   15°C down from 15°C
f   8°C up from –3°C
g   10°C down from –6°C
h   16°C up from –9°C
i   7°C down from 4°C
j   42°C down from 0°C
k   14°C down from –6°C
l   40°C down from –20°C
m   8°C up from –15°C
n   25°C up from –30°C.

11. Look carefully at your thermometer.

Can you see that 2°C is 8°C up from –6°C ?

Copy and complete these in the same way :-

a   24°C is .... from 20°C
b   3°C is .... from 17°C
c   0°C is .... from 40°C
d   15°C is .... from –10°C
e   –17°C is .... from 0°C
f   3°C is .... from –4°C
g   –21°C is .... from –4°C
h   –11°C is .... from 11°C
i   21°C is .... from –20°C
j   –35°C is .... from 35°C.

12. The temperature in the conservatory is –4°C.

The living room in the house is 23° warmer.

What is the temperature in the living room ?

13.

As a plane rose from an airport into the sky, the outside temperature fell by a **steady amount** every 1000 metres.

At ground level, the temperature was 25°C and it fell by 10°C for every 1000 metres ascent.

What was the temperature at :-

a   1000 metres
b   3000 metres
c   5000 metres
d   10 000 metres ?

Thermometer scale:
24, 22, 20, 18, 16, 14, 12, 10, 8, 6, 4, 2, 0, -2, -4, -6, -8, -10, -12, -14, -16, -18, -20, -22, -24

Adding Integers   Extension

Be able to add positive and negative integers.

When adding integers, consider a thermometer and use the following two step method :-

Example 1 :- To find (– 1) + 5 =>   • picture the first number (–1)

• then move (up) by 5 => 4

Example 2 :- To find 5 + (–9) =>   • picture the first number (5)

• then move (down) by 9 => –4

Example 3 :- To find (–6) + (–5) => • picture the first number (–6)

• then move (down) by 5 => –11

The basic rules are as follows :-

• if you add on a (+) number you move up.

• if you add on a (–) number you move down.

Exercise 2 *Draw a thermometer if you think it will help you.*

1.   Write down each question first, then the answer :-

a 8 + 9   b 5 + 11   c 0 + 29   d 11 + (–7)

e 9 + (–3)   f 5 + (–5)   g 1 + (–7)   h 4 + (–11)

i 0 + (–16)   j (–4) + 11   k (–9) + 9   l (–2) + 13

m (–8) + 5   n (–12) + 3   o 2 + (–15)   p (–7) + (–8)

q (–10) + (–10) r (–12) + (–18)   s (–13) + 5   t (–24) + (–10)

u (–50) + 20   v (–25) + (–45)   w 30 + (–55)   x (–2·6) + (–5·4).

2.   Again, use your thermometer to help here :–

a 12 + 7 + 4   b 1 + 1 + (–1)   c 2 + (–3) + 1   d 2 + (–4) + 3

e 4 + (–2) + 5   f 3 + (–11) + (–1) g 0 + (–4) + (–2)   h (–1) + (–2) + (–3)

i (–6) + (–4) + 9   j (–3) + 7 + (–5)   k (–11) + 24 + (–5) l (–1) + (–25) + 30.

3.   What happens when you take away a **negative** number like (6 – (–2)) ? Discuss.

1. State what temperatures are represented on these thermometers :-

   a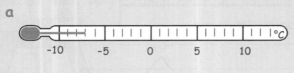

   b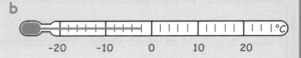

   c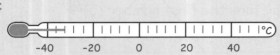

   d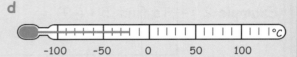

2. On 29th January, Alex's bank balance read –£455.

   a Describe "a balance of –£455" another way.

   His monthly salary of £1475 was paid in the next day.

   Alex then sent off a cheque for £175 for his season ticket.

   b Write down Alex's new balance.

3. a In an experiment, a scientist cooled a flask of liquid from 5°C down to –32°C.

   By how much had the liquid's temperature dropped ?

   b Senator Rovicus arrived in Britain in 23 BC.

   He sailed back to Rome in the year 19 AD.

   For how long had Rovicus been away ?

   c  A submarine was on the ocean bed at a depth of –155 metres.

   It rose to a depth of –68 metres.

   It then dropped by a further 52 metres.

   How far above the ocean bed was the submarine at that time ?

4. Find the temperature that is :-

   a   8°C up from –5°C   b   3°C down from 1°C

   c   11°C up from –18°C   d   9°C down from –12°C.

5. Find :-

   a   5 + (–7)   b   –4 + (–3)   c   –5 + 5   d   –6 + (–6)

   e   11 + (–8)   f   –2 + (–2)   g   –6 + 10   h   –20 + (–20).

Chapter 3

Drawing Triangles

Given 2 sides and the included angle, be able to draw a triangle.

Given 3 relevant pieces of information about a triangle, you should be able to draw it accurately.

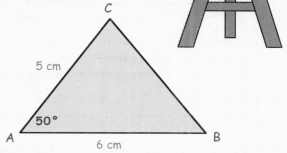

Two Sides and the Included* Angle

(* *the angle between the 2 sides*)

Here is a rough sketch of △ABC.

To draw it accurately :-

Step 1 :- Draw a line AB = 6 cm.

A ———————————— B
6 cm

Step 2 :- Place your protractor at A and mark an angle of 50°.

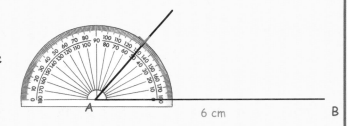

Step 3 :- Draw a line AC, from A through the X, to point C.

Make sure it is 5 cm long.

Step 4 :- Join B to C to form the triangle ABC.

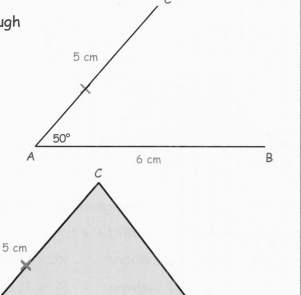

You will require :- a **RULER**, a **PROTRACTOR** and a **PAIR** of **COMPASSES**.

1. Shown is a rough **sketch** of △DEF.

    Follow these instructions to draw it accurately :-

    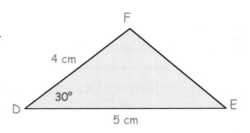

Step 1 :-	Draw line DE = 5 cm.
Step 2 :-	Put your protractor at D and mark (*with an X*) an angle of 30°.
Step 3 :-	Draw line DF, from D through the X, to point F. (*Make sure it is 4 centimetres long*).
Step 4 :-	Join E to F to make the triangle.

2. Make an accurate drawing of this triangle :-

    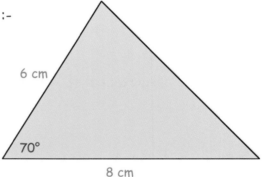

3. Make accurate drawings of these two triangles :-

    a 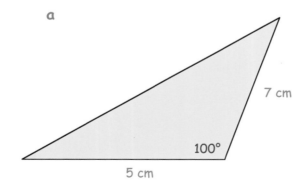   b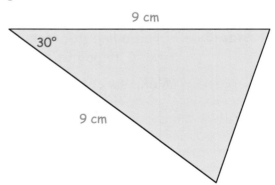

4. Make accurate drawings of the following triangles :-

    (*Make rough sketches of the triangles first before drawing them accurately*).

    a   Draw △KLM where   KL = 10 cm,   KM = 8 cm and ∠MKL = 60°.

    b   Draw △PUT where   PU = 11 cm,   UT = 6 cm and ∠PUT = 120°.

    c   Draw △XYZ where   XY = 8·5 cm,   XZ = 8·5 cm and ∠YXZ = 60°.

Two Angles and a Side

Shown opposite is a sketch of ΔSUD.

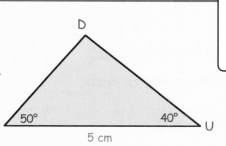

To draw it accurately :-

Step 1 :-   Draw line SU = 5 cm.

Step 2 :-   Now put your protractor at S and mark an angle of 50°.

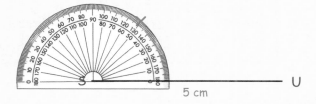

Step 3 :-   Draw line from S through the point X.

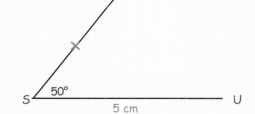

Step 4 :-   Now put your protractor at U and mark an angle of 40°.

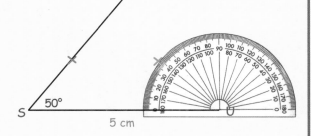

Step 5 :-   Finally, draw the line from U through your new X point.

   (Mark the point where the two lines meet with the letter D).

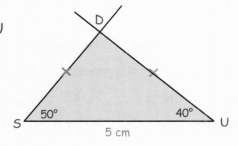

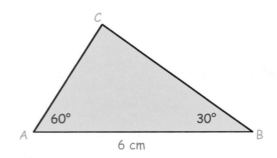

Exercise 2

1. Shown is a rough **sketch** of △ABC.

   Follow these instructions to draw it accurately :-

Step 1 :-	Draw line AB = 6 cm.
Step 2 :-	Put protractor at A and mark (*with an X*) an angle of 60°.
Step 3 :-	Draw a line from A through the X.
Step 4 :-	Put protractor at B and mark (*with an X*) an angle of 30°.
Step 5 :-	Draw a line from B through X, to meet the first line at point C.

2. Make an accurate drawing of this triangle :-

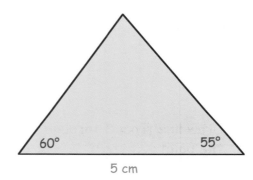

3. Make accurate drawings of these two triangles :-

   a   b

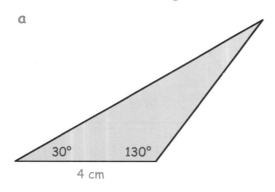 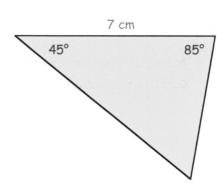

4. Make accurate drawings of the following triangles :-

   (*Make rough sketches of the triangles first before drawing them accurately*).

   a   Draw △PLJ where   PL = 9 cm,   ∠JPL = 55° and ∠PLJ = 65°.

   b   Draw △HMV where   HM = 6 cm,   ∠VHM = 120° and ∠HMV = 25°.

Knowing the Lengths of all Three Sides

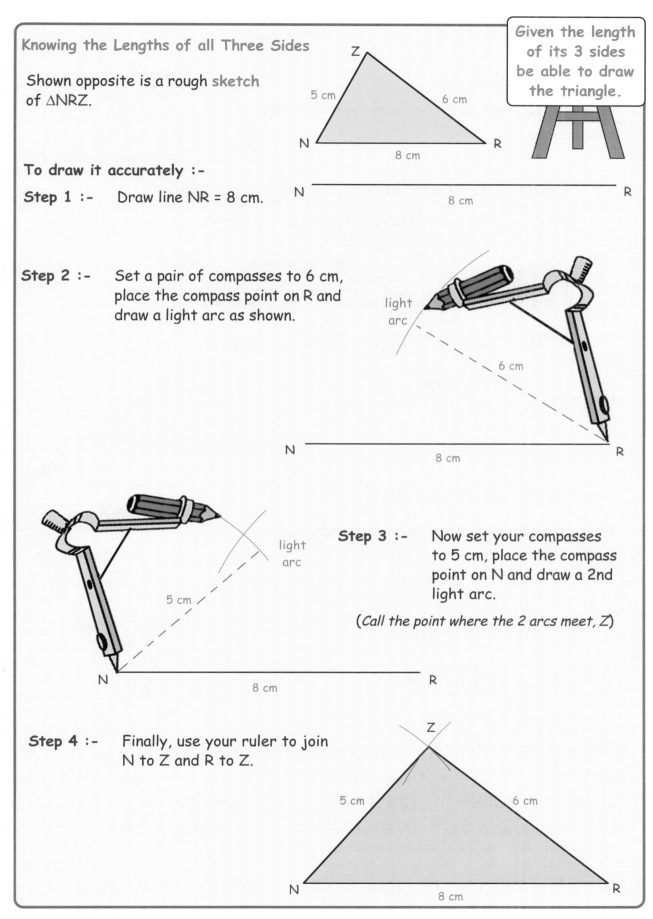

Given the length of its 3 sides be able to draw the triangle.

Shown opposite is a rough **sketch** of △NRZ.

To draw it accurately :-

Step 1 :- Draw line NR = 8 cm.

Step 2 :- Set a pair of compasses to 6 cm, place the compass point on R and draw a light arc as shown.

Step 3 :- Now set your compasses to 5 cm, place the compass point on N and draw a 2nd light arc.

(Call the point where the 2 arcs meet, Z)

Step 4 :- Finally, use your ruler to join N to Z and R to Z.

1. Shown is a sketch of ΔPOW.

   Draw it accurately using the following instructions :-

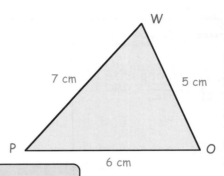

Step 1 :-	Draw line PO = 6 cm.
Step 2 :-	Set your compasses to 5 cm, place the compass point on O and draw a light arc.
Step 3 :-	Now set your compasses to 7 cm, place the compass point on P and draw a 2nd arc.
Step 4 :-	Call this point where the arcs meet W and join W to P and to O.

2. Make an accurate drawing of this triangle :-

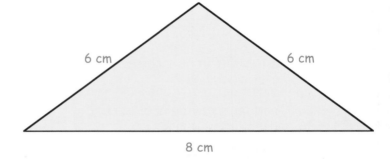

3. Make accurate drawings of these two triangles :-

   a

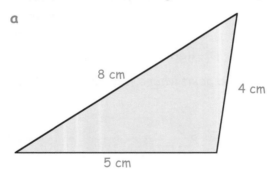

   b

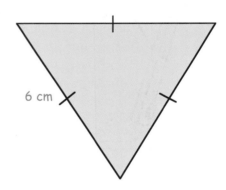

4. Make accurate drawings of the following triangles :-

   (*Make rough sketches of the triangles first before drawing them accurately*).

   a Draw ΔIJK where IJ = 11 cm, JK = 7 cm and IK = 7 cm.

   b Draw ΔUVW where UV = 10·5 cm, VW = 6·5 cm and UW = 6 cm.

5. Try to draw ΔDEF where DE = 10 cm, EF = 6 cm and DF = 3 cm. What happens ?

Drawing Quadrilaterals and Regular Polygons

Be able to draw quadrilaterals and regular polygons.

Three examples using only a pair of compasses and a straight edge :-

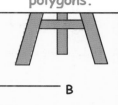

Bisecting a Line at Right Angles

We want to find the midpoint of line AB.

Step 1 :- Set your compasses to a size larger than half of AB.

Step 2 :- Draw an arc, centre A and another arc, centre B, with same radius.

Step 3 :- Join the 2 points (*C and D*) where the arcs intersect.

This line CD will bisect (*cut in half*) AB and does so at right angles. (*Discuss why*).

Bisecting an Angle

We want to cut ∠PUT in half (*bisect it*).

Step 1 :- With centre U and using any radius, draw an arc, cutting UP at Q and UT at R.

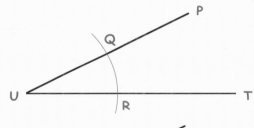

Step 2 :- With the same radius as above, draw an arc centre Q and another, centre R. These will meet at a point (*call it X*).

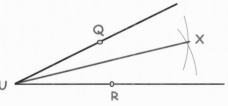

Step 3 :- Join U to X. This line will cut ∠PUT in half.

Can you see that UQXR is a rhombus ? (*Discuss why this is so*).

Drawing a 60° Angle

Step 1 :- Draw a line KL.

Step 2 :- With radius KL draw an arc centre K.

Step 3 :- Draw a 2nd arc, centre L, with the same radius.

Step 4 :- The 2 arcs intersect at a point M.

Join K to M. (∠MKL = 60°). (*Why ?*)

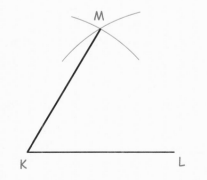

1. Draw any line PQ in your exercise book and use a method shown on the previous page to find its **mid-point**,

   (*i.e. show how to* **bisect** *the line PQ*).

2. Draw any angle ABC.

   Use the method shown earlier to **bisect** the angle.

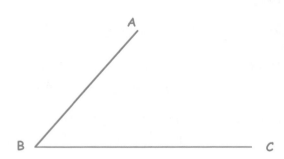

3. Draw a line KP, 8 cm long.

   Show how to create an **equilateral triangle** KPR.

4. Draw the line CD = 7 cm and create a rectangle CDEF with side CD = 7 cm and angle FDC = 60°.

   (**No** *protractor allowed here*).

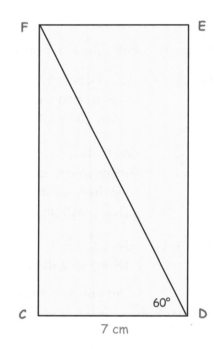

5. Draw a line CD = 7 cm again and make an accurate drawing of rectangle ADBC, (sketched opposite) with CD = 7 cm as a diagonal* this time :-

   (**No** *protractor allowed here*).

   *Remember - (a **diagonal** is any line in a figure joining 2 opposite corners).

6. a   Start with a line HI = 8 cm
        and create ∠GHI = 60°.

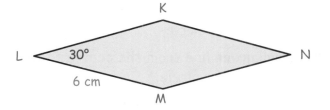

   b   Now show how to bisect ∠GHI
        to create an angle of 30°.

7. Show how to create the rhombus
   KLMN, shown opposite, using only
   a ruler and a pair of compasses.

        No protractor.

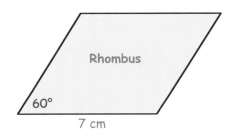

For Question 8, you can use compasses and a ruler - but NOT a protractor !

8. Make accurate drawings of these two quadrilaterals :-

   a   b

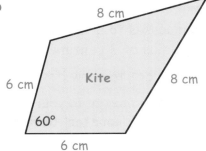

9. Shown is a regular hexagon.
   (*6 sided shape with equal sides and angles*).

   Can you see that it is made up
   from six equilateral triangles ?

   Draw a regular hexagon with side 6 cm.

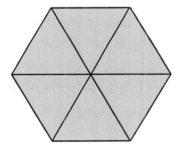

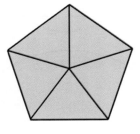

10.   a   Investigate the angles in a regular pentagon.

                                   b   Draw a regular pentagon with side 6 cm.

11. a   Investigate other regular polygons

         (*8 sided, 9 sided, 10 sided .....*).

    b   Draw some other regular polygons.

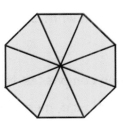

The Circle

Naming Parts of a Circle

The pink dot represents the centre of the circle.

The blue line through the centre is called a diameter of the circle.

The small green line from the centre to the edge is called the radius of the circle.

The curved edge, (*the perimeter*), is called the circumference.

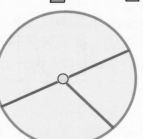

Note :-   Diameter = 2 x Radius

Exercise 5

1. Use compasses to draw a circle with a radius of 3 centimetres.

    a   Mark a dot to show its centre.

    b   Draw a diameter in your figure and write "diameter" beside it.

    c   Draw a radius in your figure and write "radius" beside your line.

    d   In your figure write the word "circumference" beside the actual circumference.

2. This is a sketch of a circle whose diameter is 14 cm.

    What must the length of its radius be ?

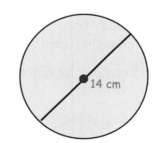

14 cm

3. The radius of a circle is 25 millimetres.

    What must the length of its diameter be ?

4. Look at this semi-circle.

    a   Use a ruler to measure its diameter.

    b   Write down what size its radius must be.

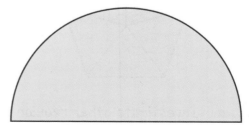

5. a   Use your compasses to draw a semi-circle with a radius of 6 cm.

    b   On your figure, measure and show what length its diameter must be.

6. Shown is a sketch of 3 touching circles surrounded by a rectangular box.

    The **radius** of each circle is 8 cm.

    Calculate the length and width of the box.   (*Do not use a ruler*).

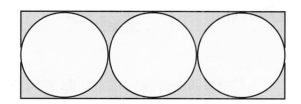

7. The length of the shape below is 40 cm.

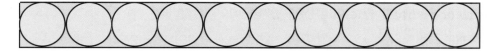

    a   What must the height of the shape be ?

    b   What must the length of the **radius** of each circle be ?

8. This shape has four identical semi-circles on top of a rectangle.

    a   Calculate the length of the diameter of **one** semi-circle.

    b   What must the **radius** be ?

    c   Now calculate the **height** of the shape.

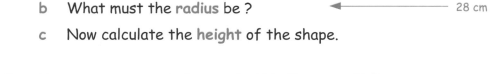

9. Use your compasses to create this flower pattern :-

    Start by drawing a circle with radius 4 cm.

    Next, put your compass point on any point (P) on the circumference and with radius still 4 cm, "step" round the circle moving from one point to the next.

    Carefully colour your design and make a class display.

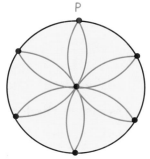

10. Here are 2 more designs created in almost the same way.

    Draw each of them using a fixed radius of 5 cm.

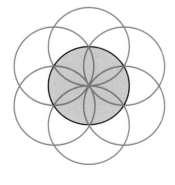

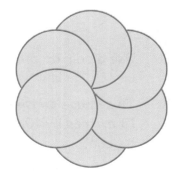

11. Try to create your own circular or semi-circular designs.

    Make a display of the most imaginative and well drawn designs.

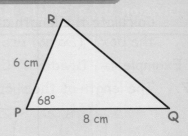

The 3 Я's — Revisit - Review - Revise

1. a   Make an accurate drawing of triangle PQR.

   b   Measure and write down the size of line RQ.

2. a   Draw accurately triangle DEF where :-

   DE = 8·5 cm   ∠DEF = 65°   ∠FDE = 25°.

   b   Measure and write down the size of :-   (i)   line DF   (ii)   angle EFD.

3.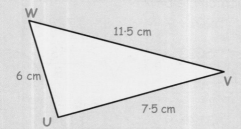

   Look at this sketch of triangle UVW.

   a   Make an accurate drawing of this triangle.

   b   Measure and mark in the sizes of each of its three angles.

4.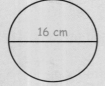

   Draw a kite with sides 5 cm, 5 cm, 8 cm and 8 cm.

   The angle between the 2 smaller sides is to be 110°.

5. a   Make a neat, accurate drawing of this trapezium.

   b   Measure the length of the 4th side.

   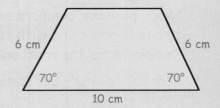

6. The diameter of a circle is 16 centimetres.

   Write down the length of its radius.

7. Use a pair of compasses to draw a circle with a radius of 3·5 cm.

8. This shape consists of a rectangle measuring 13 metres by 10 metres, with a semi-circle on its end.

   Calculate the length of the shape.
   (Do NOT measure it with a ruler).

   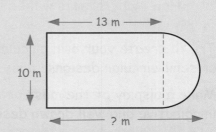

 # Chapter 4

Division by a Single Digit (Revision)

Example :- Divide 5745 by 9.

$$\begin{array}{r} 6\ 3\ 8\ r\ 3 \\ 9\,\overline{\smash{)}\,5\ 5\ 7^3 4^7 5} \end{array}$$

Be able to divide a number with up to 4 digits by a single digit.

Exercise 1

1. Set down the following in the same way as above and complete each calculation :-

   a $534 \div 6$ b $892 \div 2$ c $5901 \div 7$ d $7728 \div 8$

   e $6858 \div 9$ f $6316 \div 4$ g $\dfrac{5033}{7}$ h $\dfrac{7533}{9}$.

2. Find the remainder each time :-

   a $513 \div 8$ b $2715 \div 6$ c $4317 \div 9$ d $6134 \div 7$.

3. Eggs are packed into boxes of 6.

   How many boxes are needed to pack 4086 eggs ?

4. Nine people won a total of £5283.

   If it is shared equally amongst them, how much will each receive ?

5. Chocolate biscuits are packed into jars of 8.

   If the factory produces 7552 biscuits each day
   how many jars are needed to pack them ?

6. Blank DVDs in their cases are priced at £9 for 10.

   How many packs of 10 could a shopkeeper buy in with £3267 ?

7. A bag contains 135 sweets. They are shared equally amongst 8 children.

   a How many will each child receive ?

   b How many sweets will be left over ?

8. Tennis balls are packed into boxes of 6.

   a How many boxes are needed for 1000 balls ?

   b How many tennis balls are left over ?

9. Try this one :- $9436 \div 4 \div 7$.

Division by a Two Digit Number (No Remainder)

Be able to divide a number with up to 4 digits by a 2 digit number (no remainder).

Example 1 :- Divide 3810 by 15.

Division by a 2 digit number is normally done using long division.

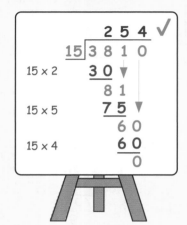

```
                2 5 4 ✓
        15 3 8 1 0
15 × 2   3 0 ▾
         8 1
15 × 5   7 5 ▾
         6 0
15 × 4   6 0
            0
```

Example 2 :- Divide 495 by 11.

Division by 11 or 12 may be done using short division.

```
        4 5 ✓
11 4 9⁵5
```

* Your teacher will explain this technique of Long Division.

Doh Me Soh- Cross Down

Divide - Multiply - Subtract Cross down the next number

Exercise 2

1. Use **short division** to complete each calculation :-

   a 11⟌154   b 11⟌649   c 11⟌3223   d 11⟌8404

   e 12⟌252   f 12⟌948   g 12⟌4248   h 12⟌9396.

2. **Copy** and **complete** :-

   a
   ```
         2..
   13 325
      26
       6..
      ....
       ..
   ```
   b
   ```
         5..
   14 756
      70
       5..
      ....
       ..
   ```
   c
   ```
         4..
   17 714
      6..
       3..
      ....
       ..
   ```
   d
   ```
         2..
   25 525
      5..
      ....
      ....
       ..
   ```

3. Use long division to work out the answer to each of these divisions :-

   a 13⟌52   b 14⟌308   c 15⟌510   d 16⟌656

   e 17⟌884   f 18⟌612   g 19⟌114   h 13⟌1586

   i 1568 ÷ 14   j 3165 ÷ 15   k 5008 ÷ 16   l 2584 ÷ 17

   m 2185 ÷ 19   n 625 ÷ 25   o 3584 ÷ 32   p 5043 ÷ 41.

4. 276 people need to use the elevator to get to a meeting on the top floor of an office building.

   If the lift can hold 12 people at a time how many up and down trips will the elevator have to make ?

5.  Miss Jones has 341 grapes.

   She manages to give each of her pupils 11 grapes each.

   How many pupils does Miss Jones have in her class ?

6. A car park attendant collected £795 in parking fees last Monday.

   If each car was charged £15 for the day, how many cars used the car park on that Monday ?

7.  A tour group paid £273 to buy rail tickets.

   Each ticket cost £13.

   How many tourists were in the group ?

8. A school library has 414 books.

   If each shelf in the library can hold 18 books, how many shelves will be needed ?

9.  A vegetable grower needs to ship 3655 lettuces to a supermarket.

   How many boxes will she need if each box can hold 17 lettuces ?

10. An estate agent has £5075 to spend on newspaper adverts.

    If each advert costs £25 how many will he be able to afford ?

11. A hotel orders 828 pork chops from its supplier.

    If the chops come in packs of 36 how many packs will have to be ordered ?

12. 360 plates were used by a catering company for a large function.

    After the event, the plates were washed, dried and stacked in piles of 24.

    How many stacks were there ?

Division by a Two Digit Number (With a Remainder)

Be able to divide a number with up to 4 digits by a 2 digit number (with a remainder).

In year 5, you saw that some division have a remainder.

The remainder can take the "r 1" form or be expressed as a fraction, a decimal or can be rounded to the nearest whole number.

This exercise is similar - only the divisor this time has 2 digits.

Example :- Divide 1729 by 14, giving the remainder :-

a as a fraction b as a decimal c rounded to the nearest whole number.

a
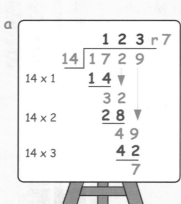

```
              1 2 3 r 7
        14 | 1 7 2 9
14 x 1      1 4
              3 2
14 x 2      2 8
              4 9
14 x 3      4 2
                7
```

b
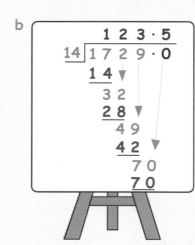

```
              1 2 3 · 5
        14 | 1 7 2 9 · 0
              1 4
              3 2
              2 8
                4 9
                4 2
                  7 0
                  7 0
```

c
Both $123\frac{1}{2}$ and $123\cdot5$ round to 124.

Answer :- $123\frac{7}{14}$ or $123\frac{1}{2}$. Answer :- $123\cdot5$.

Exercise 3

1. Carry out the divisions and write the remainder in the form "r ....".

   a 13 | 54   b 14 | 312   c 15 | 511   d 16 | 660

   e 17 | 894   f 18 | 627   g 19 | 117   h 13 | 1587 .

2. Do these divisions, writing the remainders as fractions :-

   a 14 | 63   b 12 | 162   c 15 | 515   d 16 | 550

   e 17 | 885   f 18 | 639   g 24 | 2682   h 35 | 7030 .

3. Work out these divisions, writing the remainders in decimal form :-

   a 16 | 88   b 12 | 498   c 18 | 495   d 15 | 618

   e 14 | 721   f 16 | 676   g 24 | 6036   h 25 | 7105 .

4. Set down, work out and give your answers correct to the nearest whole number :-

   a   378 ÷ 11   b   1006 ÷ 12   c   316 ÷ 13   d   360 ÷ 14

   e   478 ÷ 15   f   472 ÷ 16   g   1739 ÷ 17   h   2030 ÷ 18

   i   1920 ÷ 19   j   6920 ÷ 22   k   1255 ÷ 25   l   3835 ÷ 34.

5. Work out the answer to 7794 ÷ 72, giving your answer :-

   a   in "r...." form   b   as a fraction   c   as a decimal   d   to nearest whole no.

6. a   A machine can split mint imperials into jars of 65.

   If 1825 mints are put into the machine how many
   full jars will be produced ?

   b   Eighteen people shared a thunderball win of £4419.

   How much did they get each ?

   c   A school paid £5225 for 25 identical laptops.

   What was the cost of each laptop ?

   d      24 school children paid a total of £4182
   to go on a school trip to Rome.

   How much was that per child ?

   e   5670 litres of liquid feeding is spread over an
   area of 28 square kilometres of grassland.

   How many litres is that per square kilometre ?

   (*Give your remainder as a fraction.*)

   f      A college is planning a field trip.

   1330 students want to go and the buses booked can seat 44.

   What's the minimum number of buses required ?

   g   Findlay drives one of the buses.

   He gets paid £513 for a 36 hour shift.

   What is his hourly rate of pay ?

Addition, Subtraction, Multiplication & Division

Be able to solve problems using mathematical operations.

In the following exercise, you will have to carefully read each problem and decide whether to use +. −, × or ÷ to solve it.

Examples :-

Jason earns £20 563 per year.   Jan gets an annual salary of £24 367.

1. What is their combined pay ?

    This is a + problem.

    £20 563
    + £24 367
    £44 930   Combined pay is £44 930.

2. How much more than Jason does Jan earn ?

    This is a − problem.

    £24 367
    − £20 563
    £3 804   Jan earns £3804 more than Jason.

3. What would Jason earn over 3 years at this rate of pay ?

    This is a × problem.

    £20 563
    × 3
    £61 689   Jason would earn £61 689.

4. What did Jan earn in the first six months ?

    This is a ÷ problem.

    ÷2, as there are 2 lots of 6 months in a year.

    £12 084
    2 £24 168   Jan earns £12 084 every 6 months.

Exercise 4

Decide whether to add, subtract, multiply or divide .... then solve the problem.

1. As a bus arrived at a stop, there were 38 people on board.

    At the stop, a further 17 passengers got on.

    How many were there now on the bus ?

    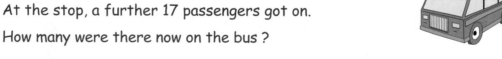

2. On January 1st 2013, I noted that my car had done 28 312 miles.

    On January 1st 2014, the reading on the odometer was 41 187.

    How many miles had my car covered over the year ?

3. A palette holds 1275 pots of noodles.

    How many pots are there altogether on 6 palettes ?

4.  A week consists of 7 days.

    How many whole weeks are there in 809 days ?

5. Arthur bought a brand new car for £8998.

   One year later, it was valued at only £7005.

   How much had the value of his car dropped over the year ?

6.  A train travelled for 14 hours at an average speed of 82 km/hr.

   How many kilometres had the train travelled ?

7. Sultana shortcakes are packed into jars of 16.

   Every day, the biscuit factory hopes to make 6840 sultana shortcakes.

   How many jars will be filled each day and how many cakes left over ?

8.  During a storm, a plane dropped in height from 35 280 feet to 29 690 feet.

   By how many feet had it dropped ?

9. An hour consists of (60 x 60) = 3600 seconds.

   How many seconds are there in a day ?

10.  Jessie works in a hat shop for 4 hours per day.

    She worked a total of 592 hours over the past year.

    How many days exactly did she turn up for work ?

11. Mr & Mrs Greig took their two children to Playdome for a day out.

    a   How much was it for 2 adult and 2 children's tickets ?

    b   They bought the Family Ticket.

         How much did they save ?

PLAYDOME
(daily ticket)
(unlimited rides)

| Adult | £9·75 |
| Child | £5·99 |

Family Ticket   £25·75
(2 adults + 2 kids)

12.  The total bill for 16 ladies who went on a golfing weekend, including the hotel and two rounds of golf, came to £4324.

    How much did each lady pay if the bill was shared evenly ?

In the following questions 13 to 20, where money is involved, you might find it easier to change any reference to pounds and pence into pence, before attempting the calculations.

13. *Alfredo's* sell boxes of mini pizzas.
    A box of 6 costs £16·50 (*1650p*) and a box of 4 costs £11·40 (*1140p*).

    Which is the better deal ? Explain your answer with working.

14. Tracy bought a pack of 12 bottles
    of carpet shampoo on the internet
    for £57·60 + post and package of £5·60.

    She saw the same shampoo in the supermarket at £5·95 per bottle.

    How much did Tracy save by ordering online ?

15.  Two packs of sandwiches and a bottle of Raspberry Cooler
    cost £7·36.
    The drink cost 80p.

    What was the price of one pack of sandwiches ?

16. Brian took his parents and in-laws for afternoon tea to Glenhawks Hotel.
    They ordered 5 slices of apple pie, 3 coffees and 2 teas.
    The total bill came to £22·80.

    If the pie slices were £2·75 each and the teas £1·60 each,
    what was the cost of a coffee ?

17. Nine friends went for a meal. If the total bill had been shared
    amongst all of them, each would have had to pay £32·88.

    As Clive had turned up with no money, the others had to split
    the bill amongst the 8 of them.

    How much did they each have to pay ?

19.   Mrs Able bought a new washing machine by paying a deposit of
    £23·95, followed by 9 monthly payments of £22·25.

    What was the total cost of the washing machine ?

19. 2 adult tickets and 6 child tickets for a train journey comes to
    exactly the same as that for 3 adults and 2 children.

    If an adult ticket is £5·20, calculate the cost of a child's ticket.

20.  John bought 10 pieces of fruit, a mixture of apples and pears.
    Each apple cost 45p and each pear cost 60p.

    If his bill came to £4·95, how many of each must he have bought ?

    (*Make a guess first, check how far out your answer is and re-guess.*)

Add, Subtract, Multiply & Divide Mentally

> Be able to use quick methods to carry out mental calculations.

Mental methods are about trying to get the correct answer in the quickest and easiest way.

We will look at addition and subtraction first.

Example 1 :-

Addition

126 + 139

(Do 126 + 140 and take 1)

= 126 + 140 – 1

= 266 – 1

= 265

Example 2 :-

Subtraction

283 – 149

(Do 283 – 150 and add 1)

= 283 – 150 + 1

= 133 + 1

= 134

Example 3 :-

Addition

257 + 324

(Do 250 + 320 add 7 + 4)

= 570 + 11

= 581

Example 4 :-

Subtraction

585 – 342

(Do 580 - 340 add 5 - 2)

= 240 + 3

= 243

YOU have to choose the quickest and easiest method.

Discuss various methods in class.

Exercise 5

1. Write down the easiest, quickest way to calculate mentally :-

   a   139 + 146   "add .... + 146, then take ...."   b   590 – 268   "590 - ...., then take ...."

   c   3900 + 2400   "add .... + 2400, then take ...."   d   787 – 534   "780 - ...., then add 7 - ...."

   e   23 000 + 45 000   "add 23 to .... , then add .... zeros at the end"

2. Choose your own mental method to find the answers to these :-

   a   39 + 58   b   53 + 66   c   19 + 85   d   38 + 88

   e   270 – 125   f   569 – 253   g   800 – 472   h   350 + 190

   i   320 + 990   j   790 – 460   k   1000 – 280   l   1820 – 1380

   m   23 000 + 45 000   n   68 000 – 23 000   o   300 000 – 200 005

   p   590 000 + 520 000   q   3 200 000 + 2 800 000   r   6 000 000 – 900 000.

3. Do these problems mentally :-

   a   245 000 tickets have been sold for the Commonwealth Games.
       Another 19 000 will be sold tomorrow.

       How many tickets will have been sold then ?

   b   Cath won a lottery prize of £4 300 000.

       What was she left with after donating £1 950 000 to charity ?

Mental Multiplication and Division methods are slightly more complicated.

Example 1 :-
Multiplication

$$370 \times 3$$

(Treat as 3 x 300 and add 3 x 70)

= 3 x 300 + 3 x 70

= 900 + 210

= 1110

*Using mental methods is about choosing the method that works best for you and the numbers you are dealing with.

Example 2 :-
Multiplication

$$23 \times £1·99$$

(Treat as 23 x £2 and take 23 x 1p)

= 23 x £2 - 23 x 1p

= £46 - 23p

= £45·77

Example 3 :-
Division

$$480 \div 3$$

(Split 480 into 300 and 180 as they both can be ÷ 3 easily, and add)

= 300 ÷ 3 + 180 ÷ 3

= 100 + 60

= 160

Example 4 :-
Division

$$228 \div 6$$

(Split 6 into 2 x 3 and do 228 ÷ 2 ÷ 3)

= 228 ÷ 2 ÷ 3

= 114 ÷ 3

= 38   Not all that easy !

4. Write down the easiest, quickest way to calculate mentally :-

   a 830 x 9   " 9 x ...., add 9 x ...."   b £5·99 x 14 "14 x £.., then take 14 x .. p"

   c £1·99 x 18   "18 x £..., then take 18 x ... p" d 420 ÷ 3 "Split 420 into 300 & 120, then ...."

   e 650 ÷ 5 "Split 650 into 500 & 150, then ...." f 174 ÷ 6   "174 ÷ .... ÷ .... = ..."

5. Choose your own easiest, quickest way to find the answers to these, mentally :-

   a 260 x 2   b 4300 x 3   c 81 000 x 5   d 104 000 x 7

   e 13 x £1·99   f 12 x £3·99   g 14 x £2·95   h 19 x £2·10

   i 540 ÷ 3   j 1260 ÷ 2   k 13 600 ÷ 4   l 720 000 ÷ 6

   m 126 000 ÷ 6   n 10 800 ÷ 4   o 1520 ÷ 8   p 126 000 ÷ 9.

6. Do these problems mentally :-

   a The owner of the Glenmore Hotel went into town to buy fifteen 3-D TV's, priced £999 each.

      What did his bill come to ?

£999

   b  Twelve people paid a total of £7320 for a week's skiing holiday.

      What did it cost each of them ?

Rounding and Estimating

Be able to round to a required level of accuracy and be able to give good approximations for answers.

By now, you should be able to **round** to a required number of decimal places, nearest whole number, 10, 100, £, kg ... etc.

You should also be able to give a **good approximation** for an answer to an addition, subtraction, multiplication and division.

The following exercise brings together all that you have learned on rounding and estimating over the past 5 years.

Exercise 6

1. Round :–

    a   248·51 to the nearest whole number

    b   204·397 kg to the nearest kilogram

    c   £156 299·89 to the nearest £

    d   3841·5 m to the nearest metre

    e   39·64 to one decimal place

    f   845·727 to two decimal places

    g   38 756 to the nearest ten

    h   87 563 to the nearest hundred

    i   65 376 to the nearest thousand

    j   77 567 to the nearest ten thousand

    k   1 352 578 to the nearest 100 thousand

    l   8 199 999 to the nearest million.

2. Round your numbers before calculating.

    Use this to decide which of the 3 given answers is most likely to be correct :–

    a   5934 + 6201   Choice of   {21 135,   12 135   or   121 355}

    b   897 678 – 310 002   Choice of   {985 878,   257 767   or   587 676}

    c   2935 × 116   Choice of   {340 460,   430 640,   or   34 046}

    d   198 445 ÷ 215   Choice of   {92 300,   9230   or   923}.

3. Round each number to 1 figure accuracy, then give an estimate for :–

    a   89 268 + 3125   b   408 712 – 197 865   c   395 × 1870   d   79 939 ÷ 2061.

4. The population of Plymouth in June 2014 was 218 198.

    Birmingham's population was 4 times that.

    Using 2 figure accuracy, estimate the population of Birmingham in June 2014.

5. Have a go at rounding :–

    a   62 to the nearest twenty

    b   131 to the nearest twenty

    c   86 to the nearest forty

    d   237 to the nearest forty

    e   682 to the nearest fifty

    f   654 915 to the nearest fifty.

BOMDAS - The Order of Operations

Be able to
+, −, ×, ÷
using the order
of operations.

Many calculations have to be completed in a **specific order**.

Example :- For 100 − 20 × 4, the answer is **not** 80 × 4 = 320.

The answer IS ...... 100 − 80 = 20.

The easy way to remember which part of a calculation
comes first is using the mnemonic BOMDAS.

• *Multiply & Divide rank equally*
• *Add & Subtract rank equally*

Example 1 :-	Example 2 :-	Example 3 :-
21 + 9 × 4	one third of 90 - 30	(27 + 33) ÷ (2 × 15)
Multiply first	*Of first*	*Brackets first*
= 21 + 36	= 30 - 30	= 60 ÷ 30
= 57	= 0	= 2

Brackets
Of
Multiply
Divide
Add
Subtract

· *Apply any **B** and **O** first, move from left to right using any **M** or **D** as you find them.*
· *Then move from left to right doing any **A** or **S** as you find them.*

Exercise 7

1. Use BOMDAS to help you calculate :-

    a   25 + 8 × 3   b   50 − 4 × 9   c   20 × 2 + 10

    d   49 − 28 ÷ 7   e   100 − 50 ÷ 10   f   74 − 48 ÷ 2.

2. Calculate :-

    a   50 − 24 + 4 − 10   b   third of 60 ÷ 5   c   quarter of 40 − 8

    d $\frac{1}{2}$ of 72 ÷ 9   e   2 + $\frac{1}{4}$ of 48   f   8 − $\frac{1}{3}$ of 21 + 5

    g   9 × 6 − 100 ÷ 4 + 1   h   7 × 8 − 5 × 9 + 28 ÷ 7   i   8 − $\frac{1}{5}$ of (44 − 9).

3. Find :-

    a   24 + (18 ÷ 3)   b   75 ÷ (18 − 13)   c   9 × (8 + 12)

    d   300 ÷ (106 + 44)   e   8 × (9 + 4) − 104   f   (7 + 3) × (9 − 1) − 78.

4. Copy each of the following and **put in brackets** to make each calculation correct :-

    a   3 + 7 × 2 = 20   b   16 − 7 × 2 = 2   c   20 + 18 ÷ 2 = 19

    d   40 + 20 ÷ 4 × 5 = 3   e   15 + 30 ÷ 12 − 3 = 5   f   5 + 8 × 6 − 2 + 5 = 57.

5. Find :-

    a   200 ÷ 4 + 5 × 10   b   a fifth of (97 + 3)   c   3 × (68 + 12)

    d   9 × 6 − 4   e   4 + 8 × 7   f   7 + (9 × 8)

    g   300 − $\frac{1}{3}$ of 60 × 10   h $\frac{1}{10}$ of ($\frac{1}{5}$ of 150)   i   ((12 ÷ 6) + 2) × 6 − (17 + 3).

1. Set down the following as divisions ($\lceil$) and complete each calculation :-

   a 623 ÷ 7   b 4269 ÷ 2   c 8765 ÷ 5   d 2247 ÷ 8.

2. The total cost for a group of 9 adults to go on holiday to Portugal was £4158.

   a What was the cost for each person ?

   b Mr Prentice paid for himself, his wife, and their
   two friends. How much did Mr Prentice have to pay ?

3. Use long division in each of these :-

   a $14\overline{)56}$ b $34\overline{)918}$ c $15\overline{)3510}$ d $28\overline{)3500}$.

4.
   A gym takes in £5250 per month from its members,
   who each pay a fee of £25 per month.

   How many members does the gym have ?

5. Work out the answer to 1636 ÷ 16, giving your answer :-

   a as a remainder   b as a fraction   c as a decimal   d to nearest whole no.

6. Round each number to 1 figure accuracy, then give an estimate for :-

   a 69775 + 4078   b 519213 – 298485   c 498 x 2954   d 58899 ÷ 3120.

7. Set down and work out :-

   a 300 ÷ 5 + 7 x 20   b a seventh of (97 – 13)   c 8 x (57 + 23)

   d 8 x 9 – 5   e 12 + 8 x 11   f (12 + 8) x 11

   g 110 – $\frac{1}{6}$ of 54 x 10   h $\frac{1}{5}$ of ($\frac{1}{6}$ of 240)   i ((28 ÷ 7) + 2) x 4 – (21 + 3).

8. A buyer for a phone store bought 60 phones for £2280.

   The store managed to sell all but 5 of them for £42 each.

   a How much money did the store take in ?

   b How much did the store make out of these sales ?

9. Choose your own easiest, quickest way to find the answers to these, mentally :-

   a £19·99 x 20   b 3015 x 3   c 28028 ÷ 4   d 1050 ÷ 25.

Chapter 5

Evaluating Expressions and Formulae

Be able to substitute numbers for letters.

Examples :-

If $p = 3$, $q = 4$ and $r = -2$, find the values of :-

1. $7p$

$= 7 \times 3$

$= 21$

2. $4p + r$

$= 4 \times 3 + (-2)$

$= 10$

3. $q^2 - p^2$

$= (4 \times 4) - (3 \times 3)$

$= 16 - 9$

$= 7$

4. $2q^3$

$= 2 \times q \times q \times q$

$= 2 \times 4 \times 4 \times 4$

$= 128$

5. $5p^2 + 6pq + r$ *pq means $p \times q$

$= (5 \times p \times p) + (6 \times p \times q) + r$

$= (5 \times 3 \times 3) + (6 \times 3 \times 4) + (-2)$

$= 45 + 72 - 2 = 115$

6. If $C = \dfrac{a + b}{4}$,

find the value of C when when $a = 10$ and $b = 18$.

$C = \dfrac{a + b}{4}$

$C = \dfrac{10 + 18}{4}$

$C = \dfrac{28}{4} = 7$

Exercise 1

1. Find the value of each of the following when $a = 3$:-

   a $a + 6$ b $a - 1$ c $8a$ d $5a - 14$

   e $2 + 4a$ f $20 - 6a$ g a^2 h a^3

   i $a^2 - 9$ j $2a^2$ k $a^2 + a$ l $a^2 - 1 \cdot 2a$.

2. Find the value of each of the following when $x = 4$:-

   a $5x$ b $7x$ c x^2 d $2x^2$

   e x^3 f $10x^2$ g $20x^3$ h $18 - x^2$.

3. Find the values of each of the following :-

   a $g + 7$ when $g = 9$ b $3h + 4$ when $h = 0$

   c $2p - 9$ when $p = 25$ d $s + t$ when $s = -9$ and $t = 4$

   e $5ef$ when $e = 4$ and $f = 2$ f $20 - 4ab$ when $a = 1$ and $b = 4$.

4. Given $p = 1$, $q = 3$ and $r = 7$, calculate the value of :-

   a $p + q + r$ b $2p + 5q + r$ c $q + p + 2r$

   d pqr e $5p + 5q + 10r$ f $pq + qr + pr$

   g $3p + 2q - r$ h $10pq - 4r$ i $5pqr - 100$.

The Square Root :-

When you square a number you multiply it by itself => $5^2 = 5 \times 5 = 25$.

In reverse :- Ask yourself, "What number, times itself, gives 25" ?

=> The answer of course is 5 (since 5 x 5 = 25).

We say that the square root of 25 is 5 and use the symbol "$\sqrt{}$" like this => $\sqrt{25} = 5$.

It reads as the square root of 25 is 5. Here are some more **examples** :-

$\sqrt{16} = 4$ (*since 4 x 4 = 16*)	$\sqrt{81} = 9$ (*since 9 x 9 = 81*)
$\sqrt{1\cdot 44} = 1\cdot 2$ (*since 1·2 x 1·2 = 1·44*)	$\sqrt{6^2 + 8^2} = \sqrt{36 + 64} = \sqrt{100} = 10$.

5. If $m = 3$ and $n = 4$, find the values of :-

    a m^2 b $m^2 + n^2$ c $(n - m)^2$ d $\sqrt{n}$

    e $(n + m)^2$ f $2m^2$ g $\sqrt{3mn}$ h $(m - 2)^2$

    i $35 - 2n^2$ j $40 - 4m^2$ k $\sqrt{m^2 + n^2}$ l $(n^2 - m^2)^2$.

6. If $x = 4$, $y = -2$ and $z = 1$, find :-

    a $5x + y$ b $y + 5z$ c x^2

    d $10 + 8z^2$ e $x^2 + 3z^2$ f $z^2 + 2x^2$

    g $5x^2 + 10z + y$ h $6z^2 + y - x$ i $3x^2 + y - 30z$.

7. Given $a = 2$, $b = 8$, $c = 10$ and $d = -4$, find :-

    a $\frac{1}{2}a$ b $\frac{1}{4}b$ c $\frac{2}{5}c$

    d $\frac{1}{5}(a + b)$ e $\frac{1}{3}(c + d)$ f $\frac{1}{8}(c - a)$

    g $\frac{1}{4}(b - 2a)$ h $\sqrt{\dfrac{b + c}{2}}$ i $2c^2 - 25b$.

8. Find the value of the letter asked :-

    a $P = q - r$ find P,   when $q = 9\cdot5$ and $r = 2\cdot5$.

    b $D = S \times T$ find D,   when $S = 60$ and $T = 1\cdot5$.

    c $V = Ah$ find V,   when $A = 40$ and $h = 2\cdot5$.

    d $D = e \times f \times g$ find D,   when $e = 100$, $f = 5$ and $g = 0\cdot5$.

    e $N = z - 100v$ find N,   when $z = 500$ and $v = 4\cdot4$.

    $P = q - r$
    $P = 9\cdot5 - 2\cdot5$
    $P = \ldots..$

Constructing and Evaluating Formulae

Examples :-

1. Julie is withdrawing money from an ATM.

   She withdraws x lots of £5 notes and y lots of £10 notes.

   a   Write down a formula in terms of x and y for W, the total amount she withdraws.

   b   When $x = 4$ and $y = 3$, find the actual amount withdrawn.

a $W = 5x + 10y$	b $W = 5x + 10y$
	$= 5 \times 4 + 10 \times 3$
	$= 50$
	£50 withdrawn.

2.   An **isosceles** triangle is shown opposite.

   a   Write a formula for its perimeter, P, in terms of m and n .

   b   Calculate its perimeter when $m = 9$ and $n = 5$.

   c   Find n when $P = 52$ and $m = 20$.

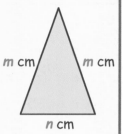

m cm m cm

n cm

a $P = 2m + n$	b $P = 2m + n$	c $P = 2m + n$
	$= 2 \times 9 + 5$	$52 = 40 + n$
	$= 23$	$n = 12.$
	Perimeter = 23 cm.	

Exercise 2

1.   A truck weighs x tonnes when empty. If rocks weighing y tonnes are lifted, its loaded weight becomes W tonnes.

   a   Write a formula for W, in terms of x and y.

   b   Find W when $x = 2 \cdot 75$ and $y = 2 \cdot 25$.

   c   Calculate y when $W = 9$ and $x = 6 \cdot 5$.

2.      A plank of wood is m metres long. When n metres have been sawn off, the remaining length is L metres.

   a   Write a formula for L, in terms of m and n.

   b   Find L when $m = 3 \cdot 75$ and $n = 1 \cdot 5$.

   c   Calculate m when $L = 10$ and $n = 2 \cdot 75$.

3. "To find the average speed (S mph) for a journey travelled, divide the distance travelled (D miles) by the time taken (T hrs)."

    a   Write a formula for S, in terms of D and T.

    b   Find S when D = 180 and T = 3.

    c   Calculate the distance travelled at a speed oF 30 mph for 4 hours.

4.

    The cost £C of hiring a shredder from a garden store is £k per day, plus a payment of £10.

    a   Write a formula for C, in terms of k , when hiring for 5 days.

    b   Find C when k = 6.

5. To change from degrees Celsius (°C) to degrees Fahrenheit (°F) use the formula :-

    "Multiply the temperature in °C by 1·8, then add 32 to the answer".

    a   Write a formula for changing from C to F. F = ... × .... + ...

    b   Use your formula to change 10°C into degrees Fahrenheit.

6. The recommended time,(T) minutes, to cook a ham joint in the oven is g minutes **per pound**, then add an extra h minutes at the end.

    a   Write a formula for T, in terms of g and h showing the time needed to cook a 10 pound joint of ham.

    b   Find T when g = 20 and h = 15.

7. a   Write down a formula, in terms of a, b and c, for finding the perimeter P of this shape.

    b   Find P when a = 5, b = 4 and c = 8.

    c   Calculate c when P = 50, a = 10 and b = 7.

    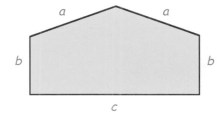

8.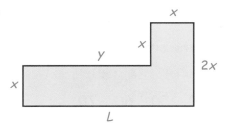

    a   Write down the length of the side marked L in terms of x and y.

    b   Write down a formula, in terms of x and y, for finding the perimeter P of this shape.

    c   Find P when x = 3 and y = 10.

9. a   Write down a formula, in terms of m and n, for finding the perimeter P of this shape.

    b   Find P when m = 8 and n = 4.

    c   Calculate n when P = 40 and m = 10.

    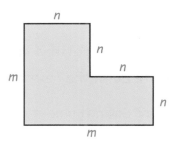

When asked to write the next three numbers in this pattern :-

$$1, \ 3, \ 5, \ 7, \ 9, \ \ldots \ldots$$

=>   you would write 11, 13, 15.

A list of numbers which come in a definite order is called a Sequence.

> The sequence 1, 3, 5, 7, 9, ... shown above is the sequence of **odd** numbers.

Rules :-   The **RULE** "add on 2" is used to allow you to move from one odd number to the next **consecutive** odd number.

In the same way, the same **RULE** "add on 2" is used to allow you to move from one **even** number to the next.

=>   the next **even** number after 54 is 56.

But... not all rules are simply "add on".

Example 1 :-   What about the sequence   3, 6, 12, 24, ... ?

Can you see here the **RULE** is "times by 2" ?

=> the next number in the sequence is 48 !

Example 2 :-

The rule for pattern 2, 7, 12, 17, 22, ... is "start at 2 and go up by 5 each time".

Exercise 3

1.   Describe the following pattern of numbers :- 6, 9, 12, 15, 18, ...

Copy :- this is the "...." times table, starting with the number "....".

2.   Describe each of these sequences using a sentence like the one shown in Question 1.

   a   4, 8, 12, 16, 20, ...   b   6, 12, 18, 24, 30, ...

   c   15, 20, 25, 30, 35, ...   d   30, 40, 50, 60, 70, ...

   e   18, 27, 36, 45, ...   f   56, 48, 40, 32, 24, ...

3. Look at the pattern in Question 2a :-   4, 8, 12, 16, 20.

Write down the next **3 numbers** in this pattern.

4. Write down the next 3 terms in the pattern shown in Question 2b. 2c, 2d, 2e and 2f.

5. Describe the following sequence of numbers :–   8, 11, 14, 17, 20, 23, ...

   Copy :–   "Begin at the number "...." and go up by "...." each time".

6. Describe each of the following sequences by saying :–

   "Begin at the number "...." and go up (down) by "...." each time".

   a   5, 7, 9, 11, 13, ...   b   4, 7, 10, 13, 16, ...

   c   8, 12, 16, 20, 24, ...   d   7, 17, 27, 37, 47, ...

   e   83, 88, 93, 98, 103, ...   f   2, 2·5, 3, 3·5, 4, ...

   g   14, 15, ..., 17, 18, ..., 20, ...   h   52, 48, 44, 40, ...

7. Write down the next 3 terms for each of the patterns in Question 65.

8. Look at this pattern made with matches.

   1 triangle   2 triangles   3 triangles

   3 matches   6 matches   9 matches

   a   Draw the pattern showing the matches needed for 4 triangles.

   b   The pattern for the number of matches needed is 3, 6, 9, 12, ...
       Copy this sequence and fill in the next 3 numbers.

   c   Copy the following and complete :–

       "Start with 3 matches for 1 triangle and add on ... matches for each extra triangle".

   d   How many matches are needed for 10 triangles ?

9. Mrs Martin makes sponge cakes which she decorates with cherries.

   1 sponge cake   2 sponge cakes   3 sponge cakes
   (6 cherries)   (12 cherries)   (18 cherries)

   a   How many cherries are needed for 4 sponge cakes ?

   b   Copy the pattern 6, 12, 18 and write down the next 3 terms.

   c   Copy the following and complete :–

       "Start with "...." cherries for 1 sponge cake and
       add on "...." cherries for each extra sponge cake.

   d   How many cherries are needed for 9 sponge cakes ?

Revisit - Review - Revise

1. Work out the value of these expressions when $a = 4$, $b = 3$ and $c = 2$:-

   a $5a + b$
   b $6b - a$
   c $a^2 + c^2$
   d abc

   e $(b - c)^2$
   f $3a^2$
   g $\sqrt{a}$
   h $\dfrac{a - c}{b}$

   i $\dfrac{3a}{bc}$
   j $\dfrac{ab^2}{c^2}$
   k $\sqrt{5a - 2c}$
   l $\sqrt{a^2 + 6b + c}$.

   > *(Remember $\sqrt{16} = 4$, since $4 \times 4 = 16$, $\sqrt{100} = 10$ since $10 \times 10 = 100$).

2. For each formula, work out the value of the capital letter :-

   a $M = c + d$ Find M, when $c = 2\cdot5$ and $d = 1\cdot75$.

   b $T = \dfrac{pq}{r}$ Find T, when $p = 6$, $q = 15$ and $r = 9$.

   c $W = \sqrt{efg}$ Find W, when $e = 1$, $f = 2\cdot5$ and $g = 10$.

   d $G = 3m^2 + n$ Find G, when $m = 5$ and $n = -25$.

3. To change a number of kilometres to miles :-

   > Multiply the kilometres by **five**, then divide your answer by **eight**.

SEASIDE HIGHWAY	
Sandy Beach	5
Bill's Lagoon	9
Sandstone Cliffs	22
Golden Blue Beach	45

   a Write a formula for changing kilometres (k) to miles (M).

   $$M = \dots \times k \div \dots$$

   b Change 320 kilometres to miles.

4. The cost of hiring a jet ski for a number of hours is given by the rule :-

   > The total cost (£C) is **ten** times the number of hours (h) **plus** a fixed payment (£p).

   a Write a formula for finding the total cost of jet skiing when you know what the cost is per hour and you know what payment you have to make at the start :-

   $$C = \dots\dots\dots\dots\dots\dots\dots$$

   b Work out the total cost of hiring a jet ski for 3 hours with a fixed payment of £25.

5.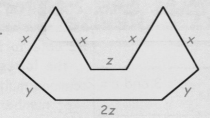

a Construct a formula for finding *P*, the **perimeter** of the shape shown opposite. (*Units are in cm.*)

b Find *P*, when *x* = 8, *y* = 6 and *z* = 5.

c Find *z*, when *P* = 136, *x* = 20 and *y* = 10.

6. Describe each pattern of numbers carefully and write down the next three numbers each time :–

a 12, 16, 20, 24, 28, ...

b 2, 16, 30, 44, 58, ...

c 74, 69, 64, 59, ...

d 2·3, 3·7, 5·1, 6·5, 7·9, ...

7. A boy is building a pattern with LEGO bricks. The first 3 patterns are shown.

a How many bricks are needed for the 4th pattern ?

b Copy the pattern "6, 12, 18, ..." and write down the next 3 terms.

c Copy the following and complete :–

> "Start with "...." bricks for pattern number 1 and add on "...." bricks for each new pattern number.

d How many bricks will there be in the 7th pattern ?

8. Jenny's rate of pay is shown in the table below.

No. of Hours (*H*)	1	2	3	4	5
Wage in £'s (*W*)	7·50	15·00	22·50	?	?

a What is Jenny's wage for :– (i) 4 hours   (ii) 5 hours ?

b Write a formula connecting *W* and *H* using symbols.

c Use your formula to find Jenny's wage for working 10 hours.

d One week, Jenny's total pay was £300. How many hours had she worked ?

Chapter 6 — Multiples and Factors

Multiples & Lowest Common Multiple

Be able to find the lowest common multiple of numbers (l.c.m.).

In Year 5, we found out the meaning of the word multiple.

Examples :-

| The 1st seven multiples of 9 :- | (0), 9, 18, 27, 36, 45, 54. |
| The 1st five multiples of 4 :- | (0), 4, 8, 12, 16. |

* Since "0" is always a multiple, *(the trivial multiple)*, in this chapter we will ignore it.

In the following exercise you will not only be finding multiples of numbers, but also the lowest common multiple (l.c.m.) of these numbers.

Exercise 1

1. List (**not** including 0) :-

   a   the first **ten** multiples of 4

   b   the first **eight** multiples of 3

   c   the first **nine** multiples of 5

   d   the first **seven** multiples of 10.

2. a   Write down all the multiples of **3** between **8** and **25**.

   b   Write down all the multiples of **6** between **29** and **61**.

   c   Write down all the multiples of **8** between **23** and **73**.

   d   Write down all the multiples of **9** between **53** and **100**.

3. a   List the first **ten** multiples of **2**.

   b   There is a special name for the "**multiples of 2**". What is it ?

   c   Subtract 1 from each of the numbers you have in part **a** and write them down.
   Is this a set of multiples ?

   d   What is the special name for this group of numbers ?

4. {14, 21, 28, 35, 42} could be described as "the multiples of 7 from 14 to 42".
   Describe the following sets of numbers in the same way :-

   a   {44, 46, 48, 50, 52, 54, 56}   b   {35, 40, 45, 50, 55, 60}

   c   {120, 130, 140, 150, 160}   d   {60, 66, 72, 78, 84, 90}

   e   {81, 90, 99, 108, 117}   f   {60, 80, 100, 120, 140}

   g   {15, 30, 45, 60, 75}   h   {600, 650, 700, 750, 800}

   i   {39, 52, 65, 78, 91}   j   {500, 750, 1000, 1250, 1500}.

5. a   List the first twelve multiples of 3.

   b   List the first twelve multiples of 4.

   c   From **a** and **b**, write down the multiples which are "**common**" to both lists.
        (*The numbers that are multiples of both 3 and 4*).

   d   What is the **lowest** number that is a multiple of both 3 and 4 ?

   This is called the "**lowest common multiple**" of 3 and 4 (*the l.c.m.*)

6. a   List the first ten multiples of 4.

   b   List the first ten multiples of 6.

   c   List the common multiples of 4 and 6.

   d   What is the l.c.m. of 4 and 6 ?

7. Find the l.c.m. of each of the following pairs of numbers :–
   (Hint :–   *go through the multiples of the larger of the two numbers until
              you reach a number into which the smaller number divides exactly*).

   a   2 and 5   b   6 and 3   c   4 and 9   d   3 and 4

   e   9 and 6   f   4 and 10   g   5 and 6   h   7 and 8

   i   10 and 6   j   9 and 8   k   9 and 12   l   4 and 11.

8. Find the l.c.m. of   a   2, 3 and 5   b   3, 4 and 8   c   2, 5 and 8

                         d   2, 5 and 10   e   2, 3 and 7   f   3, 6 and 9   g   6, 8 and 20.

9. Howard's timetable for his golf lessons is :-

   > • Driver lessons every 2 days.
   >
   > • Putter lessons every 4 days.
   >
   > • Sand Bunker lessons every 5 days.

   He had a lesson on all three on the same day.

   When will he next have all 3 lessons on the same day again ?

10. A Christmas tree's lights are set so that :-

   > • the blue lights flash every 6 seconds.
   >
   > • the green lights flash every 8 seconds.
   >
   > • the red lights flash every 10 seconds.

   When they are switched on, they all flash together.

   When will they all next flash together again ?

Factors & Highest Common Factor

Be able to find the highest common factor of numbers (h.c.f.).

1, 2, 4 and 8 are all the whole numbers which divide exactly into 8.

You already know that these numbers are called the factors of 8.

Examples :- | The factors of 6 are :- 1, 2, 3, 6.
The factors of 12 are :- 1, 2, 3, 4, 6, 12.

* The factors of any number always includes the number itself and 1.

In the following exercise, you will not only be finding factors of numbers, but also the highest common factor (h.c.f.) of these numbers.

Exercise 2

1.   The number 10 has four factors. What are they ?

2.   List all six factors of 28.

3.   List the six factors of 18.

Factors usually occur in pairs. In this example, 1 and 24 are a pair, as are 2 and 12. 3 and 8 and 4 and 6 are also pairs.

1   2   3   4   6   8   12   24

Using this pairing helps you not to miss out any of the factors.

4.   Copy and complete the following, showing all the factors of 20.

1,   2,   4, ..., ..., ...

5.   Use this method to find all the factors of :-

a	8	b	24	c	27	d	22
e	30	f	31	g	32	h	50
i	67	j	40	k	45	l	60.

*Note that in each case, there is an even number of factors.

6.   For each of these, list all the factors and state how many factors each number has :-

a	9	b	49	c	36	d	4
e	25	f	64	g	16	h	100.

7. a   Check that your answer to each question in Q6 has an **odd** number of factors.

    b   What is the special name for these numbers ?   {4, 9, 16, 25, 36, ...}

    c   Can you explain why there will always be an **odd** number of factors for
        this type of number ?

8. 36 apples are laid out in rows.

    One way is to have 4 rows of 9 apples.

    State a few other ways of laying out the
    36 apples.   (2 rows of ...., etc)

9. a   List all the factors of 12.   {1, 2. .... }

    b   List all the factors of 18.   {1, 2. .... }

    c   Make a list of the common factors of 12 and 18, (*those that appear in both lists*).

    d   What is the largest of these numbers ?

    This number is referred to as the **highest common factor** (or h.c.f.) of 12 and 18.

10. a   List all the factors of 15.   b   List all the factors of 20.

    c   Make a list of the **common factors**.

    d   What is the h.c.f. of 15 and 20 ?

11. Find the **highest common factor** for each of the following :-

    a   6 and 9   b   12 and 20   c   20 and 30   d   24 and 28

    e   24 and 36   f   40 and 100   g   17 and 34   h   18 and 42.

12. Find the h.c.f. of :-

    a   7 and 23   b   31 and 41   c   11 and 17   d   53 and 67.

13. Find the h.c.f. of :-

    a   8, 12, 20   b   10, 20, 45   c   14, 35, 56   d   24, 32, 40.

14. A full revolution is divided into 360 parts. Each part is called "1 degree".

    The choice of 360 is no accident.

    The reason is that 360 has many factors (**24** in fact) and
    this means a circle can be divided equally in lots of ways.

    Write down all 24 factors of 360.

    360°

15. There is only 1 number which is both a **multiple** and a **factor** of 1000. What number ?

What you should already know about PRIME NUMBERS :-

Every number can be divided by itself and 1.

but

Every prime number can only be divided by itself and 1.

A prime number is a number with exactly 2 factors.

Be able to list all the prime numbers up to 200.

I'm in my prime

Exercise 3

1. Write all the factors of 10. Why is 10 not a prime number ?

2. Is 2 a prime number ? Give a reason for your answer.

3. For each of the following numbers, list all of its factors, and state whether or not it is a prime number.

a	5	b	16	c	15	d	17
e	23	f	27	g	29	h	35
i	44	j	47	k	51	l	62.

4. Write down all 25 prime numbers under 100.

5. a Make a neat large copy of this number square showing all the numbers from 101 to 200.

   b Score out every multiple of 2, 3, 5 and 7.

   c Now score out every multiple of 11.

   d Lastly score out every multiple of 13.

   e Circle all the remaining numbers – these are the primes from 101 to 200.

   f Make a list of all the primes from 101 to 200. (*There are 21 of them*).

101	102	103	104	510	106	107	108	109	110
111	112	113	114	115	116	117	118	119	120
121	122	123	124	125	126	127	128	129	130
131	132	133	134	135	136	137	138	139	140
141	142	143	144	145	146	147	148	149	150
151	152	153	154	155	156	157	158	159	160
161	162	163	164	165	166	167	168	169	170
171	172	173	174	175	176	177	178	179	180
181	182	183	184	185	186	187	188	189	190
191	192	193	194	195	196	197	198	199	200

It is not difficult to check whether a number up to about 400 is a prime or not.

You simply have to check if the number can be divided by the primes 2, 3, 5, 7, 11, 13, 17 and 19 and if none of these primes divide into it, then the number must be prime.

The study of prime numbers has fascinated mathematicians for hundreds of years.

Extension

Be able to express a number as a product of primes.

Every number is either prime or composite, except for 0 which is neither.

If it is composite, like 18, it can be expressed as a "product of primes".

This means that a composite number can be rewritten as a list of prime numbers multiplied together.

$$18 = 2 \times 9 = 2 \times 3 \times 3 \qquad \text{(3 prime numbers)}$$
$$40 = 2 \times 20 = 2 \times 2 \times 2 \times 5 \qquad \text{(4 prime numbers)}$$
$$64 = 2 \times 32 = 2 \times 2 \times 2 \times 2 \times 2 \times 2 \qquad \text{(6 prime numbers)}$$

Here is an easy way of doing it for the number 40 :-

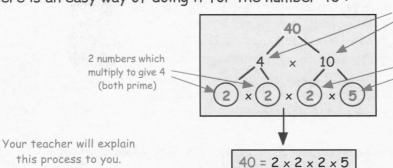

(2 numbers which multiply to give 40)

2 numbers which multiply to give 4 (both prime)

2 numbers which multiply to give 10 (both prime)

Your teacher will explain this process to you.

$$40 = 2 \times 2 \times 2 \times 5$$

This is called a Prime Factor Tree.

Exercise 4

1. Copy this diagram and complete it to show the prime decomposition of the number 60.

    So $60 = 2 \times 2 \times \ldots \times \ldots$

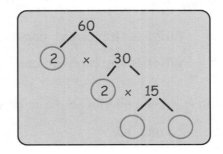

2. Copy and complete these prime factor trees :-

a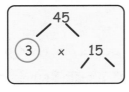

$$45 = 3 \times \ldots \times \ldots$$

b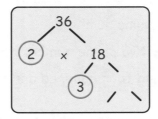

$$36 = 2 \times 3 \times \ldots \times \ldots$$

c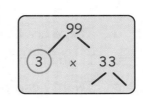

$$99 = 3 \times \ldots \times \ldots$$

3. Use a similar method to find the prime decomposition of the following numbers :-

a 16	b 18	c 20	d 27
e 30	f 54	g 45	h 48
i 68	j 98	k 100	l 162.

1. Write down :-

   a   the first ten non-zero multiples of :-   (i) 4   (ii) 5.

   b   the lowest common multiple (l.c.m.) of 4 and 5.

2. Write down the lowest common multiple (l.c.m.) of :-

   a   6 and 9   b   15 and 25   c   4, 5 and 6.

3. Write down :-

   a   the factors of 10 and of 15

   b   the highest common factor (h.c.f.) of 10 and 15.

4. Write down the highest common factor (h.c.f.) of :-

   a   18 and 24   b   20 and 70   c   27, 45 and 108.

5. a   Write down all the numbers, under 10, that have exactly two factors.

   b   Write down three numbers with exactly three factors.

6. a   What is the lowest common multiple of the numbers 2, 3, 4, 5, 6 and 7 ?

   b   What is the highest common factor of the numbers 95, 96, 97, 98 and 99 ?

7. Write down all the prime numbers between :-

   a   20 and 30   b   80 and 110   c   140 and 160.

8. Write down TRUE or FALSE for each of the following statements :-

   a   There are no even prime numbers.

   b   If you multiply any two prime numbers, the answer you get is always a prime.

   c   Twenty one thousand four hundred and forty five is NOT a prime number.

9. Write down why each of these numbers are definitely not prime numbers :-

   a   483 792   b   sixteen million   c   99 999.

10. a   Write down the highest common factor (h.c.f.) of 17 and 23.

    b   Make a statement about the highest common factor of ANY two prime numbers.

Chapter 7

Equivalent Fractions   Revision

Be able to find an equivalent fraction.

Remember

A fraction consists of two parts :-

$$\frac{3}{5} \longleftarrow \text{numerator}$$
$$\phantom{\frac{3}{5}} \longleftarrow \text{denominator}$$

You can obtain an **equivalent** fraction by multiplying the top and bottom of a fraction by the same number.

Example :-

$$\frac{3}{5} \text{ can become } \frac{3}{5} \begin{array}{c} \times 2 \\ \times 2 \end{array} = \frac{6}{10}$$

You can **simplify** a fraction by dividing the top and bottom of the fraction by a suitable number.

Example :-

$$\frac{12}{15} \text{ simplified is } \frac{12}{15} \begin{array}{c} \div 3 \\ \div 3 \end{array} = \frac{4}{5}$$

Exercise 1

1. Find **two** equivalent fractions for each of the following :-

   a $\frac{1}{2}$ b $\frac{1}{3}$ c $\frac{3}{4}$ d $\frac{2}{3}$

   e $\frac{1}{10}$ f $\frac{2}{5}$ g $\frac{5}{7}$ h $\frac{1}{100}$

   i $\frac{9}{20}$ j $\frac{7}{11}$ k $\frac{8}{19}$ l $\frac{17}{21}$

   m $\frac{34}{35}$ n $\frac{3}{311}$ o $\frac{107}{115}$ p $\frac{11}{8}$.

2. Simplify **fully** (*where possible*) :-

   a $\frac{6}{8}$ b $\frac{16}{18}$ c $\frac{12}{15}$ d $\frac{15}{30}$

   e $\frac{18}{24}$ f $\frac{36}{72}$ g $\frac{39}{52}$ h $\frac{39}{51}$

   i $\frac{135}{150}$ j $\frac{35}{42}$ k $\frac{13}{131}$ l $\frac{1200}{1500}$

   m $\frac{180}{3600}$ n $\frac{60}{900}$ o $\frac{108}{909}$ p $\frac{17}{51}$.

Be able to convert
between improper
fractions and
mixed numbers.

Remember ..

Example :- Changing an improper fraction to a mixed number :-

$\frac{23}{4}$ really means $23 \div 4$ => $4\overline{)23}$ $\begin{smallmatrix}5\end{smallmatrix}$ (remainder 3) => $5\frac{3}{4}$

note :- the 3
is divided by
the 4

$\frac{23}{4}$ = ?

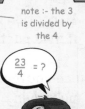

Example :- Changing a mixed number to an improper fraction :-

$6\frac{2}{3}$ = ((6 × 3) + 2) thirds = 20 "thirds" = $\frac{20}{3}$

Exercise 2

1. Copy and complete the following :-

   a $\frac{11}{2}$ really means $11 \div 2$ => $2\overline{)11}$ (.... remainder ....)   => $5\frac{..}{2}$

   b $\frac{17}{3}$ really means .... ÷ ....   => $3\overline{)...}$ (.... remainder ....)   =>   .... .

2. Change each of the following to mixed numbers and **simplify** where possible :-

   a $\frac{17}{4}$ b $\frac{23}{5}$ c $\frac{34}{4}$ d $\frac{34}{10}$

   e $\frac{76}{6}$ f $\frac{68}{8}$ g $\frac{75}{30}$ h $\frac{55}{3}$

   i $\frac{39}{9}$ j $\frac{50}{16}$ k $\frac{51}{17}$ l $\frac{275}{100}$.

3. Copy and complete :-

   a $4\frac{2}{3}$ = ((3 × 4) + 2) "thirds" = 14 "thirds" = $\frac{..}{3}$

   b $8\frac{1}{9}$ = ((... × ...) + ...) "ninths" = ... "ninths" = $\frac{..}{..}$.

4. Change each of the following mixed numbers to improper fractions :-

   a $2\frac{1}{2}$ b $4\frac{1}{5}$ c $7\frac{2}{3}$ d $10\frac{2}{5}$

   e $15\frac{3}{7}$ f $8\frac{8}{9}$ g $7\frac{9}{10}$ h $20\frac{19}{20}$.

Comparing Fractions   Revision

To decide which is the larger of two fractions, you sometimes need to change one or more of the fractions to an equivalent fraction *(so that the denominators become the same)*.

Example 1 :-

Which is larger $\frac{1}{2}$ or $\frac{5}{8}$?

If we change $\frac{1}{2}$ to $\frac{4}{8}$ we can easily compare the two fractions.

$\frac{4}{8} < \frac{5}{8}$ which means $\frac{1}{2} < \frac{5}{8}$.

Remember :-
> means greater than.
< means smaller than.

Example 2 :-

Write these in order *(smallest first)* :-

$$\frac{3}{5}, \qquad \frac{7}{10}, \qquad \frac{1}{2}$$

Change all to tenths * :-

$$\frac{3}{5} = \frac{6}{10}, \qquad \frac{7}{10}, \qquad \frac{1}{2} = \frac{5}{10}$$

answer $\frac{1}{2}, \frac{3}{5}, \frac{7}{10}$.

* this is the lowest number 5, 10 and 2 will divide into - *(the l.c.m. of 2, 5 and 10)*

Exercise 3

1. Use <, > or = to fill in the missing symbol between each pair of fractions :-

   a $\frac{1}{2} \dots \frac{1}{4}$ b $\frac{3}{5} \dots \frac{7}{10}$ c $\frac{11}{18} \dots \frac{2}{3}$ d $\frac{9}{11} \dots \frac{27}{33}$.

2. Use <, > or = to fill in the missing symbol between each pair of fractions :-
   (This time you need to change both fractions !)

   a $\frac{1}{2} \dots \frac{2}{3}$ *(change both to $\frac{..}{6}$'s)*   b $\frac{3}{4} \dots \frac{5}{6}$ *(change both to $\frac{..}{12}$'s)*

   c $\frac{3}{8} \dots \frac{1}{3}$ d $\frac{4}{5} \dots \frac{5}{7}$ e $\frac{6}{27} \dots \frac{2}{9}$ f $\frac{5}{12} \dots \frac{4}{9}$.

3. Write each set of fractions in order *(starting with the smallest)* :-

   a $\frac{1}{2}, \quad \frac{2}{5}, \quad \frac{2}{3}$ *(change all to $\frac{..}{30}$'s)*   b $\frac{2}{3}, \quad \frac{3}{4}, \quad \frac{4}{5}$ *(change all to $\frac{..}{60}$'s)*

   c $\frac{7}{2}, \quad \frac{21}{8}, \quad \frac{8}{3}, \quad \frac{27}{12}$ d $\frac{17}{20}, \quad \frac{9}{10}, \quad \frac{3}{4}, \quad \frac{3}{5}$.

4. Three friends wanted to share their lottery win.

   Bill wanted $\frac{2}{5}$, Tim wanted $\frac{3}{8}$ and Archie wanted $\frac{5}{16}$ of the winnings.

   Can they do this ? *(Explain your answer)*

Adding and Subtracting Fractions

Be able to add or subtract any two or more fractions.

Remember the Golden Rule :-

The denominators MUST be the same if you wish to add or subtract.

Question :- What do we do if the denominators are not the same ?

Answer :- Change each fraction so that they do have the same denominator.

Example 1 :-   Find $\frac{2}{3} + \frac{1}{2}$.   [they do not add to give $\frac{3}{5}$ ✗]

- the denominators 3 and 2 are not the same.

- what is the l.c.m. (*lowest common multiple*) of 3 and 2 —> 6.

- we must change $\frac{2}{3}$ and $\frac{1}{2}$ to $\frac{1}{6}$'s.

$$\frac{2}{3} + \frac{1}{2}$$

note —> $$\frac{4}{6} + \frac{3}{6}$$ <— note

$$= \frac{7}{6} = 1\frac{1}{6}$$

$$(\frac{2}{3} = \frac{?}{6}) —> ? = 4$$

$$(\frac{1}{2} = \frac{?}{6}) —> ? = 3$$

Example 2 :-

(8 and 5 divide into 40)

$$\frac{5}{8} - \frac{1}{5}$$

$$\frac{?}{40} - \frac{?}{40}$$

$$= \frac{25}{40} - \frac{8}{40}$$

$$= \frac{17}{40}$$

Example 3 :-

(6 and 4 divide into 12)

$$\frac{5}{6} + \frac{3}{4}$$

$$\frac{?}{12} + \frac{?}{12}$$

$$= \frac{10}{12} + \frac{9}{12}$$

$$= \frac{19}{12} = 1\frac{7}{12}$$

Exercise 4

1.   Copy each of the following and complete :-

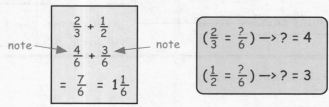

a $\frac{1}{7} + \frac{2}{3}$

$$= \frac{?}{21} + \frac{?}{21}$$

$$= \frac{?}{21}$$

b $\frac{4}{5} - \frac{2}{3}$

$$= \frac{?}{15} - \frac{?}{15}$$

$$= \frac{?}{15}$$

c $\frac{7}{8} - \frac{3}{4}$

$$= \frac{7}{8} - \frac{?}{8}$$

$$= \frac{?}{8}$$

d $\frac{3}{4} + \frac{1}{3}$

$$= \frac{?}{12} + \frac{?}{12}$$

$$= \frac{?}{12} = 1\frac{?}{12}$$

2.   Show how to simplify the following :-

a $\frac{2}{3} + \frac{1}{5}$ b $\frac{3}{4} - \frac{1}{2}$ c $\frac{5}{8} + \frac{2}{3}$ d $\frac{4}{5} + \frac{1}{2}$

2. e $\frac{5}{6} - \frac{1}{3}$ f $\frac{3}{4} - \frac{2}{3}$ g $\frac{7}{10} + \frac{2}{5}$ h $\frac{7}{9} - \frac{1}{2}$.

3. Show your working here :-

   a $\frac{1}{2} + \frac{1}{3} + \frac{1}{4}$ b $\frac{5}{6} - \frac{1}{2} - \frac{1}{3}$ c $\frac{2}{3} + \frac{3}{5} - \frac{1}{2}$.

Mixed Fractions :-   Deal with the whole numbers first - then the fractions.

Example 4 :-

$$2\frac{1}{2} + 3\frac{2}{3}$$
$$= 5 + (\frac{1}{2} + \frac{2}{3})$$
$$= 5 + (\frac{3}{6} + \frac{4}{6})$$
$$= 5\frac{7}{6}$$
$$= 6\frac{1}{6}$$

Example 5 :-

$$7\frac{7}{8} - 4\frac{2}{3}$$
$$= 3 + (\frac{7}{8} - \frac{2}{3})$$
$$= 3 + (\frac{21}{24} - \frac{16}{24})$$
$$= 3\frac{5}{24}$$

Example 6 :-

$$4\frac{3}{4} + 3\frac{5}{6}$$
$$= 7 + (\frac{3}{4} + \frac{5}{6})$$
$$= 7 + (\frac{9}{12} + \frac{10}{12})$$
$$= 7\frac{19}{12}$$
$$= 8\frac{7}{12}$$

---

4. Copy and complete the following :-

   a $8\frac{1}{3} + 2\frac{1}{2}$ b $4\frac{3}{4} - 2\frac{1}{3}$ c $5\frac{7}{8} - 3\frac{1}{4}$ d $9\frac{1}{2} + 1\frac{3}{5}$

   e $2\frac{5}{6} - 1\frac{2}{3}$ f $9\frac{2}{3} + 11\frac{5}{8}$ g $17\frac{1}{5} + 12\frac{1}{4}$ h $51\frac{9}{10} - 50\frac{1}{2}$

   i $16\frac{1}{3} + \frac{7}{9}$ j $14\frac{4}{5} + 10\frac{3}{4}$ k $1\frac{1}{10} + 2\frac{2}{5}$ l $15\frac{1}{4} - 15\frac{1}{6}$

   m $11\frac{5}{6} - 10\frac{1}{4}$ n $12\frac{1}{2} - 10\frac{1}{3}$ o $1\frac{3}{5} - \frac{1}{4}$ p $47\frac{1}{4} - 46\frac{1}{12}$.

5. Copy and complete the following :-

   a
   $$7 - 4\frac{1}{3}$$
   $$= 3 - \frac{1}{3}$$
   (7 – 4) $= 2\frac{..}{3}$

   b
   $$15 - 13\frac{2}{5}$$
   $$= 2 - \frac{2}{5}$$
   $$= 1\frac{..}{5}$$

   c
   $$20 - 17\frac{5}{8}$$
   $$= 3 - \frac{..}{8}$$
   $$= 2\frac{..}{8}$$

   d
   $$14 - 13\frac{3}{5}$$
   $$= ... - \frac{..}{5}$$
   $$= \frac{..}{5}.$$

6. Use the above method to find :-

   a $4 - 1\frac{1}{5}$ b $6 - 3\frac{4}{7}$ c $10 - 5\frac{5}{6}$ d $6 - 4\frac{3}{5}$

   e $5 - 4\frac{7}{10}$ f $35 - 29\frac{3}{8}$ g $12 - 6\frac{5}{7}$ h $8 - 3\frac{1}{3}$.

7. From a 6 metre length of cable, the engineer cut off a piece which was $3\frac{3}{8}$ metres long.

   What was the length of the remaining piece of cable ?

A Problem with Subtraction :- $4\frac{1}{3} - 1\frac{3}{5}$?

- **Step 1 :-**   Subtract whole numbers first —> 3 and $(\frac{1}{3} - \frac{3}{5})$
- **Step 2 :-**   Change both fractions to $\frac{1}{15}$ ths => 3 and $(\frac{5}{15} - \frac{9}{15})$

         (* you cannot take $\frac{9}{15}$ from $\frac{5}{15}$!!!!)

- **Step 3 :-**   Take 1 whole number from the 3 and write it as $\frac{15}{15}$ (= 1)

       —> $3 + (\frac{5}{15} - \frac{9}{15})$

     becomes $2 + \frac{15}{15} + (\frac{5}{15} - \frac{9}{15}) = 2 + \frac{20}{15} - \frac{9}{15}$

                $= 2\frac{11}{15}$

Example 7 :-

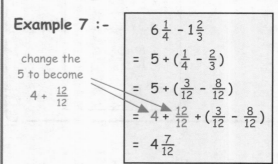

change the
5 to become

$4 + \frac{12}{12}$

$6\frac{1}{4} - 1\frac{2}{3}$

$= 5 + (\frac{1}{4} - \frac{2}{3})$

$= 5 + (\frac{3}{12} - \frac{8}{12})$

$= 4 + \frac{12}{12} + (\frac{3}{12} - \frac{8}{12})$

$= 4\frac{7}{12}$

Example 8 :-

$5\frac{3}{5} - 1\frac{5}{6}$

$= 4 + (\frac{3}{5} - \frac{5}{6})$

$= 4 + (\frac{18}{30} - \frac{25}{30})$

$= 3 + \frac{30}{30} + (\frac{18}{30} - \frac{25}{30})$

$= 3\frac{23}{30}$

8.   Copy and complete the following :-

a $5\frac{2}{5} - 1\frac{1}{2}$

$= 4 + (\frac{2}{5} - \frac{1}{2})$

$= 4 + (\frac{4}{10} - \frac{5}{10})$

$= 3 + \frac{10}{10} + (\frac{4}{10} - \frac{5}{10})$

$= 3\frac{..}{10}$

b $4\frac{3}{8} - 2\frac{3}{5}$

$= 2 + (\frac{3}{8} - \frac{3}{5})$

$= 2 + (\frac{15}{40} - \frac{24}{40})$

$= 1 + \frac{40}{40} + (\frac{15}{40} - \frac{24}{40})$

$= 1\frac{..}{40}$

c $6\frac{1}{5} - \frac{3}{4}$

$= 6 + (\frac{1}{5} - \frac{3}{4})$

$= 6 + (\frac{4}{20} - \frac{15}{20})$

$= 5 + \frac{..}{20} + (\frac{4}{20} - \frac{15}{20})$

$= 5\frac{..}{20}$.

9.   Show all your working here :-

a $4\frac{1}{5} - 1\frac{1}{2}$ b $4\frac{1}{4} - 2\frac{1}{2}$ c $6\frac{3}{8} - 4\frac{3}{4}$ d $6\frac{3}{5} - 1\frac{5}{6}$

e $10\frac{1}{3} - 7\frac{1}{2}$ f $6\frac{1}{7} - 1\frac{1}{2}$ g $8\frac{1}{3} - 3\frac{7}{10}$ h $8\frac{1}{6} - 5\frac{2}{5}$.

10.   What is the difference in each of the following hat sizes :-

a $7\frac{3}{4}$ and $6\frac{1}{2}$ b $6\frac{1}{2}$ and $6\frac{5}{8}$ c $8\frac{3}{4}$ and $6\frac{7}{8}$?

11.      I had flown $4\frac{3}{4}$ hours of a $7\frac{1}{2}$ hour flight to New York. How much longer had I still to travel ?

1. Write down **three equivalent fractions** for :-

   a $\frac{1}{4}$ b $\frac{2}{5}$ c $\frac{4}{9}$ d $\frac{1}{15}$.

2. Find and **simplify** where possible :-

   a $\frac{4}{7} + \frac{1}{7}$ b $\frac{7}{10} - \frac{1}{5}$ c $\frac{3}{4} + \frac{3}{8}$ d $\frac{1}{2} + \frac{1}{8}$

   e $\frac{1}{3} + \frac{1}{2}$ f $\frac{1}{4} - \frac{1}{5}$ g $\frac{2}{3} + \frac{5}{6}$ h $\frac{4}{5} - \frac{3}{7}$.

3. Find :-   a $\frac{1}{2} + \frac{1}{3} + \frac{1}{5}$ b $\frac{1}{5} + \frac{1}{6} + \frac{1}{2}$ c $\frac{5}{6} - \frac{1}{7} - \frac{1}{2}$.

4. Change each of the following to an **improper fraction** :-

   a $2\frac{1}{4}$ b $5\frac{2}{3}$ c $11\frac{5}{8}$ d $17\frac{3}{10}$.

5. Change each of the following to a **mixed number** :-

   a $\frac{9}{2}$ b $\frac{17}{5}$ c $\frac{47}{7}$ d $\frac{176}{10}$.

6. Find each of the following, leaving your answer as a **mixed number** :-

   a $\frac{9}{10} + \frac{7}{10}$ b $1\frac{2}{7} + 2\frac{4}{7}$ c $5\frac{9}{10} - 1\frac{3}{10}$ d $4\frac{4}{5} - 2\frac{1}{5}$

   e $8\frac{1}{4} + \frac{5}{8}$ f $6\frac{5}{6} - 5\frac{1}{3}$ g $12\frac{3}{4} - 7\frac{1}{3}$ h $11\frac{8}{9} + 1\frac{1}{2}$

   i $5\frac{1}{4} - 1\frac{1}{6}$ j $4\frac{1}{3} - 2\frac{4}{7}$ k $9 - 2\frac{9}{10}$ l $11\frac{1}{2} - 10\frac{4}{7}$.

7. Wendy set out to run a marathon which was approximately $26\frac{1}{5}$ miles long.

   She pulled a hamstring muscle after $17\frac{1}{2}$ miles and stopped.

   How far short of the finishing line was she then ?

8.    Calculate the **perimeter** of this triangle.

   $4\frac{1}{3}$ cm $3\frac{1}{4}$ cm $5\frac{1}{5}$ cm

9. Rewrite this set of fractions in order, **smallest first** :- $\frac{5}{8}$, $\frac{3}{4}$, $\frac{9}{16}$, $\frac{1}{2}$.

 # Chapter 8

 **Coordinates in 4 Quadrants**

Be able to plot a point with given coordinate in any quadrant.

Revision :– You should know what a Coordinate diagram, (or a **Cartesian** diagram), looks like.

Remember :–

- x–axis (*or horizontal axis*).

- y–axis (*or vertical axis*).

- The **origin** (O).

P is 3 (*right*) and 4 (*up*) from the origin.

=> P(3, 4),   has x-coordinate 3 and y-coordinate 4.

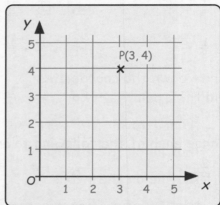

If we now extend the set of x and y axes **backwards** and **downwards**, we create four areas where we can plot points. These are called the **4 QUADRANTS**.

Look at the numbers on the x–axes and y–axes.

They now include **NEGATIVE** values.

The point Q is 4 (*to the right*) and 2 (*down*) from the origin

—> Q(4, –2).

The point R is 2 (*to the left*) and 3 (*up*) from the origin

—> R(–2, 3).

The point S is 4 (*to the left*) and 1 (*down*) from the origin

—> S(–4, –1).

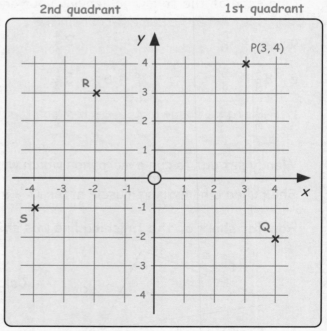

Exercise 1

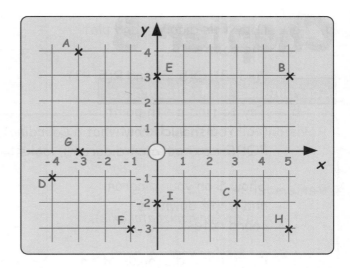

1. Look at this coordinate diagram.
   The coordinates of A are

   A(–3, 4).

   Write down the coordinates
   of the other 8 points.

2. Write down the coordinates
   of all the points :–

   a   from J to T

   b   that lie on the *x*-axis

   c   that lie on the *y*-axis

   d   that have an *x*-coordinate of :-

      (i)   4   (ii) –2

   e   that have a *y*-coordinate of :-

      (i)   3   (ii) –1

   f   that have the same *x*-coordinate

   g   that have the same *x* and *y*-coordinate.

3. a   Copy the Cartesian coordinate grid from Question 2.

   b   Plot the following points on your diagram :–

   A(4, 1),   B(–2, 3),   C(–1, –1),   D(0, 3),   E(–5, 0),   F(–4, –3),

   G(0, –3), H(6, –3),   I(–2, –3),   J(5, –1),   K(–3, 3),   L(–3, –3).

4. Draw a large set of axes (–10 to 10 on both scales).

   Plot each set of points, join them up and state what shape is formed each time :–

   a   A(3, 3) B(5, 4) C(7, 3) D(5, –2)

   b   E(–7, 5) F(–5, 8) G(2, 8) H(0, 5)

   c   I(–10, 3) J(–8, 3) K(–9, –3)

   d   L(1, –5) M(–4, –4) N(–5, 1) O(0, 0)

   e   P(4, –5) Q(6, –7) R(5, –9) S(3, –9) T(2, –7)

   f   U(–8, –3) V(–6, –3) W(–5, –5) X(–6, –7) Y(–8, –7) Z(–9, –5).

5. a Copy this diagram and plot the points :-

P(–3, 2), Q(5, 2) and R(5, –3).

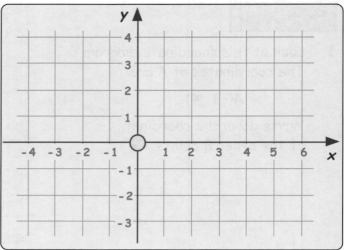

b Try to find a 4th point, (call it S) , such that PQRS is a rectangle.

Show S on your diagram, and write down its coordinates.

c Draw the 2 diagonals of the rectangle and state the coordinates of the point where these two lines meet.

Remember - a diagonal is a line joining opposite corners in a 2-D figure.

6. a Draw a coordinate diagram and plot the points A(1, 3), B(5, -1) and C(1, -5).

b If ABCD is a **square**, find the coordinates of D.

c Draw in the diagonals AC and BD of ABCD and write down the coordinates of where the two diagonals meet.

7. EFGH is a **kite** with E(0, 2), F(3, 2), G(3, -1) and H(-2, ?).

a State the missing value in H.

b State two possible coordinates for K such that EFGK is also a **kite**.

8. A **parallelogram** has 3 of its vertices (*corners*) at (–2, 4), (5, 3) and (2, –2).

a Plot these points on a Cartesian diagram.

b Find the coordinates of the other vertex.

c State where the diagonals of this **parallelogram** meet.

9. A **kite** RSTU has vertices at R(-2, 4), S(-6, 0), T(-2, -4) and U(6, ?).

a State the missing value in U.

b State two possible coordinates for V such that RSTV is also a kite.

c What does the kite become when V is the point with coordinates (2, 0) ?

10. A regular **hexagon** GHIJKL has vertices at G(-4, 1), H(1, 1), I(4, -3) and J(1, -7).

a Find the coordinates of the vertices K and L.

b Find the coordinates of the point where the 3 diagonals GJ, HK and IL meet.

Translation and Reflection in 4 Quadrants

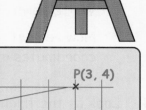

Be able to translate or reflect points in a coordinate diagram.

Remember :-

Translation is the movement of a point or shape from one position to another.

Reflection uses symmetry to reflect a point or shape over a line to give an image of the original point(s).

Translation and reflection can be applied in all 4 quadrants.

Examples :-

P(3, 4) can be translated left 5 and down 1 to give P'(–2, 3).

Q(4, –2) can be reflected over the y-axis to give Q'(–4, –2).

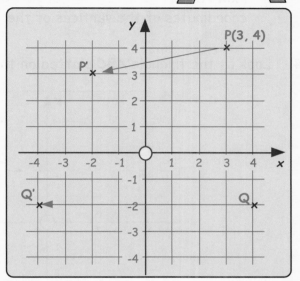

Exercise 2

1. a Copy this coordinate diagram.

   b Plot the points :-

   A(2, 1),   B(3, –2),   C(–4, 0)

   D(–3, –2), E(–2, 0)   F(–4, 4).

   c State the coordinates of the points A, B, C, D, E and F under a translation of left 2 and up 1.

   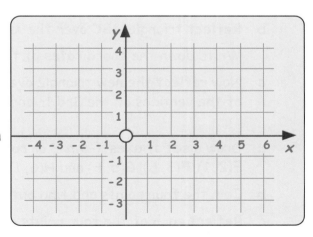

   d State the coordinates of the images A', B', C', D', E' and F' when ABCDEF, is reflected over the y-axis.

   e State the coordinates of the images A", B", C", D", E" and F" when ABCDEF is reflected over the x-axis.

2. a Plot the points G(1, 5) H(6, –4), I(–3, 0), and J(–5, –3).

   b Find the coordinates of G', H', I' and J' when G, H, I and J are reflected over the x-axis then over the y-axis.

   c Would you end up with the same points if you reflected G, H, I and J over the y-axis first, then over the x-axis ?

3. A rectangle has vertices at A(2, 1), B(5, 1), C(5, 3) and D(2, 3).

    a   Plot the above 4 points on a Cartesian coordinate diagram.

    b   **Reflect** (*Flip*) rectangle ABCD over the *x*-axis.

        Write down the coordinates of the 4 new points A', B', C' and D'.

    c   Now **reflect** your new rectangle over the *y*-axis and write down the
        coordinates of the vertices of the 3rd rectangle (A" B" C" D").

4. Look at the triangle ABC plotted on this coordinate diagram :-

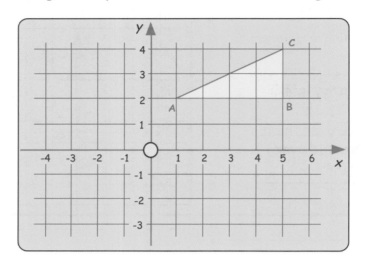

    a   Write down the coordinates of the 3 points, A, B and C.

    b   **Reflect** triangle ABC over the *x*-axis.

        Write down the coordinates of the vertices of the new triangle A' B' C'.

    c   Now **reflect** the new triangle over the *y*-axis and write down the coordinates
        of the vertices of the 3rd triangle A" B" C".

5. a   Draw a set of axes, (*-8 to 8 on both scales*) and plot the four points :-
        E(2, 1), F(3, 6), G(5, 6) and H(6, 1).

    b   Join the four points and find out what the shape EFGH is called.

    c   **Reflect** each of the four points over the *x*-axis to form a new four-sided
        shape, E'F'G'H'.

    d   Write down the coordinates of the four vertices of this new reflected shape.

6. Draw a new set of axes from −8 to 8 on both scales.

    a   Plot the 4 points P(0, 1), Q(−1, 6), R(−4, 7) and S(−5, 2) and join them up.

    b   **Reflect** your shape over the *y*-axis and write the coordinates of your new shape.

    c   **Reflect** the original shape over the *x*-axis and write the new coordinates.

7. a   Copy the set of axes shown :−

    b   Plot the square with points
        I(3, 2) J(5, 2) K(5, 4) and L(3, 4).

    c   Reflect the square over the red
        dotted line (use I′, J′ etc).

    d   Write down the coordinates of the
        vertices of the new square I′ J′ K′ H′.

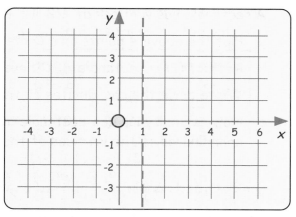

8. a   Copy this coordinate diagram.

    b   Plot the 4 points P(3, 2), Q(4, 3),
        R(3, 4) and S(-2, 3) to form a kite.

    c   Reflect the kite over the blue
        dotted line (use P′, Q′ etc).

    d   Write down the coordinates of the
        vertices of the new kite P′ Q′ R′ S′.

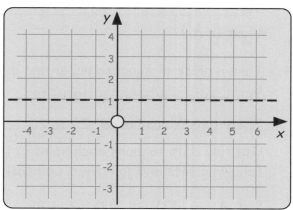

9.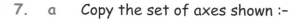

    a   Copy this coordinate diagram and
        plot the triangle MNP, where
        M(−3, 3), N(−3, −2) and P(−5, 3).

    b   Reflect the triangle over the pink
        dotted line to triangle M′N′P′.

    c   Write down the coordinates of the
        vertices of the new triangle M′N′P′.

10. A square has vertices at E(2, 2), F(2, −2), G(−2, −2) and H.

    Plot the image of EFGH when the square is firstly reflected over the x-axis, and
    is then reflected over the y-axis. State the coordinates of E′. F′. G′ and H′.

11. A point D is translated "left 4 and down 1" to a new point D′.

    If the new coordinates are D′(4, −2), find the coordinates of the original point D.

12. Another point T is translated "right 2 and down 3" to T′.

    T′ is then reflected over the x-axis to T″(5, -3).

    Find the coordinates of the original point T.

13. Draw an axes grid with both *x* and *y* axis numbered from –18 to 18.
Use tiny dots to mark each point in the following sets and join them up neatly.

> (9, 2), (8, 4), (9, 4), (9, 6), (10, 5), (11, 5), (9, 0), (10, 0), (8, -3), (9, -3),
> (5, -6), (3, -7), (2, -9), (3, -11), (3, -12), (-2, -17), (-3, -16), (-4, -17),
> (-4, -15), (-5, -15), (-3, -13), (-2, -14), (-1, -11), (-2, -8), (-3, -8), (-5, -10),
> (-7, -11), (-8, -11), (-8, -10), (-9, -10), (-8, -9), (-9, -8), (-6, -8), (-5, -6),
> (-2, -5), (-3, -2), (-10, -4), (-11, -4), (-11, -3), (-12, -3), (-11, -2), (-12, -1),
> (-10, -1), (-9, -2), (-6, 0), (-9, 1), (-10, 4), (-12, 4), (-11, 5), (-12, 7), (-11, 7),
> (-11, 8), (-9, 7), (-9, 5), (-8, 3), (-4, 2), (-3, 5), (-5, 5), (-5, 6), (-3, 6),
> (-5, 7), (-6, 9), (-3, 9), (-2, 11), (2, 11), (4, 13), (4, 10), (6, 7), (4, 7), (5, 5),
> (3, 5), (4, 3), (8, 3), (4, 1), (3, 1), (3, -5), (4, -5), (7, -2), (7, 0), (5, -1), (9, 2).

What is it ?

14. Take a piece of squared paper and in the **middle**, draw a set of axes **lightly** in pencil.

The *x*–axis is numbered –12 to 12.

The *y*–axis is numbered –20 to 20.

Use tiny dots to mark each point in the following sets and join them up neatly.

Set A (-6, -17) (-4, -17) (-6, -12)
     (-4, -8) (8, -2) (9, 1) (-4, -8)
     (-8, -8) (-9, -2) (-9, 4) (-10, 6)
     (-9, 9) (-7, 9) (-7, 13) (-10, 14)
     (-8, 15) (-5, 15) (-6, 17) (4, 13)
     (3, 16)

Set B (5, 16) (4, 13) (8, 13) (10, 12)
     (8, 11) (6, 12) (7, 13) (5, 11)
     (3, 10) (3, 11) (1, 13) (2, 10)
     (-2, 13) (-7, 14)

Set C (5, 11) (6, -1)

Set D (3, 6) (5, 6) (3, 4)

Set E (-6, -17) (-8, -15) (-6, -12)
     (-8, -8) (-10, -7) (-9, -6)

Set F (-5, -6) (-7, -2) (-5, -2) (0, 1) (-1, 5) (1, 0)
Set G (-9, 4) (-7, 3) (-4, 4) (-2, 7) (2, 2) (1, -4)

Set H (-7, 11) (-4, 8)

Set I (-3, 9) (-2, 8) (0, 5)

Set J (-5, 12) (-6, 10) (-5, 9) (-4, 11) (-5, 12)

Set K (-2, 12) (-3, 10) (-2, 9) (-1, 10) (-2, 12).   Have Fun !!!!!   — Who is it ?

Revisit - Review - Revise

1. From the coordinate diagram :-

   a   Write the coordinates of all the points.

   b   Which points have the same x and y coordinate ?

   c   State the coordinates of each of these :-

   (i)   Translate I right 3 and up 2

   (ii)   Translate J left 1 and up 2

   (iii) Translate G left 6 and down 12.

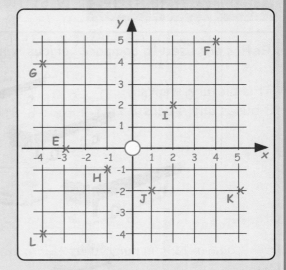

2. Draw a set of axes similar to Question 1, but this time make both axes -8 to 8.

   a   Plot the following points and join them up in order to reveal a geometric shape.

   > A(-3, 5),   B(3, 4),   C(5, -2),   D(1, -6),   E(-5, -5),   F(-7, 1),   A(-3, 5).

   b   What is the name of the shape you have just formed ?

   c   Join A to D, B to E and C to F and write the coordinates of the point where these three lines AD, BE and CF cross.

3. Draw another set of axes (-6 to 6 on both scales).

   a   Plot the points P(-4, 2), Q(1, 3) and R(4, -6).

   b   Plot a 4th point (S) so that figure PQRS is a kite with PR a line of symmetry, and write down the coordinates of point S.

4. Copy the set of axes shown opposite.

   a   Plot R(1, 0), S(5, -2) and T(3, -4).

   b   What kind of triangle is △RST ?

   c   Reflect △RST over the y-axis, showing its new position in your diagram, (R'S'T').

   d   Now give your new triangle a reflection over the blue dotted line, showing its final position on your diagram, (R"S"T").

   e   After both reflections, what is the coordinates of the new point S" ?

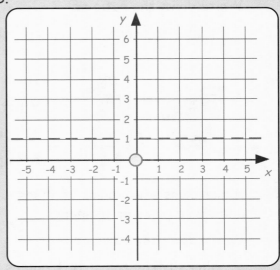

Chapter 9

Understanding Ratio

Be able to compare different quantities using ratio.

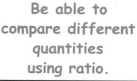

Ratios are used to compare various numbers of objects.

This picture shows 3 buses and 4 cars.

We say that :-

"the ratio of buses to cars" is 3 to 4,

or for short :-   buses : cars = 3 : 4.

Note :-

The ratio of cars to buses is 4 : 3.

Exercise 1

1. Look at this picture. Write down the ratio of :-

    a   butterflies : birds

    b   birds : butterflies.

2.

    a   Write down the ratio of mice : cats.

    b   Write down the ratio of cats : mice.

3. In a cafe there are 9 tables and 19 chairs.

    Write down the ratio of :-

    a   tables to chairs

    b   chairs to tables.

4.

    In an orchard, there are 23 apple and 29 pear trees.

    What is the ratio of :-

    a   pear trees to apple trees

    b   apple trees to pear trees ?

5. A man owns seven pairs of shoes and three pairs of trainers.

    Write down the ratio of :-

    a   shoes : trainers   b   trainers : shoes.

6.	In her bag, Granny Smith has 2 onions and 15 potatoes.

	What is the ratio of :-

	a	onions to potatoes		b	potatoes to onions

	c	onions to vegetables		d	vegetables to potatoes ?

7.	In a shop window, there are apples, oranges, pears, bananas and pineapples.

	What is the ratio of :-

	a	apples : oranges		b	bananas : pears		c	pears : apples

	d	oranges : bananas		e	pineapples : bananas		f	pears : oranges

	g	bananas : other fruit ?

8.	Shown is a framed picture of Ben the Rottweiler.

	It is 43 cm long and 27 cm broad.

	a	Write down the ratio,	length : breadth.

	b	Write down the ratio,	breadth : length.

	c	Write down the ratio,	length : perimeter.

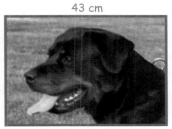

43 cm

27 cm

9.		A mother seal is fed 20 fish for every 3 fish for its baby.

	Write down the ratio of :–

	a	fish for mother : fish for baby.

	b	fish for baby : number of fish for both.

10.	During September and October, there were 50 days of recorded rainfall.

	Write down the ratio of :–

	a	wet days : total days.		b	wet days : dry days.

Simplifying Ratio

Be able to simplify fully any given ratio.

"Simplifying" a ratio is much the same as "simplifying" a fraction.

Remember :-   The fraction $\frac{9}{12}$ can be simplified, since 9 and 12 are part of the "3 times" table.

$$\frac{9}{12} \Rightarrow \frac{9 \div 3}{12 \div 3} = \frac{3}{4}.$$

Similarly, the ratio **9 : 12** can be simplified to give :- $\boxed{3 : 4}$

(It cannot be "simplified" any further - this is called its "simplest form").

Exercise 2

1.   By dividing both numbers by 2, simplify the ratio 10 : 6.

2.   By dividing both numbers by 9, simplify the ratio 54 : 63.

3.   Copy the following ratios and simplify each as far as possible :-

a	4 : 6	b	15 : 18	c	13 : 26	d	12 : 32	e	5 : 5	f	36 : 6
g	18 : 9	h	36 : 24	i	36 : 18	j	35 : 49	k	30 : 45	l	50 : 80
m	90 : 40	n	77 : 55	o	81 : 6	p	11 : 99	q	6 : 600	r	400 : 8
s	27 : 81	t	54 : 24	u	17 : 1700	v	3 : 12 000 000.				

4.   Write down each **ratio** from the picture, then write it in its simplest form :-
   (*e.g. ratio of burgers to hot-dogs is 4:2 = ... : ...*)

   a

   b

   c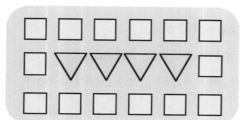

   d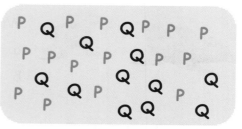

5.   At a football match, there were 4 stewards for every 200 fans.

   a   What was the ratio of fans to stewards ?

   b   Give this ratio in its **simplest form**.

6.   There are 15 pipers and 5 drummers in a pipe band.

    a   Write down the ratio of pipers : drummers.

    b   Simplify this ratio **as far as possible**.

7.   A school trip has 36 pupils and 9 teachers.
    Write, in its **simplest form**, the ratio of :-

    a   pupils : teachers   b   teachers : pupils.

8.   Of the 36 pupils on the bus, 16 are girls.

    a   Write down the ratio of boys : girls.

    b   Simplify this as far as possible.

9.   The crowd capacity of a football stadium in the Premier League is 80000.
    A smaller stadium in Division 1 can hold up to 16 000 people.

    a   Write down the ratio of **larger** capacity : **smaller** capacity.

    b   Simplify this as far as possible.

10.  Ari the dentist charges £55 per hour for a private consultation.
    Ena charges £44 for the same period.

    a   Write down the ratio of their charges :- Ena : Ari.

    b   Simplify this as far as possible.

11.   The small square has each of its sides 12 mm long.

    The larger square has its sides 44 mm long.

    a   Write down the ratio of their **perimeters** :- small : large.

    b   Express this ratio in its simplest form.

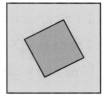

12. A large rectangle measures 8 m by 9 m. A smaller rectangle measures 6 m by 10 m.

    a   Write down the ratio of their **areas** :- larger : smaller.

    b   Simplify this ratio as far as possible.

13. Write each of these ratios in its simplest form :-

    a   1 millimetre : 1 cm   b   1 gram : 1 kilogram   c   20 secs : 1 minute

    d   40p : £8   e   1 month : 1 year   f   50 cm : 4 m

    g   £2·50 : £10   h   days in a week : days in a leap year

    i   minutes in an hour : minutes in a day.

Ratio Calculations

Example 1 :-

In Granton Tennis Club, the
ratio of juniors to seniors is :-

juniors : seniors = 2 : 5.

If there are 40 junior members,
how many seniors are there ?

Set down like this :-

| since 40 = 20 x 2 |
| then seniors = 20 x 5 = 100 |

Be able to determine a missing quantity in a given ratio.

	juniors	seniors	
x 20	2	5	x 20
	40	**100**	

Example 2 :-

To obtain a particular strength of plant food,
Gerry has to mix fertiliser and water in the ratio :-

fertiliser : water = 2 : 3.

Gerry actually uses 10 measures of fertiliser.

How many measures of water is required ?

	fertiliser	water	
x 5	2	3	x 5
	10	**15**	

Set down like this :-

| since 10 = 5 x 2 => then water = 5 x 3 = 15 |

Exercise 3

1. In a classroom, the ratio of boys to girls = 1 : 3.

    There are 7 boys in the classroom.

    How many girls are there ?

	boys	girls	
x ?	1	3	x ?
	7	......	

2. To make a Summer Punch, I use 1 litre of
    apple juice to 4 litres of orange juice.

    => the ratio of apple to orange juice is 1 : 4.

    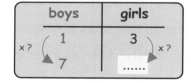

    If I use 8 litres of apple juice, how many litres of orange juice should I use ?

3. Flavoured chew sweets are sold in lemon and strawberry flavours in a 2 : 3 ratio.

    a   How many strawberry sweets should there be if there are :-

    (i)   12 lemon   (ii)   32 lemon sweets ?

    b   How many lemon sweets would there be if there are :-

    (i)   12 strawberry   (ii)   81 strawberry sweets ?

    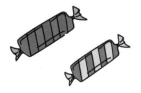

4. Some people recommend that in hospitals a decent ratio of nurses to doctors is 9 : 2.

How many doctors would be required for hospitals with :-

a   18 nurses   b   45 nurses

c   72 nurses   d   135 nurses ?

5. One evening at the local cinema, the ratio of males to females was 3 : 4.

There were 120 men in the cinema.

How many women were there ?

Males	Females
× ? (3	4) × ?
120	....

6. In a large crate, the ratio of red peppers to green peppers is 3 : 5.

If there are 102 red peppers in the crate, how many green peppers are there ?

7.
In a box of chocolates, the ratio of soft : caramel is 2 : 7.

a   If there are 4 soft chocolates, how many caramels will there be ?

b   If there are 35 caramels, how many soft chocolates will there be ?

8. The ratio of "Hard" questions to "Easy" questions in a test is 1 : 4.

a   If the test consists of 13 hard questions, how many easy ones are there ?

b   A second test consists of 28 easy questions.

(i)   How many hard ones are there ?

(ii) How many questions are there altogether in this test ?

9.
Ann and Jo compare the money they earn selling cosmetics.

The ratio of their weekly commission is

Ann : Jo = 2 : 5 - (every £2 Ann earns, Jo earns £5)

a   If Ann earned £20, how much must Jo have earned ?

b   If Jo earned £250, how much must Ann have earned ?

c   If Ann earned £1000, how much did they earn altogether ?

10. A South of England Golf Championship was made up of boys from Devon and boys from Cornwall.

The ratio of Devon boys : Cornwall boys = 8 : 7.

   a   If 49 entries were from Cornwall, how many were from Devon ?

   b   How many entries were there in total ?

11.

The ratio of new to used cars for sale in a showroom is :- new : used = 3 : 5.

   a   If there are 35 used cars, how many new cars are there ?

   b   How many cars are there in the showroom ?

12. At a school disco, the ratio of pupils to teachers is 20 : 1.

If 360 pupils turn up at a disco, how many **people** in **total** should there be at that disco ?

13. A wizard is making his secret potion.

Which **strength** of potion does he get if he mixes :–

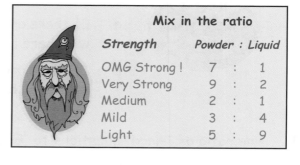

Mix in the ratio		
Strength	**Powder** :	**Liquid**
OMG Strong !	7 :	1
Very Strong	9 :	2
Medium	2 :	1
Mild	3 :	4
Light	5 :	9

   a   840 grams of powder with 120 ml of liquid ?

   b   800 grams of powder with 400 ml of liquid ?

   c   600 grams of powder with 800 ml of liquid ?

   d   550 grams of powder with 990 ml of liquid ?

   e   1080 grams of powder with 240 ml of liquid ?

14. The ratio of **cats** : **dogs** : **mice** in a pet shop is 2 : 1 : 5.

   a   How many cats are there if there are 4 dogs ?

   b   How many mice are there if there are 10 cats ?

   c   How many cats are there if there are 35 mice ?

   d   How many cats and dogs **in total** are there if there are 20 mice ?

   e   If there are 3 dogs, how many animals are there **altogether** ?

Proportion

If you know the total cost of several items, you can easily find the cost per item.

Be able to use basic proportion to find the value of one item.

Example :-   The cost of 5 pies is £4·00.

The cost of **1** pie = (400p ÷ 5) = **80p** – (*simply divide*).

Exercise 4   *Oral Exercise*

1.   The cost of 6 cakes is £6·30. Find the cost of one cake.

2.   Find the cost per item : -

a	5 sweets costing 35p	b	9 shirts costing £108
c	7 DVDs costing £63	d	11 ice-creams costing £6·60
e	12 carrots costing £2·40	f	10 rabbits costing £210.

3.   It took a truck 60 trips to move 1200 tonnes of rubble.

How many tonnes did the truck move each trip ?

4.    A soldier can march 36 kilometres in 6 hours.

Calculate the rate in kilometres per hour.

5.   Jill exchanges £40 for 44 euros. What is the rate of € per £.

6.    A 4 kilogram bag of carrots costs £2.

What is the weight per £ ?

7.   A hamster rotates a running wheel 90 times in a minute.

Calculate the number of rotations per second.

8.    Alf's team ran the 4 by 100 metres relay race in 50 seconds.

What was the team's average speed ?

(*How many metres were run in 1 second ?*)

9.   David bought a set of 4 new tyres from *Slow-Fit* for a total of £192.

Tim bought a set of 5 similar tyres from *Tyres 'R Us* for £220.

Who got the better deal ?

Direct Proportion

Be able to use direct proportion to solve problems.

Two quantities, (*for example, the number of cakes and the total cost*), are said to be in **direct proportion**, if : -

"... when you **double** (treble, quadruple, half) the number of one item you **double** (treble, quadruple, half) the number of the other".

Example :- The cost of 6 cakes is £4·20.

Find the cost of 5 cakes.

Set down like this : -

Cakes		Cost
6	—>	£4·20
1	—>	420p ÷ 6 = 70p
5	—>	5 × 70p = £3·50

5 cakes cost £3·50

Exercise 5

1. The cost of 7 books is £65·80.

   Find the cost of 6 books.

Books		Cost
7	—>	£65·80
1	—>	6580p ÷ 7 = ...p
6	—>	

2. Nine sheets of high gloss photo paper costs £7·29 (*729p*).

   How much would it cost for 10 sheets ?

   (*Find the cost of 1 sheet first*).

3. On holiday, Bronte exchanged £80 for $120.

   How many dollars would Bronte have got for £50 ?

   (*Find how much for £1 first*).

4. a It takes a cement mixer 2 minutes to mix 1·2 cubic metres of cement.

   What volume of cement could the mixer do in 9 minutes ?

   b A wheel turns 500 times in 4 minutes.

   How many turns would it make in 5 minutes ?

5. a Five air-mail letters cost £4 to post.

   How much would it cost to post 6 letters ?

   b Nine cakes cost £18·36. How much would ten cakes cost ?

6. A machine makes 3000 staples every 6 seconds. How many staples will it make in : -

        a   1 second   b   7 seconds   c   one minute   d   an hour ?

7. Which of the following are examples of **direct proportion** ?

    a   Five iced doughnuts cost £3. Six of them cost £3·50.

    b   9 sweets cost 72p. Ten cost 81p.

    c   3 DVDs cost £42. 4 DVDs cost £52.

    d   11 pies cost £11·99. 5 pies cost £5·45.

8.    A bricklayer can lay 35 bricks in seven minutes.

    a   How many bricks could he lay in an hour ?

    b   How long would it take to build a wall with 250 bricks ?

9. A computer programmer writes 30 lines of computer code in an hour.

    a   How long would it take to write 25 lines of code ?

    b   It took 1 hour and 48 minutes to write a computer programme.

        How many lines of code were in this programme ?

Sometimes it is easier to find the cost of 10, or 100, or 1000 items first - not just 1 !

Example : -   500 coloured crayons cost £20. How much would it cost for 700 crayons ?

This time it would be easier to find the cost of 100 first, then multiply by 7.

Crayons		Cost
500	—>	£20
100	—>	£20 ÷ 5 = £4
700	—>	£4 × 7 = £28

---

10. a   200 litres of olive oil costs £30. Find the cost of 300 litres.

    b   100 matches take 50 minutes to burn, lighting them one at a time.

        How long would it take 70 matches to burn ?

    c   It takes 5000 bees a week to make 35 kg of honey.

        What weight of honey would you get in a week from 4000 bees ?

    d   600 ml of strawberry concentrate costs £2·40.

        How much would it cost for one litre ?

The 3 Я's

Revisit - Review - Revise

1. Write down the ratio of :-

   a   cows : sheep

   b   sheep : pigs

   c   pigs : other animals.

2. In Jim's toolbox, he found 8 screws, 11 nuts, 5 bolts and 3 washers.

   a   Write down the ratio of   bolts : screws.

   b   Write down the ratio of   washers : nuts.

3. Of a 28 km journey, Tom cycled 16 km and walked the rest.

   a   Write down the ratio of :-   distance cycled : distance walked.

   b   Simplify this ratio as far as possible.

4. Express each of the following ratios in its simplest form :-

   a   10 : 15   b   30 : 50   c   33 : 22   d   16 : 22

   e   55 : 35   f   35 : 49   g   39 : 26   h   23 : 31

   i   1·5 : 3   j   125 : 75   k   2·4 : 3·6   l   1000 : 650.

5.    The ratio of baby boys : baby girls in a maternity hospital is 4 : 5.
   There are 16 baby boys. How many baby girls are there ?

6. Cans of cola and diet cola were bought for a party.

   The ratio of cola : diet cola was 3 : 4.

   a   If there were 15 cans of cola, how many
       cans of diet cola were there ?

   b   There were 32 cans of diet cola.

       How many cans were there altogether ?

7.  In April 2014, the ratio of wet days to dry days was 2 : 3.

A weatherman claimed there were 14 wet days in April.

Explain why the weatherman's statement must be incorrect.

8. Simplify each ratio as far as possible :-

   a   4·5 : 6

   b $3\frac{1}{3}$: 5.

9. The cost of 6 pies is £12. Find the cost of one pie.

10. Find the cost (or the weight) of 1 item : -

   a   5 comics costing £20

   b   9 paperweights costing £72

   c   7 apples weighing 420 g

   d   11 glasses weighing 2200 g

   e   12 turnips costing £12·60

   f   10 chinchilla costing £440.

11.  It took a truck 40 deliveries to deliver 1200 fridges.

How many fridges did the truck deliver on each trip, assuming the truck carried the same number each time ?

12. a   Five shirts cost £45. Find the cost of 4 shirts.

   b   Eight identical parcels weigh 72 kg. What would be the weight of 3 parcels ?

   c   Ten blank DVDs cost £6. What would be the cost of 9 DVDs ?

   d   It takes 3600 g of dough to make twelve buns.

   How much dough would you need for a baker's dozen (13) ?

13. a   300 litres of oil costs £60. How much would it cost for 200 litres ?

   b   150 cans of soup weigh 9 kg. How much would 100 cans weigh ?

14. **Difficult**   It takes 20 litres of weedkiller to cover a rectangular garden 8 m by 6 m.

How many litres of weedkiller should I use for a square garden with side 6 m ?

Chapter 10

Be able to do some percentage calculations without a calculator.

Calculating a Percentage without a Calculator

Many percentages can be reduced into simple fractions for calculations **without** using a calculator.

Many percentages can be calculated **without** a calculator.

Examples :-

1. Find 3% of ...
   • Find 1%
   • then times by 3.

2. Find 70% of ...
   • Find 10%
   • then times by 7.

3. Find 11% of ....
   • Find 10%, find 1%
   • then add your two answers.

Exercise 1

1. Make a copy of the list shown below and **LEARN** it :-

percentage	50%	25% 75%	$33\frac{1}{3}$ % 66$\frac{2}{3}$ %	20% 40% 60% 80%	10% 30% 70% 90%
fraction	$\frac{1}{2}$	$\frac{1}{4}$ $\frac{3}{4}$	$\frac{1}{3}$ $\frac{2}{3}$	$\frac{1}{5}$ $\frac{2}{5}$ $\frac{3}{5}$ $\frac{4}{5}$	$\frac{1}{10}$ $\frac{3}{10}$ $\frac{7}{10}$ $\frac{9}{10}$

note   note

2. Do the following, using their fractional equivalents instead of the percentages :-

   a   10% of £120
   b   20% of £120
   c   40% of £120

   d   10% of £40
   e   5% of £40 (*half of 10%*)
   f   75% of £240

   g $33\frac{1}{3}$ % of £15
   h $66\frac{2}{3}$ % of £15
   i   25% of £140

   j   30% of £140
   k   20% of £760
   l   60% of £350

   m $33\frac{1}{3}$ % of £93
   n $66\frac{2}{3}$ % of £93
   o   50% of £3

   p   75% of £36
   q   10% of £180
   r   5% of £180

   s   1% of £700
   t   2% of £700
   u   3% of £700

   v   75% of £480
   w $33\frac{1}{3}$ % of £3900
   x   5% of £120.

3. Harder !! (no calculator). Discuss how, without a calculator, you might find :-

   a   15% of something
   b $2\frac{1}{2}$ % of something
   c $7\frac{1}{2}$ % of something.

4. Find :-
   a   15% of £80
   b   15% of 160 km

   c $2\frac{1}{2}$ % of 1400 km
   d $2\frac{1}{2}$ % of £4
   e $7\frac{1}{2}$ % of 480 ml

   f $12\frac{1}{2}$ % of 1600 mm
   g   12·5% of 80 cm
   h   7·5% of 1200 litres.

5. A school has 420 pupils. 40% of the pupils are on a trip.

   How many pupils are there on the trip ?

6.  Five hundred trees are planted in a town.

   15% of them are planted in a park.

   How many trees are planted in the park ?

7. A recipe requires 680 g of flour.

   30% of the flour is self-raising.

   How much of the flour is self-raising ?

8.  A Cat and Dog home have 114 animals. $33\frac{1}{3}$% are cats.

   How many cats are there ?

9. a Abbie had £220. She spent 25% on a weekend spa break.

   How much did Abbie pay for her break ?

   b Ellie weighed 85 kilograms.

   She went to a health resort for a month and lost 20% of her weight.

   (i) How many kilograms did she lose ?

   (ii) How much did she weigh after her visit to the health resort ?

   c Dara paid a 75% deposit on a £360 mountain bike.

   How much was his deposit ?

   d Arnie does 150 sit-ups every day.

   He does 60% in the morning and the rest at night.

   (i) How many sit-ups does he do in the morning ?

   (ii) What percentage of the sit-ups does he do at night ?

   e 75% of the animals in a farm yard are chickens.

   If there are 96 animals in the yard,
   how many are **not** chickens ?

10. *Very Difficult.*   A book price has been increased by 20% and now costs £24.

   How much was the book **before** the increase ?

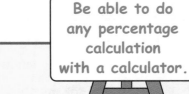
Be able to do
any percentage
calculation
with a calculator.

Remember –   When using a calculator make sure you show **all** your working.

Example :–   Find 17% of £1860.

$$\frac{17}{100} \times £1860 = (17 \div 100) \times £1860$$
$$= 316 \cdot 2$$
$$= £316 \cdot 2\underline{0}$$

Exercise 2   *(The exercise over the next 3 pages requires a calculator.)*

1.   Find the following using a calculator :–

   a   13% of £1500   b   72% of 520 km   c   28% of £50·50

   d   81% of 420 ml   e   22·5% of 120 kg   f   33% of 480 mm

   g   79% of £60   h   14% of 120 cm   i   60% of 12 000 km

   j   18% of 7 cm   k $66\frac{2}{3}$ % of 28·5 km   l   23% of £0.25 million

   m   101% of £800   n   125% of 150 km   o   150% of £5.

2.   a   On red nose day, 24% of pupils at Leeds Academy wore a red nose.
          If there were 1400 pupils, how many wore a red nose ?

   b   43% of 1600 people asked in a survey preferred cats to dogs.
          How many people in the survey preferred cats ?

   c      There were 5850 people using a ski slope yesterday.
          32% of them had never been skiing before.
          How many had never been skiing before ?

   d   The cost of using the ski slope was £45 per day.
          A 12% **discount** was given yesterday.
          How much money was taken off the price yesterday ?

   e   Jake weighed 87 kg and wanted to **lose** 8%.
          How much did Jake want to weigh ?

3. a   Zara, who weighed 70 kg, found that after training
         for a Marathon her weight had dropped by 13%.

         (i)   By how much had Zara's weight dropped ?

         (ii)   How much did Zara weigh then ?

    b   Zara's last Marathon time was exactly 3 hours.

         She wanted to beat this time by at least 10%.

         What time did she want to achieve in this Marathon ?

4. a

         A shopkeeper sells TIKTOK watches at £120 each.

         He decides to raise the price by 15%.

         (i)   How much is the increase ?

         (ii)   How much does the watch now cost ?

    b   Leather watch straps cost £18 each.

         Find the cost if the price is reduced by 11%.

5. a   Peter poured 12 litres of juice into a large punch bowl
         for his *Save The Children* fundraising party.

         After the party, there was only 8% of the juice left.

         How many millilitres had been drunk at the party ?

    b   Peter beat last year's fundraising total (£1850) by 18%.

         How much money did he raise this year ?

6.

         Shop A had a football strip priced at
         £70 but had a 12% discount sticker.

         Shop B had the strip marked £75 but with
         a 21% discount sticker.

         Which shop had the cheaper football strip ?
         (*Explain*).

7. Two flats each cost £80 000.

    A year later, Flat 1 had an increased valuation of 12%.

    Flat 2 had its value decreased by 9%.

    a   What profit did Flat 1 make on its property ?

    b   What was the difference between the two Flats' prices then ?

8. a   A bank charges 14% interest for a £6400 car loan.

How much interest did the bank charge for the loan ?

$$\frac{14}{100} \times 6400$$

$$= 14 \div 100 \times 6400$$

b   Only 55% of bugs are killed by a bug spray.

If there were 8600 bugs, how many were killed ?

c   Hayley's council tax last year was £960. This year, there is a 7% **increase**.

How much is the increase ?

d   Last month, a house was valued at £120 000.

This month the house is valued at 3·5% **less**.

How much less is the value of the house ?

9.  The storm yesterday had winds of 60 mph.

The wind speed is expected to **increase** by 15% today.

What is the expected wind speed today ?

10. a   A bus service is to **increase** its Zone Card price by 11%.

How much will I pay for my £28 Zone Card after the increase ?

b   A bus driver gets a **pay rise** of 6%.

How much will a bus driver earning £325 a week now earn ?

c   Tyre pressure on a bus should be at 56 p.s.i. (*pounds per square inch*).

If the pressure **drops** by 25%, what would the p.s.i. be ?

11. a    Avia offers a 17·5% **discount** on their hire cars.

Find the cost to hire a car originally costing £124.

b   A garage has a car priced £12 800 for sale.

The *Manager's Special* **discount** is 7·25%.

How much will the car cost with the *special* **discount** ?

12. a   A pick-up truck was given a 10% **discount** and was sold for £9000.

How much was the pick-up before the **discount** ? (*not £9900*) !

b   Ally had £2000 left of his lottery win after spending 80% of his money.

How much did he win on the lottery ?

Revisit - Review - Revise

1. Write each percentage as a fraction in its simplest form :-

   a 50%   b 25%   c 10%   d 75%

   e 20%   f 5%   g $33\frac{1}{3}$%   h 80%.

2. Do the following by using the fractional equivalents instead of the percentages :-

   a 10% of £90   b 20% of £45   c 40% of £45

   d 10% of £160   e 5% of £160   f 75% of £36

   g $33\frac{1}{3}$% of £21   h $66\frac{2}{3}$% of £21   i 25% of £6

   j 30% of £60   k 20% of £750   l 60% of £750

   m $33\frac{1}{3}$% of £6·30   n $66\frac{2}{3}$% of £6·30   o 50% of £7

   p 75% of £40   q 10% of £220   r 5% of £220

   s 1% of £900   t 2% of £900   u 3% of £900.

3. a Kev bought a second hand pickup for £3500.

   He sold it 6 months later at 10% less than what he paid for it.

   How much did Kev sell the pickup for ?

   b  Mrs Woods bought in 150 apples for the nursery children.

   She discovered 60% of them were bad.

   How many of the apples was she then able to use ?

   c RyanJet's flight prices have risen by 25% this year.

   I flew to Rome last year for £84.

   How much will it cost this year ?

   d   My weight on Friday was 150 pounds.

   After over-indulging at the weekend, my weight rose by 2%.

   How much did I weigh on Monday morning ?

Chapter 11

Simple Linear Patterns

Be able to identify a pattern from a table and make up a rule for extending it.

It is easy to spot a **number pattern** from a diagram or a table.

Example :- Each chocolate sponge has 4 candles.

Drawing up a table helps you see the pattern :-

No. of Sponges (S)	1	2	3	4	5	6
No. of Candles (C)	4	8	12	?	?	?

4   4   4

Can you see that for every new sponge => the number of candles rises by 4 ?

=> We can write, in words :-

> Number of Candles = 4 x no. of Sponges

=> or in symbol form :-

> $C = 4 \times S$

* For **12 sponges**, you would need $C = 4 \times 12 = 48$ candles.

Exercise 1

1. In a school library, the tables are set out so that 3 children sit around each table.

1 table
3 children

2 tables
6 children

3 tables
9 children

a Draw the next pattern of children sitting around 4 tables.

b Copy the following table and complete it :-

No. of Tables (T)	1	2	3	4	5	6
No. of Children (C)	3	6	9	?	?	?

?   ?   ?

c For every extra table, how many extra children are seated ?

1. d   Copy and complete the formula :-

   Number of children = ... × **Number of tables.**

   e   Now write down the formula using symbols :- C = ... × T.

   f   Use your formula to decide how many children the library can take if there are 20 tables in it.

2.   Look at the star shapes with circles at each end point.

 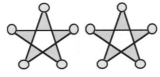 

   1 star   2 stars   3 stars
   5 circles   10 circles   15 circles

   a   Draw the next pattern of stars and circles.

   b   Copy the following table and complete it :-

No. of Stars (S)	1	2	3	4	5	6
No. of Circles (C)	5	10	?	?	?	?

   ?   ?   ?

   c   For every extra star, how many extra circles are needed ?

   d   Copy/complete the formula :- **number of circles** = ... × **number of stars.**

   e   Write down the formula using symbols C = ... × S.

   f   Use your formula to decide how many circles are needed for 40 stars.

3.   Here is a glass of strawberry juice which needs 6 strawberries per glass to make it.

 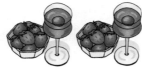

   a   Copy and complete the table listing the number of strawberries per 1 glass :-

No. of Glasses (G)	1	2	3	4	5	6
No. of Strawberries (S)	6	?	?	?	?	?

   ?   ?   ?

   b   How many strawberries are needed for 7 glasses ?

   c   Copy/complete :- "**number of strawberries** = ... × **number of glasses**".

   d   Write the formula using symbols connecting S and G.

   e   Use your formula to say how many strawberries would be needed to make 10 glasses of the juice.

4. Look at the price DJ Sports are charging for World Cup footballs :-

1 ball   2 balls   3 balls
£7   £14   £21

a   Copy and complete the table below showing the cost of buying the footballs :-

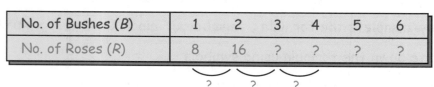

No. of Footballs (F)	1	2	3	4	5	6
Cost in £'s (C)	7	?	?	?	?	?

? ? ?

b   Copy and complete :- Cost = ... x the number of footballs.

c   Write the formula using symbols connecting C and F.

d   Use your formula to find the cost to a football club wanting to buy 30 footballs.

5. Copy and complete this table which shows how many roses are expected to flower on each rose bush in early spring :-

No. of Bushes (B)	1	2	3	4	5	6
No. of Roses (R)	8	16	?	?	?	?

? ? ?

a   Copy and complete :- number of roses = ... x the number of bushes.

b   Write a formula using symbols connecting R and B.

c   Use your formula to find how many roses should flower from 50 rose bushes.

6. Copy and complete the following table which shows the number of marigolds in a pot :-

No. of Pots (P)	1	2	3	4	5	6
No. of Marigolds (M)	10	20	30	?	?	?

a   Copy and complete :- number of marigolds = ... x the number of pots.

b   Write a formula using symbols connecting M and P.

c   Use your formula to find the total number of marigolds in 15 pots.

7. The table below the number of full minibuses and the number of pupils, arriving at Belloch Academy each school day.

No. of Buses (B)	3	4	5	6	7	8
No. of Pupils (P)	60	80	100	?	?	?

a 3 school minibuses can carry 60 pupils in total.

How many pupils are allowed on one bus ?

b Write a formula linking the number of pupils (P) and the number of buses (B).

c 18 minibuses, like those used by Belloch Academy, arrive at Ainsley High School each school day. Use your formula to calculate how many pupils in total are on these buses.

8. For each of the tables below, find a formula (or rule) connecting the two letters :-

a

No. of Newspapers (N)	1	2	3	4	5	6
No. of Pages (P)	30	60	90	?	?	?

$P = ? \times N$

b

No. of Trees (T)	1	2	3	4	5	6
No. of Pineapples (P)	18	36	54	?	?	?

$P = ? \times T$

c

No. of Days (D)	1	2	3	4	5	6
No. of Hours (H)	24	48	72	?	?	?

$H = ? \times D$

d

No. of Pounds (N)	2	3	4	5	6	7
No. of Pence (p)	200	300	400	?	?	?

$p = ? \times N$

e

No. of Muffins (M)	2	3	4	5	7	8
Cost in £'s (C)	2·50	3·75	5·00	?	?	?

$C = ? \times \ldots$

f

No. of Tubes (T)	2	4	6	8	10	12
Cost in £'s (C)	7	14	21	?	?	?

$\ldots = ? \times \ldots$

More Difficult Linear Patterns

Identify a more complicated pattern from a table and find a rule to extend it.

Here is a pattern, showing children sitting around tables in their school dining area.

 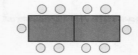 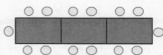

1 table	2 tables	3 tables
6 children	10 children	14 children

Drawing up a table will help you see a pattern.

No. of Tables (T)	1	2	3	4	5	6
No. of Children (C)	6	10	14	?	?	?

For each additional table => the number of children rises by 4.

But ..... No. of Children = 4 x no. of Tables   or   C = 4 x T   doesn't work here !

Check :- 4 x 1 ≠ 6,   4 x 2 ≠ 10,   4 x 3 ≠ 14,   4 x 4 ≠ 18,   4 x 5 ≠ 22

but   4 x 1 + 2 = 8   4 x 2 + 2 = 10   4 x 3 + 2 = 14 etc. does work

A **correction number** is required to make the pattern work.

In this example, that number is 2.   =>   C = 4 x T + 2.

* With 10 tables, you can seat C = 4 x 10 + 2 = **42** children.

Exercise 2

1.   Here is a pattern made with circles and squares.

  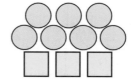

1 square	2 squares	3 squares
3 circles	5 circles	7 circles

a   Draw the next pattern of circles and squares.

b   Copy the following table and complete it :-

No. of Squares (S)	1	2	3	4	5	6
No. of Circles (C)	3	5	7	?	?	?

c   For every extra square, how many extra circles are needed ?

1. d Write down the formula using **symbols** for calculating the number
       of circles needed if you know the number of squares. | C = ... x S + ... |

    e Use your formula to decide how many circles are needed with 10 squares.

2. In another school, the dining area tables are set out differently :-

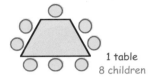
1 table
8 children

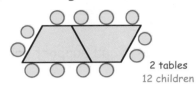
2 tables
12 children

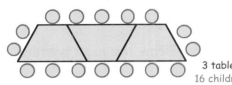
3 tables
16 children

    a Draw the next pattern, showing children sitting around 4 tables.

    b Copy and complete :-

No. of Tables (T)	1	2	3	4	5	6
No. of Children (C)	8	12	16	?	?	?

                                                  ?   ?   ?

    c For every extra table, how many extra children can be seated ?

    d Write down the formula using symbols C = ... x T + ...

    e Use your formula to decide how many children can sit around 20 tables.

3. This table shows the cost of hiring a safety deposit box in a hotel :-

No. of Days Hired (D)	1	2	3	4	5	6
Cost in £'s (C)	8	11	14	17	....	....

                             ?   ?   ?

    a How much will it cost to hire the safe for :-   (i) 5 days   (ii) 7 days ?

    b How much extra does it cost for each additional day of hire ?

    c Write down the formula for determining the cost of hiring the safe

                    C = ... x D + ...

    d How much will it cost to hire the safe for 2 weeks ?

4. The weight of a truck carrying identical photocopying machines is given in the table.

No. of Photocopiers (P)	1	2	3	4
Total weight in kilograms (W)	1250	1300	1350	1400

    a How much does each extra photocopier weigh ?

    b What is the total weight of a truck carrying 5 photocopiers ?

    c Find a formula for the total weight W = ... x P + ...

    d What is the total weight of a truck with 10 photocopiers ?

5. Look at the pattern of fence posts and support panels.

 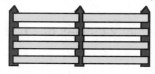 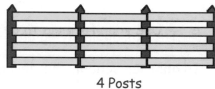

| 2 Posts | 3 Posts | 4 Posts |
| 4 Panels | 8 Panels | 12 Panels |

a   Draw the next pattern of fence posts and support panels.

b   Copy the table below and complete it :-

No. of Posts (*P*)	2	3	4	5	6	7
No. of Supports (*S*)	4	8	12	?	?	?

           ?   ?   ?

c   For every extra post, how many extra support panels are needed ?

d   Write down the formula using symbols $S = ... \times P - ...$

e   Use your formula to decide how many support panels are needed with 20 posts.

> * note the correction number has to be *subtracted*

6. The designs below are made up of triangles and circles.

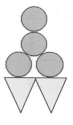 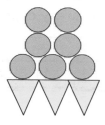 

| 2 triangles | 3 triangles | 4 triangles |
| 4 circles | 7 circles | 10 circles |

a   Draw the next pattern of triangles and circles.

b   Copy the table below and complete it :-

No. of Triangles (*T*)	2	3	4	5	6	7
No. of Circles (*C*)	4	7	10	?	?	?

           ?   ?   ?

c   For every extra triangle, how many extra circles are needed ?

d   Write down the formula using symbols $C = ... \times T - ...$

e   Use your formula to work out how many circles sit on 50 triangles.

f   How many triangles are required if we have :-

    (i)   22 circles   (ii)   34 circles   (iii)   58 circles   (iv)   88 circles ?

7. Shown below are some tables connecting pairs of values.

Determine a **formula** or rule connecting the 2nd letter in the table to the 1st letter.

a   Tubs of apples lying on a wagon.

Tub (*T*)	1	2	3	4
Weight (*W*) kg	10	13	16	19

$$W = ... \times T + ...$$

b   Fares for boat trips.

No. km (*K*)	1	2	3	4
Fare £'s (*F*)	2	7	12	17

$$F = ... \times K - ...$$

c   Bees appear as flowers bloom.

No. Flowers (F)	1	2	3	4
No. Bees (*B*)	15	25	35	45

$$B = ... \times F ....$$

d   Time taken to grill chops on a BBQ.

No. Chops (*C*)	1	2	3	4
Grilling (*G*) min	7·5	8	8·5	9

$$G = ... \times C ....$$

e   Circles round triangles.

Triangles (*T*)	1	2	3	4
Circles (*C*)	12	16	20	24

$$C = ... \times T ....$$

f   Time taken to print pages.

No. Pages (*P*)	1	2	3	4
Time (*T*) seconds	30	36	42	48

$$T = ... \times P ....$$

g   Hiring a cement mixer.

Days hired (*D*)	1	2	3	4
Cost in £'s (*C*)	7	16	25	34

$$C = ... \times D ....$$

h   Filling a paddling pool using a hose.

Time mins (*T*)	1	2	3	4
Depth (*D*) cm	1·3	2·1	2·9	3·7

$$D = ... \times T ....$$

i   Weight of plant pot and daffodil bulbs.

No. of bulbs (*B*)	1	2	3	4
Weight (*W*) g	240	300	360	420

$$W = ... \times B ....$$

j   A stamp collection grows each year.

No. Years (*Y*)	1	2	3	4
No. Stamps (*S*)	100	350	600	850

$$S = ... \times Y ....$$

Revisit - Review - Revise

1. A girl is building a pattern with rectangular wooden building bricks.

Pattern 1   Pattern 2   Pattern 3   Pattern 4
Bricks 3   Bricks ...   Bricks ...   Bricks ...

   a   Draw pattern number 5 and count the number of bricks.

   b   Copy and complete this table :-

Pattern no. (P)	1	2	3	4	5
Bricks needed (B)	3	...	...	...	...

   c   Write a formula connecting B and P using symbols.

   d   Use the formula to find how many bricks are needed for pattern 10.

   e   What pattern number has 48 bricks ?

2. A joiner bills his customers with an initial call out charge plus an hourly rate.

Examples of his charges are shown in the table :-

No. of Hours (H)	1	2	3	4	5	6
Charge in £'s (C)	42	52	62	?	?	?

   a   How much will it cost to call out the joiner for 4 hours ?

   b   How much extra does he charge for each additional hour ?

   c   Write down the formula for determining the cost of calling him out :-

$$C = \ldots \times H + \ldots$$

   d   What is his call out fee ?

   e   What does he charge for a job lasting 7 hours ?

   f   One job had to be done over 2 days, the total bill coming to £132.
        How many hours did this job take ?

3. Shown below are two tables of values connecting pairs of letters.

Write down a formula connecting the second letter to the first letter.

   a

P	1	2	3	4
M	50	55	60	65

$$M = \ldots \times P + \ldots$$

   b

W	1	2	3	4
Z	9	13	17	21

$$Z = \ldots \times W + \ldots$$

Chapter 12

Area of a Right Angled Triangle

Be able to work out the area of a right angled triangle.

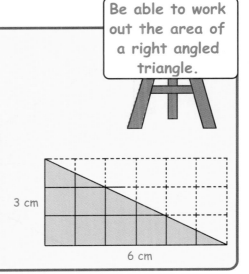

To calculate the **area** of a **Right Angled Triangle**, use **two steps** as follows :-

Step 1 – | Calculate the area of the surrounding rectangle

=> Area = 6 x 3 = 18 cm^2.

Step 2 – | Now simply **halve** the answer you obtained

=> Area = $\frac{1}{2}$ of 18 = 9 cm^2

3 cm

6 cm

Exercise 1   *Each box in this exercise represents 1 cm^2.*

1. a   Make an accurate drawing of this right angled triangle.

   b   Complete the figure by drawing the surrounding rectangle.

   c   Calculate the **area** of the **rectangle**.

   d   Now write down the **area** of the **triangle**.

4 cm

5 cm

2.

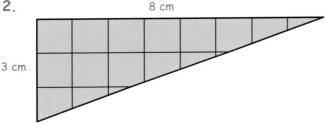

8 cm

3 cm

   a   Make an accurate drawing of this right angled triangle.

   b   Complete the figure by drawing the surrounding rectangle.

   c   Calculate the **area** of the **rectangle**.

   d   Now write down the **area** of the **triangle**.

3. a   Make an accurate drawing of this right angled triangle.

   b   Complete the figure by drawing the surrounding square.

   c   Calculate the **area** of the **square**.

   d   Now write down the **area** of the **triangle**.

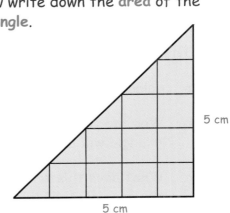

5 cm

5 cm

4. Use 1 cm squared paper to draw these right angled triangles :–

    (i)   Make an accurate drawing   (ii)   Draw the surrounding rectangle

    (iii) Find the area of the rectangle   (iv) Calculate the **area** of the **triangle**.

a

5 cm

8 cm

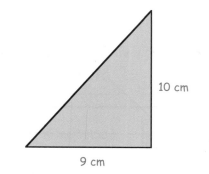

Area (*rectangle*) = $L \times B$ = 8×5

                      = 40 cm²

Area (*triangle*) = $\frac{1}{2}$ of 40 = ... cm²

b

5 cm

10 cm

c

10 cm

9 cm

d

12 cm

4 cm

e

8 cm

11 cm

f

11 cm

6 cm

g

2 cm

14 cm

5. This is **not** a right angled triangle.

    a   Calculate the area of the dotted rectangle.

    b   What do you think the area of the shaded triangle will be ?

    c   What does this tell you about finding the area of **ANY** triangle ? (*Investigate*).

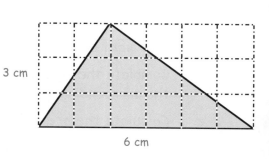

3 cm

6 cm

Area of a Triangle (any triangle)

Be able to use a formula to work out the area of any triangle.

The Formula for the Area of a Triangle, given its base and height.

height

base

*Note - the base and the height (*altitude*) of a triangle must meet at right angles.

$$\text{AREA of TRIANGLE} = \tfrac{1}{2} \times \text{ BASE } \times \text{ HEIGHT}$$

Example 1 :-

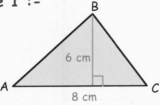

B

6 cm

A   8 cm   C

Area $\triangle ABC = \tfrac{1}{2} \times B \times H$

$= \tfrac{1}{2} \times 8 \times 6$

$= 24 \text{ cm}^2$

Example 2 :-

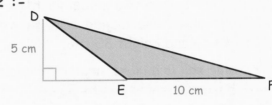

D

5 cm

E   10 cm   F

Area $\triangle DEF = \tfrac{1}{2} \times B \times H$

$= \tfrac{1}{2} \times 10 \times 5$

$= 25 \text{ cm}^2$

Remember :-   If the length and breadth are in cm =>   Area is in cm^2.

If the length and breadth are in mm =>   Area is in mm^2.

If the length and breadth are in m   =>   Area is in m^2.

Exercise 2

1.   Use the formula Area $= \tfrac{1}{2} \times B \times H$ to calculate the areas of these triangles :-

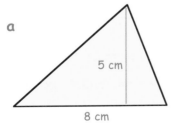

a

5 cm

8 cm

b

4 cm

9 cm

c

10 cm

12 cm

d   14 cm

6 cm

e

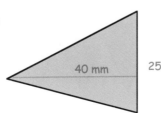

40 mm   25 mm

f

102 mm

80 mm

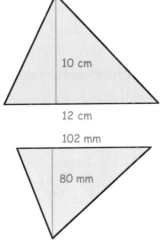

2. Three identical metal brackets are used to support a shelf.

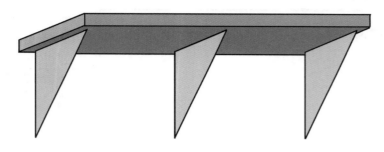

18 cm

25 cm

Each bracket is a right-angled triangle, as shown opposite.

Calculate the total **area** of metal needed to make **all** three brackets.

3. The yellow sail of this model yacht is in the shape of an **obtuse angled triangle** with base 80 cm and height 35 cm.

The blue sail is a **right angled triangle**, with base 40 cm and height 55 cm.

Calculate total **area** of the sails, in cm².

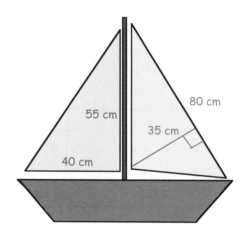

55 cm

80 cm

35 cm

40 cm

4. Calculate the **area** of each of these triangles :-

a

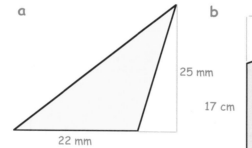

25 mm

22 mm

b

20 cm

17 cm

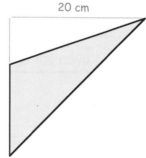

c

8 m

$6\frac{1}{2}$ m

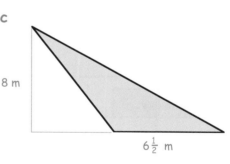

5. A joinery company uses the logo below to advertise the sharpness of their saws.
Each triangle measures 8 cm wide with a 12 cm drop. The rectangle is 4 cm by 90 cm.
Calculate the total **area** of the logo.

90 cm

4 cm

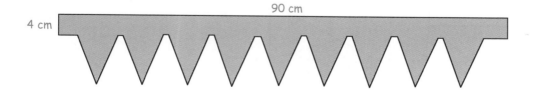

8 cm

12 cm

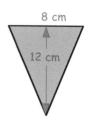

Perimeter/Area of a Square, Rectangle & Triangle

Be able to use a formula to find the Perimeter and Area of a shape.

Examples :- Calculate the **Perimeter** and **Area** of each shape :-

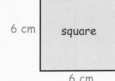

square — 6 cm, 6 cm

rectangle — 4 cm, 8 cm

triangle — 8 cm, 4·8 cm, 6 cm, 10 cm

Perimeter = 6 + 6 + 6 + 6

= 24 cm

Area = $L \times L$

= 6 × 6

= 36 cm²

Perimeter = 4 + 8 + 4 + 8

= 24 cm

OR $P = 2(L + B)$

= 2(4 + 8)

= 2 × 12 = 24 cm

Area = $L \times B$

= 4 × 8

= 32 cm²

Perimeter = 10 + 8 + 6

= 24 cm

Area = $\frac{1}{2} \times B \times H$

= 0·5 × 10 × 4·8

= 24 cm²

Exercise 3

1. For each shape below, calculate :- (i) its perimeter   (ii) its area :-

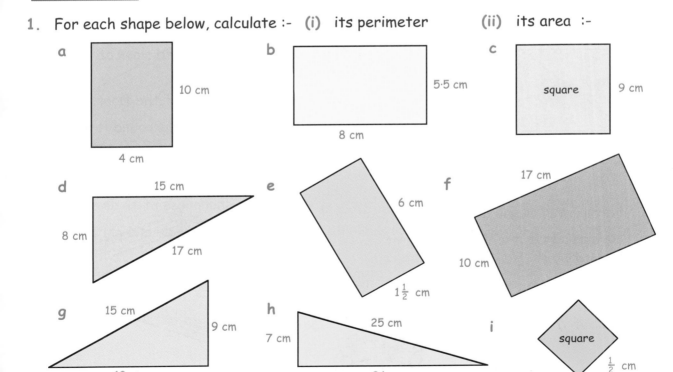

a — 10 cm, 4 cm

b — 5·5 cm, 8 cm

c — square — 9 cm

d — 15 cm, 8 cm, 17 cm

e — 6 cm, $1\frac{1}{2}$ cm

f — 17 cm, 10 cm

g — 15 cm, 9 cm, 12 cm

h — 25 cm, 7 cm, 24 cm

i — square — $\frac{1}{2}$ cm

2. Calculate the areas of the objects shown, using an appropriate formula :-

a  Sponge Bob's Square Head side 11 cm

b  Kiltie Photo 200 mm 120 mm

c  Union Jack 2 m $2\frac{1}{2}$ m

d 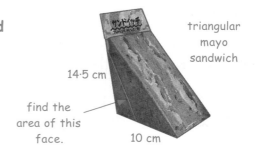 triangular mayo sandwich 14·5 cm find the area of this face. 10 cm

3. Donnie decides to varnish his Youth Club Hall floor.

   a Calculate the area of the floor.

   b A litre of varnish covers 16 m². How many litres will be needed for one coat of varnish ?

   c If a litre tin costs £8, what will it cost to cover the floor with two coats of varnish ?

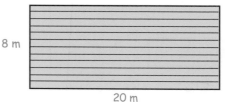 8 m 20 m

4. 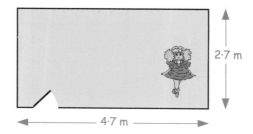 2·7 m 4·7 m

   The diagram shows the carpeted floor of Mandy's bedroom.

   a Calculate the perimeter of the floor.

   b How much will it cost to surround it with new skirting board costing £2·50 per metre ?

   (The door is 0·80 metre wide).

5. Farmer McDougall owns a rectangular field.

   He surrounds it with 3 strands of barbed wire.

   If the wire costs 50p per metre, calculate the total cost of the wire.

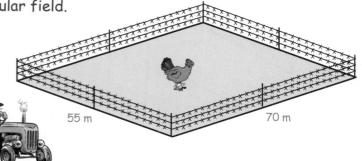 55 m 70 m

The Area of a Parallelogram

Be able to use a formula to find the Area of a Parallelogram.

It should be easy to see why ....

the Area of a Parallelogram   =   the Area of a Rectangle.

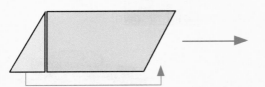

Remember :-   (Area of Rectangle = Length × Breadth)

A difference in notation :-

> AREA of Parallelogram = Base × Height

Example :-

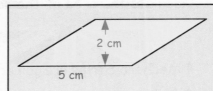

Area   =   B(ase) × H(eight)

=   5 × 2

=   10 cm²

Exercise 4

1.   Calculate the area of each parallelogram using the formula *Area = B × H* :-

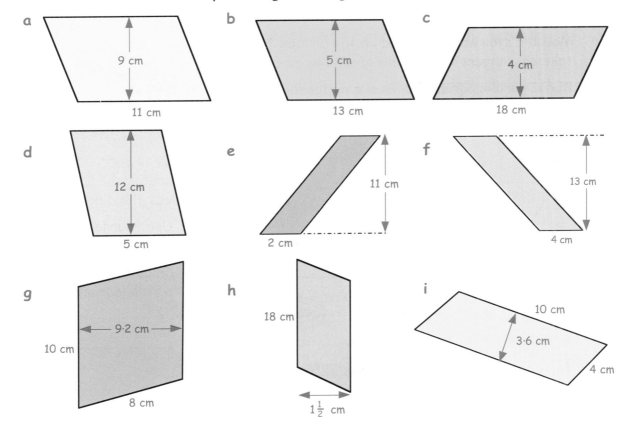

a

9 cm
11 cm

b

5 cm
13 cm

c

4 cm
18 cm

d

12 cm
5 cm

e

11 cm
2 cm

f

13 cm
4 cm

g

9·2 cm
10 cm
8 cm

h

18 cm
1½ cm

i

10 cm
3·6 cm
4 cm

2. This light switch is in the shape of a parallelogram. Calculate its **area**.

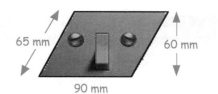

65 mm   60 mm

90 mm

3.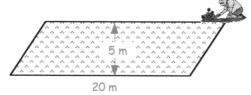

5 m

20 m

Mr Roy has a lawn in the shape of a parallelogram. Calculate the **area** of his lawn.

4. The ramp in this garage is the shape of a parallelogram. Calculate the **area** of the gap shown.

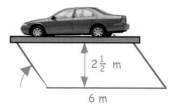

$2\frac{1}{2}$ m

6 m

5. 4 Mechano Strips are joined to make a parallelogram shape. Calculate the **area** of the shape formed.

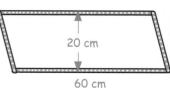

20 cm

60 cm

6.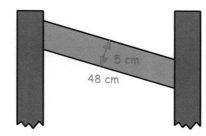

5 cm

48 cm

A sloping wooden plank is used to help strengthen 2 upright posts.

Calculate the **area** of the sloping plank.

7. Movable stairways are used on the London Tube to take passengers from below ground up to street level.

Again, parallelogram shapes are noticeable.

Find the **area** of the large parallelogram.

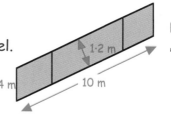

1·2 m

1·4 m   10 m

8.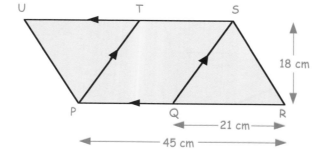

U   T   S

18 cm

P   Q   R

21 cm

45 cm

Look at the diagram opposite.

a   Use four letters each time to name 2 parallelograms.

b   Calculate the **area** of each parallelogram.

9. The **area** of this parallelogram is 325 mm². Calculate its height.

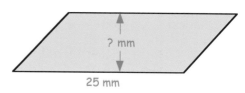

? mm

25 mm

Mixed Exercise

Be able to compare areas and perimeters

1. a Calculate the **area** of each of these 6 shapes.

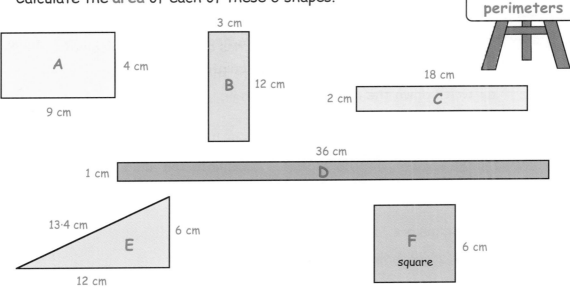

b Now, calculate the **perimeter** of each shape.

c Copy and complete ...

"Though the areas of shapes are ..., it does ... mean that their ..... are also ...".

2. a Work out the **perimeter** of each shape.

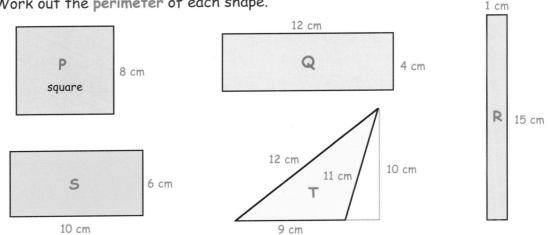

b Work out the **area** of each shape.

c If two shapes have the same perimeter, does that mean they will also have the same area ?

3. A rectangle measures 4 cm by 6 cm.

Is it possible to draw another rectangle with the same area, (*with sides having only whole number values*), but with a **smaller** perimeter ? *Explain your reasoning* !

Revisit - Review - Revise

1. a   With your ruler, make an accurate drawing of this right angled triangle.

    b   Draw a surrounding rectangle and calculate its area.

    c   Now write down the area of the triangle.

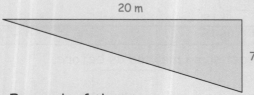

4 cm

8 cm

2.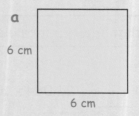

    20 m

    7 m

    Calculate the area of this right angled triangle, in m².

3. For each of these :-

    (i)   Name the shape or shapes involved.

    (ii) State what formula or formulae should be used to find the area.

    (iii) Calculate the area in cm², mm² or m².

    a   6 cm

        6 cm

    b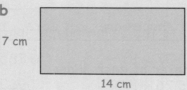

        7 cm

        14 cm

    c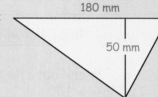

        180 mm

        50 mm

    d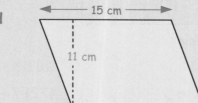

        ← 15 cm →

        11 cm

    e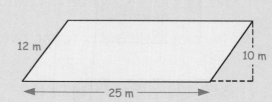

        12 m

        25 m

        10 m

4. Mrs Tweet intends to put a border round the edge of her treasured humming bird painting.

    Bordering costs £14 per metre length in the Art Shop.

    How much will it cost Mrs Tweet to get it done there ?

    155 cm

    95 cm

5. A rectangle measures 3 cm by 8 cm.

    State the measurements of another 2 rectangles with the same area as this one but with a larger perimeter.

Chapter 13

Decimals

Multiplying/Dividing Decimals by 10, 100, 1000

> Be able to multiply/ divide a number with up to 3 decimal places by 10, 100, 1000.

- To multiply by 10, 100 or 1000, you move the figures one, two or three places to the left.

- To divide by 10, 100 or 1000 you move the figures one, two or three places to the right.

We will now look at examples involving 3 decimal places.

The multiplication or division is done using the exact same method as before.

Examples :–

$3.254 \times 10 = 32.54$	$21.328 \times 100 = 2132.8$	$19.004 \times 1000 = 19004$
$4.87 \div 10 = 0.487$	$3.2 \div 100 = 0.032$	$3475 \div 1000 = 3.475$

Exercise 1

1. Write down the answers to the following multiplications :–

   a 2.5×10 b 3.97×10 c 6.285×10 d 48.006×10

   e 6.2×100 f 5.76×100 g 7.965×100 h 23.084×100

   i 1.8×1000 j 0.77×1000 k 5.439×1000 l 17.308×1000

   m 121.34×10 n 220.342×100 o 59.008×1000 p 200.999×1000.

2. Write down the answers to the following divisions :–

   a $5.2 \div 10$ b $7.27 \div 10$ c $24.68 \div 10$ d $118.53 \div 10$

   e $3.5 \div 100$ f $14.1 \div 100$ g $116.5 \div 100$ h $4721.7 \div 100$

   i $9 \div 1000$ j $35 \div 1000$ k $765 \div 1000$ l $18432 \div 1000$

   m $0.05 \div 10$ n $0.3 \div 100$ o $12006 \div 1000$ p $318444 \div 1000$.

3. a A piece of card is 0·015 centimetres thick.

      How thick is a pack of 1000 ?

   b Joe travels to his office and home again 5 times per week.

      He covers a total of 17·25 km each week.

      How far does Joe live from his office ?

   c If a block of plastic weighs 0·059 kg what will 100 blocks weigh ?

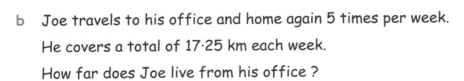

Multiplication by a Single Digit

Those multiplication tables AGAIN !!!

Example :-   37·26 × 4.

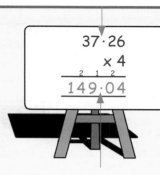

$$\begin{array}{r} 37\cdot26 \\ \times\ 4 \\ \hline {}_2{}_1{}_2\ \ \\ \hline 149\cdot04 \end{array}$$

Be able to multiply a decimal by a single digit.

note that the decimal points should line up.

Exercise 2

1. Copy the following and complete the calculations :-

    a   3·9
         × 4
    _____

    b   9·89
         × 2
    _____

    c   15·7
         × 5
    _____

    d   53·42
         × 7
    _____

    e   60·78
         × 8
    _____

    f   150·34
         × 9
    _____

    g   567·8
         × 3
    _____

    h   253·76
         × 6
    _____

2. Rewrite each of these in the above form and complete the calculations :-

    a   8·7 × 6

    b   19·3 × 4

    c   8·75 × 5

    d   12·98 × 9

    e   8 × 30·37

    f   3 × 8·38

    g   116·8 × 7

    h   6 × 407·14.

3. Show your working in answering the following questions :-

    a   A packet of gums weighs 32·7 grams.
        What is the weight of 8 packets ?

    b   Henry the heating engineer earns £48·49 per hour.
        How much does he earn for working one day from 8.30 am till 2.30 pm ?

    c    Baby Joe gained 28·9 grams per week over the past 7 weeks.
        How much is this weight increase in total ?

    d   By how much is 7 × 0·82 less than 6 × 0·97 ?

    e   The weight of a bar of chocolate is 102·4 grams.
        How much will 9 bars weigh ?

    f    A fully laden cargo ship covered 12·86 km in 1 hour.
        At this speed, how far will it travel in 6 hours ?

Division by a Single Digit

Multiplication Tables ???

Example :-   19·32 ÷ 7

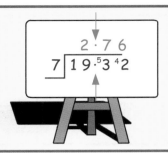

note that the
decimal points
line up.

Exercise 3

1. Copy the following and complete the calculations :-

   a   3) 16·47   b   2) 27·46   c   4) 50·76   d   5) 79·15

   e   8) 0·56   f   6) 0·96   g   7) 111·58   h   9) 50·76 .

2. Rewrite each of these in the above form and complete the calculation :-

   a   9·8 ÷ 2   b   51·8 ÷ 7   c   9·06 ÷ 3   d   38·34 ÷ 6

   e   1·36 ÷ 4   f   81·06 ÷ 6   g   78·3 ÷ 9   h   0·16 ÷ 8.

3. Show your working in answering the following questions :-

   a   9 packets of chews weigh 433·8 grams.

      What is the weight of 1 packet ?

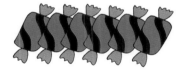

   b   Sambuka is paid £52·64 for working 8 hours as a secretary.
      How much does she earn each hour ?

   c   A 7 mile taxi journey costs Walter £17·43.

      What does that work out at per mile ?

   d   I needed 6 whole packets of moss killer to use on my lawn.

      If the area of the lawn is 72·84 square metres,
      what area did one packet of the moss killer cover ?

   e   To find a "fifth" of anything, you simply divide by 5.

      (i)   What is a fifth of 27·85 ?   (ii)   What is a quarter of 51·36 ?

      (iii) What is a third of 24·27 ?   (iv)   What is a sixth of 172·74 ?

      (v)   What is an eighth of 76·56 ?   (vi)   What is a ninth of 1·53 ?

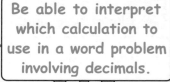

Be able to interpret which calculation to use in a word problem involving decimals.

In this exercise, you must decide whether to

add, subtract, multiply or divide.

then proceed to do the calculation.

Exercise 4

1. Lee bought a shirt, a tie and a pair of trousers from *The Trendy Shop* and the bill came to £87·49.

   He remembered that the trousers were £45·75 and the shirt was £23·99.

   What must the tie have cost him ?

2.

PEDRO'S ZOO	
Admission Prices	
Adult	€20·45
Child	€10·95
Special *	€39·50
(*1 adult + 2 children)	

While on holiday in Spain, Mrs Davies took her two children to *Pedro's Zoo*.

a   How much did it cost, in euros, to buy 1 adult and 2 children's tickets ?

b   How much would she have saved by buying the "Special" ticket ?

3. I bought 8 metres of fencing at £6·54 per metre.

   How much did it cost me altogether ?

4.

   Meryl got paid £1798·20 for 6 months work.

   What did that work out at per month, correct to the nearest one pence ?

5. Paula hires a carpet cleaning machine from a hardware shop.

   She pays £12·50 straight away and then £4·25 per hour of use.

   How much had she to pay in total when she returned the machine after using it for 5 hours ?

6. *Computer Games Store* is selling packs of 3 SD cards for £59·97.

   PC Palace sells the same cards in packs of 5 for £97·50.

   Which store is cheaper per card and by how much ?

7. Elaine buys eight coffees costing £2·25 each, five slices of cake at £2·75 each and three pieces of shortbread at 80p each.

   What change does she get from £35 ?

8.  A group of 7 retired school teachers met up for a reunion dinner.

   The total cost of the meal came to £315·87, which they split equally.

   How much did each have to pay to cover the cost of the meal ?

9. Two fish suppers and a sausage supper cost me £15·25.

   If the sausage supper was priced at £3·55, what was the price of one fish supper ?

10. The total bill for 6 girls going abroad for a two day hen party was £1493·82, food and room only.

   How much did each girl have to pay if the bill was shared evenly ?

11. *Benson the Bakers*, sells delicious cup cakes.

   A box of 8 costs £12·08 and a pack of 6 costs £9·24.

   Which is the better deal ? (*Explain your answer with working*).

12.  A cardboard box weighs 0·886 kg when empty.

   Each tin of peas weighs 0·415 kg.

   What is the combined weight of a box containing 9 tins ?

13. Six friends went for a meal. If the total bill had been shared equally amongst the 6 of them, each would have had to pay £25·45.

   Because it was Martha's birthday, the other five decided to treat her and the bill was split only 5 ways.

   How much did each person really have to pay ?

14. A policeman is out on his rounds. In his first hour, he covers 4·05 miles.

   Every hour after that, as he tires, he walks one third of the distance he walked in the previous hour.

   How far will he have walked altogether in 3 hours ?

Changing a Fraction into a Decimal

Be able to change a fraction into a decimal rounded to 3 dec. pl. when necessary.

Remember :- $\frac{2}{5}$ really means $2 \div 5 = 0 \cdot 4$.

$$5 \overline{\smash{)}2 \cdot 0} \quad \substack{0 \cdot 4}$$

We can change **any fraction** to a **decimal**, in the exercise below, but going no further than 3 decimal places.

Examples :-

Change the following fractions to a decimal, rounding to 3 dec. pl. when necessary :-

1. $\frac{3}{4} = 3 \div 4 = 0 \cdot 75$.

   $$4 \overline{\smash{)}3 \cdot 0\,\overset{2}{0}} \quad \substack{0 \cdot 7\,5}$$

2. $\frac{2}{7} = 2 \div 7 = 0 \cdot 286$ to 3 dec. pl.

   $$7 \overline{\smash{)}2 \cdot 0\overset{6}{0}\overset{4}{0}\overset{5}{0}\,^{1}} \quad \substack{0 \cdot 2\,8\,5\,7\,..}$$

Exercise 5

1. Copy and complete each of the following :-

   a $\frac{3}{5} = 3 \div 5 = 0 \cdot ....$

   b $\frac{1}{4} = 1 \div ... = 0 \cdot ....$

   c $\frac{5}{8} = ... \div ... = 0 \cdot ...$

   d $\frac{437}{1000} = ... \div ... = 0 \cdot ...$

2. Change each fraction to a decimal, rounding to 3 decimal places when necessary :-

   a $\frac{3}{8}$ b $\frac{4}{5}$ c $\frac{5}{7}$ d $\frac{1}{6}$ e $\frac{7}{12}$ f $\frac{2}{11}$.

3. Change each fraction to a decimal and then put them in order (**smallest** first) :-

   a $\frac{2}{3}, \frac{5}{6}, \frac{7}{9}, \frac{5}{7}$

   b $\frac{69}{100}, \frac{2}{3}, \frac{31}{50}, \frac{7}{12}$.

4. Change the following top heavy fractions to decimal numbers, rounding to 3 decimal places when necessary :-

   a $\frac{11}{3}$ b $\frac{17}{6}$ c $\frac{31}{8}$ d $\frac{15}{7}$.

5. A container holds 20 litres of water. An equal quantity of water is poured into 6 jugs such that each holds the same amount.

   How much water will be in each jug ? (*Answer as a decimal to 3 dec. pl.*)

Revisit - Review - Revise

1. Write down the answers to :-

   a 0·34 x 10   b 10 x 21·358   c 100 x 0·456   d 2·9 x 100

   e 0·507 x 1000   f 1000 x 2·96   g 35·1 ÷ 10   h 0·47 ÷ 10

   i 450 ÷ 100   j 1·45 ÷ 100   k 5690 ÷ 1000   l 98·1 ÷ 1000.

2. Set down and find :-

   a 3·45 x 7   b 6 x 4·58   c 9·45 ÷ 5   d 11·37 ÷ 3.

3. How much change from a £5 note will I receive if I buy
   a comic at £1·75 and a can of juice at 57 pence ?

4.
   One tin of creosote paint covers
   9 square metres of fencing.

   a   How many tins will I need to buy for a fence
       with an area of 76·5 square metres ?

   b   At £6·50 per tin, what will I have to pay ?

5. Mr Fitter bought a new set of 4 tyres for £215·20.

   What was the cost of 1 tyre ?

6.
   A carton of apple juice contains 1·42 litres.

   Cyril buys 12 cartons for his party.

   How many litres of juice did he buy ?
   (*Round your answer to 1 decimal place*).

7. *Laser Computers* are selling boxes of 20 disks for £1·44.

   Print Out Computers are selling disks in tubs of 300 for £21·90

   Which computer shop is more expensive per disk and by how much ?

8. Change each of these fractions to a decimal, rounding to 3 decimal places
   when necessary :-

   a $\frac{1}{5}$ b $\frac{7}{8}$ c $\frac{5}{6}$ d $\frac{11}{4}$.

Chapter 14

Solving (Basic) Equations

Be able to solve basic equations.

Remember - we can solve equations by **cover up** (using a finger).

$$x + 5 = 9$$
$$x = 4$$

$$p - 3 = 12$$
$$p = 15$$

$$y - 7 = 1$$
$$y = 8$$

We can also use our *cover up* method for these type of equations :-

$3x$ means 3 times x.

$$3x = 12$$
$$x = 4$$

$$2k = 10$$
$$k = 5$$

$$7y = 56$$
$$y = 8$$

There are various other ways of solving equations :-

3 times "what" equals 12 ?

- the "cover up" method
- the method of "equal addition"
- the "change side <—> change sign" rule.

$$3 \times \qquad = 12$$

You may come across these alternative methods later.

Exercise 1

1. Copy and solve each equation by finding the value of the letter :-

    a $x + 3 = 7$ b $x + 9 = 12$ c $x + 1 = 17$

    d $y + 11 = 21$ e $y - 3 = 6$ f $y - 1 = 21$

    g $p - 10 = 0$ h $p - 50 = 10$ i $p + 6 = 6$

    j $k - 18 = 0$ k $h + 15 = 30$ l $g - 40 = 40$

    m $5 - q = 1$ n $8 + w = 11$ o $9 - z = 0$

    p $71 + f = 111$ q $145 - x = 77$ r $515 + y = 761.$

2. Copy each equation and find the value of the letter :-

    a $3x = 6$ b $4m = 20$ c $5p = 30$

    d $7q = 28$ e $6t = 36$ f $6a = 60$

    g $3b = 36$ h $8d = 48$ i $2x = 24$

    j $2p = 22$ k $4p = 56$ l $6m = 54$

    m $10x = 110$ n $8t = 64$ o $14p = 42$

    p $2b = 5$ q $2c = 9$ r $2n = 19$

    s $4x = 21$ t $10x = 34$ u $5x = 24.$

Harder Equations

Be able to solve an equation.

Look at these equations which involve both addition/subtraction and multiplication.

Example 1 :-

$$2x + 1 = 7$$
$$2x = 6$$
$$x = 3$$

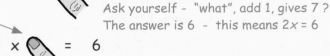

___ + 1 = 7

Ask yourself - "what", add 1, gives 7 ?
The answer is 6 - this means $2x = 6$

2 × ___ = 6

Now ask yourself - 2 times "what", gives 6 ?
The answer is 3 - this means $x = 3$

Examples :-

$$3x - 2 = 25$$
$$3x = 27$$
$$x = 9$$

$$4x - 6 = 6$$
$$4x = 12$$
$$x = 3$$

Can you see we can still use the cover up method ?

Discuss each of these examples with your teacher.

Exercise 2

1. Find the value of x by solving each equation below. **Copy** and **complete** :-

a
$$2x + 5 = 11$$
$$2x = 6$$
$$x = ...$$

b
$$3x + 1 = 13$$
$$3x = ...$$
$$x = ...$$

c
$$4x - 5 = 15$$
$$4x = ...$$
$$x = ...$$

2. Find the value of x :- (*Set down your 3 lines of working carefully*).

a $2x + 3 = 5$ b $3x + 6 = 21$ c $4x + 7 = 23$

d $5x + 2 = 42$ e $2x - 4 = 6$ f $3x - 3 = 24$

g $4x - 1 = 35$ h $3x - 6 = 0$ i $6x - 1 = 53$

j $7x - 2 = 68$ k $8x + 4 = 28$ l $9x - 2 = 61$

m $2x - 12 = 2$ n $4x + 10 = 22$ o $5x + 20 = 20$

p $5x - 1 = 24$ q $5 + 2x = 12$ r $6x - 3 = 12.$

3. Look at the picture showing 2 rods end to end.

x cm   8 cm

a   Write down an expression, in terms of x, for the total length of the 2 rods.

b   Given that the total length of the rods is actually 21 centimetres :-

(i)   make up an equation involving x.

(ii)   solve it to find the value of x.

4. Tony has £8 and Bob has £x. Together they have £17.

 a   Make up an equation using this information.

 b   Now solve it to determine how much Bob has.

5. There were x marbles in a bag. 7 were removed.

 I then found that there were 14 left.

 a   Make up an equation about the marbles.

 b   Now solve it to determine how many there were to begin with.

6. For each of the following :–   (i) make an equation and   (ii) solve it.

 a      Chad has x pencils in his case. Harry has 14 pencils.

 Altogether they have 31 pencils.

 b   Eliose has to cycle 2·3 kilometres to school.

 Franz has to walk y kilometres.

 They travel a total of 3·1 kilometres.

 c      Tom cycles from his house to the park then to the beach, a total of 34 kilometres.

 From his house to the park is 20 km.

 The park to the beach is p kilometres.

7. To find the area of a rectangle you **multiply** its length by its breadth.

 a   Write down an expression for the area of this rectangle in terms of x.

 b   If the actual area is 24 cm²,

  (i)   write down an equation involving x,

  (ii)   solve it to find the value of x.

4 cm

x cm

8. Have a go at these. Find the value of x in each case :–

 a $\frac{1}{2}x = 7$ b $\frac{1}{3}x = 9$ c $\frac{1}{4}x = 20$

 d $\frac{1}{5}x = 10$ e $\frac{1}{10}x = 5$ f $\frac{1}{8}x = 2$

 g $\frac{1}{6}x = 11$ h $\frac{1}{5}x = 20$ i $\frac{1}{2}x = 3\frac{1}{2}$

 j $\frac{1}{2}x + 1 = 6$ k $\frac{1}{3}x - 4 = 2$ l $\frac{1}{4}x - 2 = 10$.

Solving Equations with 2 Unknowns

Be able to solve an equation with 2 unknowns.

Until now, you have been asked to solve an equation which has only 1 unknown letter. Sometimes, there are 2 "unknowns" to be found.

Example 1 :- Instead of $x + 3 = 5$ we are now asked for

$$\boxed{x + y = 5}$$

and require 2 answers, one for x and one for y.

> $x + y = 5$
> You choose a value for x, say $x = 3$.
> $3 + y = 5$
> $y = 2$
> So .... $x = 3$ and $y = 2$

* There are more answers :-
$x = 0, y = 5, \quad x = 1, y = 4, \quad x = 2, y = 3, \quad x = 4, y = 1, \quad x = 5, y = 0$
and even more, as you will find out in the exercise

Example 2 :-

> $2x + y = 6$
> You choose a value for x, say $x = 1$.
>
> $2 \times 1 + y = 6$
> $2 + y = 6$
> $y = 4$
>
> So .... $x = 1$ and $y = 4$

* There are more answers :-
$x = 0, y = 6, \quad x = 2, y = 2, \quad x = 3, y = 0$
are just a few.

Exercise 3

1. Replace $x = 5$ in these three equations and work out the value of y each time.

    Copy and **complete** :-

    a
    > $x + y = 8$
    > $5 + y = 8$
    > $y \quad = ...$

    b
    > $x - y = 1$
    > $... - y = 1$
    > $y \quad = ...$

    c
    > $2x + y = 12$
    > $2 \times ... + y = 12$
    > $... + y = 12$
    > $y \quad = ...$

2. You now carefully choose a value of x and then work out the relevant value of y.
    Set down your working. (*There are several pairs of acceptable answers here*).

    a $x + y = 4$ b $x + y = 9$ c $x + y = 12$

    d $x - y = 2$ e $x - y = 8$ f $x - y = 14$

    g $2x + y = 8$ h $3x + y = 7$ i $5x + y = 11$

    j $2x - y = 5$ k $4x - y = 0$ l $6x - y = 1$.

3. Do Question **2** again, this time choosing a different value for x and obtaining a different answer for y.

---

4. Do Question 2 yet again, choosing a value for x which you have not used and find yet another answer for y.

5. Write down as many whole number (0, 1, 2, 3, ...) answers for x and y as you can for these equations :-

    a $x + y = 20$ b $2x + y = 20$ c $y = 10 - x$.

> Answers which are fractions are now going to be permitted.
>
> $x + y = 5$ Can you see that $x = 2\frac{1}{2}$ and $y = 2\frac{1}{2}$ works ?
>
>   Can you see that $x = 4\frac{1}{4}$ and $y = \frac{3}{4}$ works ?

6. Write down **three** values for x and the relevant answers for y for each of the following equations, using a fraction for the x or y :-

    a $x + y = 2$ b $x + y = 9$ c $x + y = 1$

    d $x - y = 3$ e $x - y = 5$ f $x - y = 10$

    g $2x + y = 6$ h $12x - y = 1$ i $y = 8 - x$.

> Answers which are negative numbers are now going to be permitted.
>
> $x + y = 5$ Can you see that $x = 6$ and $y = -1$ works ?
>
>   Can you see that $x = -10$ and $y = 15$ works ?

7. Write down **three** values for x and the relevant answers for y for each of the following equations with either (or both) of x or y being a negative number :-

    a $x + y = 1$ b $x + y = 7$ c $x + y = -2$

    d $2x + y = 0$ e $4x + y = 2$ f $y = 2 - 5x$.

8. In Worked **Example 1**, we found the answers to the equation $x + y = 5$ to be :-

    $x = 0, y = 5$ $x = 1, y = 4$ $x = 2, y = 3$ $x = 3, y = 2$ $x = 4, y = 1$ $x = 5, y = 0$.

These can be written in coordinate form :- (0, 5), (1, 4), (2, 3), (3, 2), (4, 1) and (5, 0).

Plot the points on a coordinate diagram and state what happens when they are joined.

9.   (i)   Find 3 values for x and y each time

    (ii)   Write them in coordinate form (x, y)

    (iii)   Plot them on separate diagrams and join them up.

         a $x + y = 4$ b $x + y = 8$

         c $x - y = 1$ d $y = x + 2$.

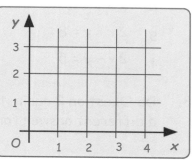

1. Solve these equations to find the value of x.

   a $x + 3 = 11$ b $x - 5 = 5$ c $x + 15 = 25$

   d $x - 7 = 0$ e $9 + x = 22$ f $35 - x = 3$

   g $2x = 14$ h $13x = 39$ i $6x = 33$

   j $2x + 7 = 9$ k $3x - 3 = 18$ l $4x + 8 = 26$

   m $8x - 1 = 41$ n $\frac{1}{2}x = 10$ o $\frac{1}{5}x - 1 = 2.$

2. There were 30 people on a train.

   After x people got off there were 21 left on the train.

   a   Make up an equation about the people on the train.

   b   Solve the equation to find how many people must have got off.

3.

Last week, George earned £x as a barber.

This week he earned **double** that amount **plus** tips of £40.

In fact, George earned £440 this week.

Make up an equation using x and solve it to find out how much George must have earned **last week**.

4. Solve to find a value for x and for y. Both x and y must be **positive** in this question.

   a $x + y = 9$ b $x - y = 3$ c $2x + y = 10.$

5. Find a value for x and y. Either x or y (or both) must be a **negative** number here :-

   a $x + y = 3$ b $x - y = 0$ c $2x + y = 2.$

6. Find a value for x and for y. Either x or y (or both) must be a **fraction** here.

   a $x + y = 5$ b $x - y = 2$ c $y = 2x + 1.$

7. a   Find 6 values for x and for y in :- $x + y = 6.$

   b   Write them in coordinate form (x, y).

   c   Plot them on a coordinate diagram and join them up.

   d   What did you get ?

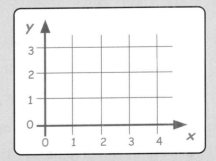

Chapter 15

Angles   Revision

Exercise 1

1. Use right, straight, acute, obtuse or reflex to describe each of these angles :-

    a 105°   b 180°   c 33°   d 303°   e 90°.

2. Use a protractor to draw each of the angles in Question 1.

3. What is the :-

    a complement of 70°   b complement of 4°

    c supplement of 110°   d supplement of 5° ?

4. Copy and complete each diagram below, filling in **all** missing angles :-

    a   b   c

    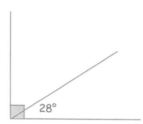      

    d   e   f

          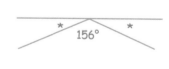

5. Shown is a rectangle ABCD.

    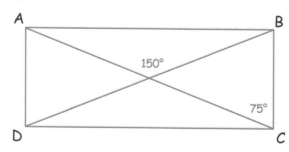

    a Make a large sketch of ABCD (*You do NOT need to be accurate*).

    b Show all parallel lines and equal sides.

    c Fill in the sizes of all the missing angles.

Angles Round a Point

Be able to calculate a missing angle round a point.

The **angles round a point** must total **360°**. (2 straight angles).

In the diagram shown

$$a + b + c + d = 360.$$

Examples :-

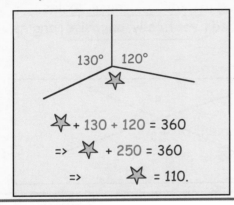

$$\bigstar + 130 + 120 = 360$$
$$\Rightarrow \bigstar + 250 = 360$$
$$\Rightarrow \bigstar = 110.$$

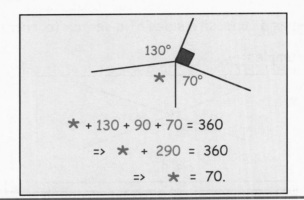

$$\ast + 130 + 90 + 70 = 360$$
$$\Rightarrow \ast + 290 = 360$$
$$\Rightarrow \ast = 70.$$

Exercise 2

1. Calculate the value of the angles marked ○ :-

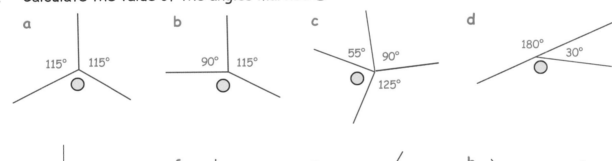

a   115°   115°

b   90°   115°

c   55°   90°   125°

d   180°   30°

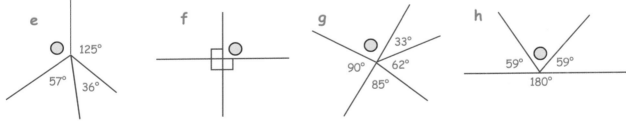

e   125°   57°   36°

f

g   33°   90°   62°   85°

h   59°   59°   180°

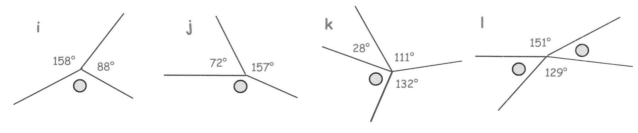

i   158°   88°

j   72°   157°

k   28°   111°   132°

l   151°   129°

2. Sketch some diagrams similar to Question 1.

   Get your partner to find the missing angles.

Be able to find
missing angles
using vertically
opposite angles.

In the diagram shown, angles
a and *b* must be the same.

Discuss why *a* = *b*.
(*Hint* :- *supplementary angles*).

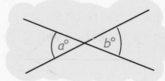

Angles at opposite sides of a vertex (corner) are called **vertically opposite** angles.

Examples :-

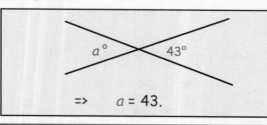

=>   *a* = 43.

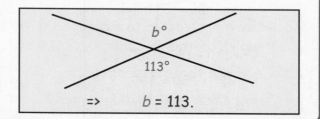

=>   *b* = 113.

Exercise 3

1.   Write down the value of the angles marked ◯ :-

a

122°

b

35°

c

53°

d

$25\frac{1}{2}$ °

e

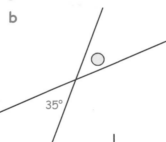

f

139°

g

58°

h

88°

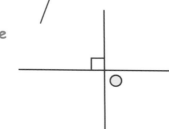

i

101·5°

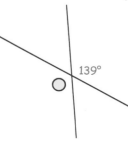

2.   Sketch all the diagrams above and fill in **all** the missing angles.

3.   Sketch some diagrams similar to Question 1.

       Get your partner to find the missing angles.

Angles in Triangles and Polygons

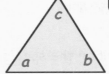

Be able to find missing angles in triangles and polygons.

In maths, no matter how big a triangle is, if you add all three angles together you always get 180°.

=> **a + b + c = 180**

Exercise 4   (You will need a protractor for questions 1 and 2)

1. a Use a protractor to measure the three angles of this triangle.

   b Add the three angles together.

   c How close to 180° did you get ?

2. a Draw a triangle of your own - any size, any shape. (*Make it about half the size of your page*).

   b Measure the 3 angles and check that the total comes to (*about*) 180°.

3. a In this triangle, what is the value of 40° + 55° ?

   b If all 3 angles add to 180°, what must the 3rd angle be (marked *****) ?

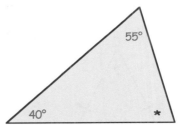

4. For each triangle, add the given angles, then calculate the size of the 3rd angle :-

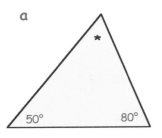
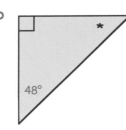
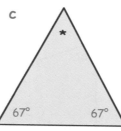
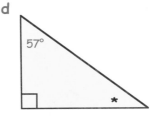

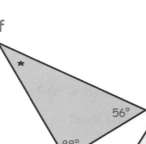
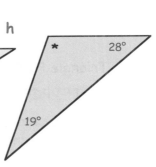

---

5. a Use the 140° to help you calculate the size of the angle marked *a*.

    b Now use triangle ∆**PQR** to help you find the value of *b*.

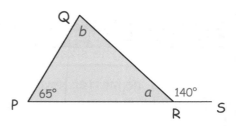

6. Can you remember the special name for this type of triangle ?

    > • The two sides (**PR** and **QR**) are equal.
    >
    > • The two angles (∠**RPQ** and ∠**RQP**) are equal.

    It is called an **ISOSCELES** triangle.

    Look at the word, cover it up and learn to spell it.

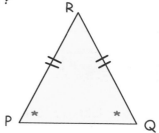

7.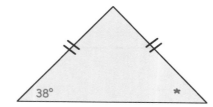

    An **isosceles** triangle has 2 angles the same size.

    a Write down the value of the angle marked *.
       (*Do NOT measure it*).

    b Now calculate the size of the 3rd angle.

8. Make a small neat sketch of each of these isosceles triangles.

    Calculate the sizes of the two missing angles in each triangle :–

    a 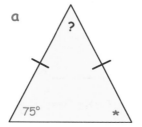   b 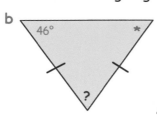   c 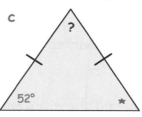   d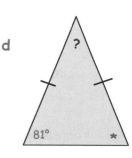

    e   f 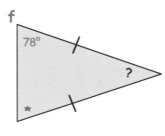   g 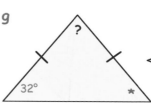   h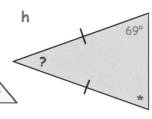

9. Triangle **PQR** is **isosceles**.

    a If ∠**PQR** = 130°, what is the value of (*a* + *b*) ?

    b Since *a* and *b* are both the same, what must both *a* and *b* be ?

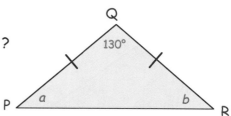

10. Make a neat sketch of each of these isosceles triangles.

Calculate the sizes of the two missing angles in each triangle :–

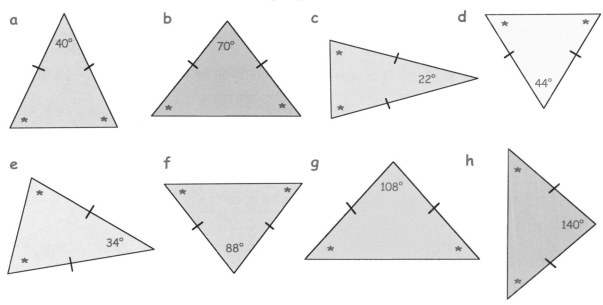

11. Triangle GFH is isosceles.   ∠HGT = 125°

   a   Calculate the size of ∠HGF.

   b   State the size of ∠HFG.

   c   Now calculate the size of ∠GHF.

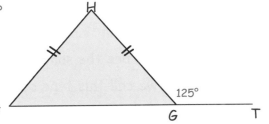

12. Copy each of the following.

Calculate and fill in the sizes of all the missing angles :–

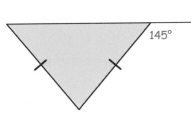
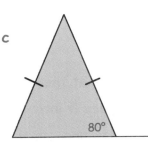

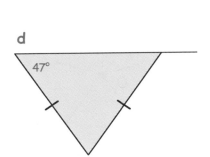
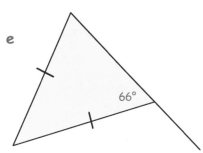
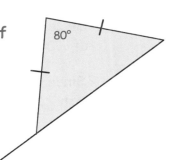

13. Make up some of your own diagrams similar to Question 12 and test your friends.

14.

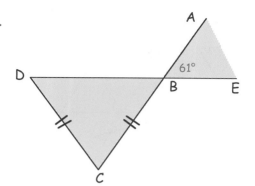

Triangle BCD is isosceles.

BC = DC. ∠ABE = 61°.

a   State the size of ∠DBC.

b   Write down the size of ∠BDC.

c   Finally, what is the size of ∠BCD ?

15.   Copy the following figures and fill in all the missing angles.

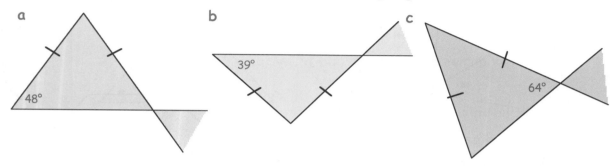

16.   This is a very special triangle.

All 3 of its sides are the same length.

a   What do we call this type of triangle ?

All 3 angles are also the same size.

b   Calculate the size of each of
the 3 angles in this triangle.

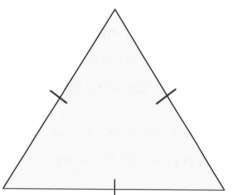

17.   Look at this regular **pentagon** with centre O.

Trace it into your exercise book.

Copy and complete statements **a** to **d** :-

a   "Since a whole turn is 360°, the size
of ∠DOC must be (360° ÷ 5) = ...°".

b   "Since DOC is an isosceles triangle,
both ∠OCD and ∠ODC must be .....°".

c   "Since ∠OCD and ∠OCB are the same size, then
the **Interior** (shaded) ∠BCD must = ...°".

d   "If you add all five angles of a pentagon together the answer you get is ....°".

18. Look at this regular **hexagon** with centre O.

Trace it into your exercise book.

Copy and complete **a** to **d** :-

a "Since a whole turn is 360°, the size of ∠DOC must be (360° ÷ 6) = ...°".

b "Since DOC is an isosceles triangle, both ∠OCD and ∠ODC must each be .....°".

c "Since ∠OCD and ∠OCB are the same size, then the **Interior** (*shaded*) angle ∠BCD must be .....°".

d "The six angles of a hexagon add to give .....°".

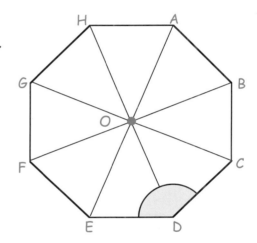

19. The polygon this time is an **octagon**. Trace it.

Go through the same 4 steps as shown in Questions **17** and **18** to find :-

a the size of each of the eight **interior** angles of the octagon.

b the **sum** of all eight angles of the octagon.

20. Trace each of these and go through the similar steps as shown in Question 18.

a nonagon

b decagon.

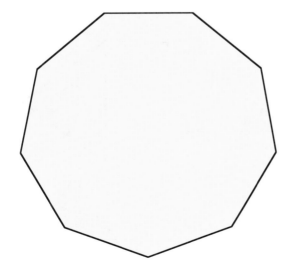

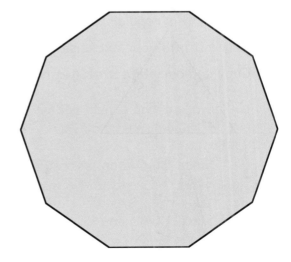

Mixed Exercise

Copy and complete each diagram below, filling in **all** missing angles :-

1. **a** 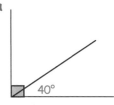   **b** 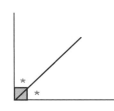   **c** 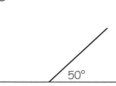   **d**

e 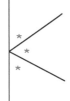   **f** 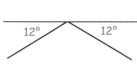   **g** 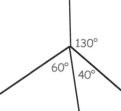   **h**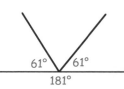

i 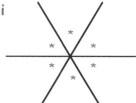   **j**    **k** 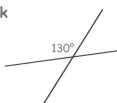   **l**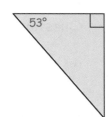

m 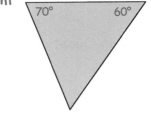   **n** 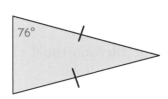   **o**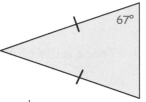

p 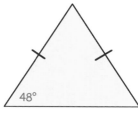   **q** 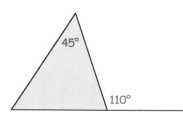   **r**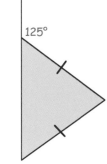

s 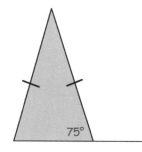   **t** 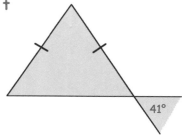   **u**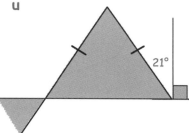

Revisit - Review - Revise

1. What is the :-   a   complement of 40°   b   supplement of 40° ?

2. Copy and complete each diagram below, filling in **all** missing angles :-

a
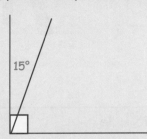
15°

b
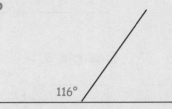
116°

c
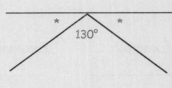
*   130°   *

d
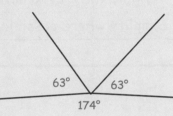
63°   63°
174°

e

124°

f
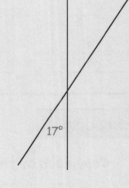
17°

g
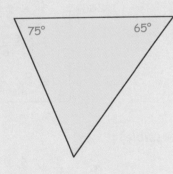
75°   65°

h
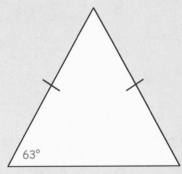
63°

i
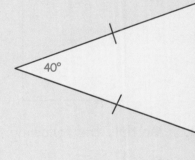
40°

j
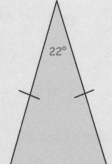
22°

k
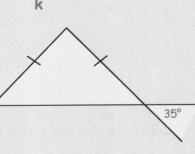
35°

l
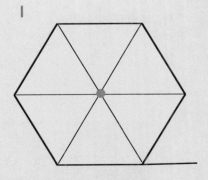

Chapter 16

Multiplying Fractions

Be able to multiply one fraction by another.

The rule for **multiplying** two proper fractions is very simple.

To multiply $\frac{3}{5} \times \frac{4}{7}$ $\longrightarrow$ $\frac{3}{5} \times \frac{4}{7} = \frac{3 \times 4}{5 \times 7} = \frac{12}{35}$.

Example 1 :-

$\frac{3}{4} \times \frac{3}{5}$

$= \frac{3 \times 3}{4 \times 5}$

$= \frac{9}{20}$

Example 2 :-

$\frac{4}{5} \times \frac{5}{6}$

$= \frac{20}{30} \left(\frac{4 \times 5}{5 \times 6} \right)$

$= \frac{2}{3}$ *(simplified)*

Example 3 :-

$\frac{8}{9} \times \frac{3}{4}$

$= \frac{24}{36}$

$= \frac{2}{3}$

Basic Rule :-

- Multiply the 2 numerators.
- Multiply the 2 denominators.
- Simplify where possible.

Exercise 1

1. Copy each of the following and complete :-

   a $\frac{3}{4} \times \frac{4}{5}$

   $= \frac{3 \times 4}{4 \times 5}$

   $= \frac{?}{20} = \frac{?}{?}$

   b $\frac{5}{6} \times \frac{1}{3}$

   $= \frac{5 \times 1}{6 \times 3}$

   $= \frac{?}{?}$

   c $\frac{3}{4} \times \frac{5}{6}$

   $= \frac{3 \times 5}{4 \times 6}$

   $= \frac{?}{24} = \frac{?}{8}$.

2. **Multiply** the following fractions and simplify (*where possible*) :-

   a $\frac{4}{5} \times \frac{2}{3}$

   b $\frac{5}{6} \times \frac{7}{10}$

   c $\frac{3}{5} \times \frac{4}{9}$

   d $\frac{4}{7} \times \frac{5}{6}$

   e $\frac{5}{8} \times \frac{4}{5}$

   f $\frac{7}{12} \times \frac{6}{7}$

   g $\frac{11}{16} \times \frac{2}{3}$

   h $\frac{2}{9} \times \frac{9}{10}$

   i $\frac{2}{3} \times \frac{4}{5} \times \frac{3}{4}$

   j $\frac{4}{5} \times \frac{1}{2} \times \frac{5}{6}$

   k $\frac{1}{2} \times \frac{3}{5} \times \frac{2}{3}$

   l $\frac{2}{3} \times \frac{3}{4} \times \frac{1}{5}$.

3.  Calculate the **area** of a rectangular sheet of metal measuring $\frac{5}{6}$ metre by $\frac{3}{8}$ metre.

Dividing Fractions by a Whole Number

Be able to divide a fraction by a whole number.

Imagine you have a quarter of a pizza and you want to share it with one other person.

This means you want to divide your quarter pizza by 2, (*or find a half of the quarter*).

Can you see from the picture that this means you end up with an *eighth* of a pizza ?

To divide by 2, is the same as finding a $\frac{1}{2}$:-   => $\frac{1}{4} \div 2 = \frac{1}{2} \times \frac{1}{4} = \frac{1}{8}$

> To divide by 3, is the same as multiplying by a $\frac{1}{3}$.
>
> To divide by 4, is the same as multiplying by a $\frac{1}{4}$.
>
> To divide by 5, is the same as multiplying by a $\frac{1}{5}$, and so on ....

Example 1 :-

$$\frac{1}{2} \div 2$$
$$= \frac{1}{2} \times \frac{1}{2}$$
$$= \frac{1}{4}$$

Example 2 :-

$$\frac{1}{5} \div 3$$
$$= \frac{1}{3} \times \frac{1}{5}$$
$$= \frac{1}{15}$$

Example 3 :-

$$\frac{2}{3} \div 4$$
$$= \frac{1}{4} \times \frac{2}{3}$$
$$= \frac{2}{12} = \frac{1}{6}$$

Exercise 2

1. I have $\frac{1}{2}$ a pizza. It is cut into 4 equal bits. What fraction of pizza is each bit ?

2. I have $\frac{1}{4}$ of a pizza cut into 4 bits. What fraction of pizza is each bit ?

3. Copy and complete :-   a $\frac{1}{4} \div 5 = ...$ b $\frac{3}{4} \div 2 = ...$ c $\frac{4}{3} \div 2 = ...$

4. Find :-

    a $\frac{1}{2} \div 4$ b $\frac{1}{4} \div 4$ c $\frac{1}{3} \div 5$ d $\frac{2}{3} \div 2$

    e $\frac{5}{6} \div 5$ f $\frac{5}{8} \div 3$ g $\frac{3}{4} \div 5$ h $\frac{3}{5} \div 3$

5. Billy and his three friends won an equal share in the lottery.

    Billy decided to give his portion of the winnings equally to his 3 daughters.

    What **fraction** of the lottery win will each daughter receive ?

Mixed Exercise using all 4 operators.

1. Change to a **mixed number** :-

    a $\frac{17}{3}$ b $\frac{24}{5}$ c $\frac{42}{8}$ d $\frac{45}{4}$.

2. Rewrite as an **improper fraction** :-

    a $2\frac{3}{4}$ b $4\frac{5}{6}$ c $10\frac{2}{7}$ d $15\frac{5}{6}$.

3. How many $\frac{1}{3}$ pizza slices can by sold from $6\frac{2}{3}$ pizzas ?

4. Copy and complete :-

    a $\frac{3}{7} + \frac{2}{7}$ b $\frac{1}{2} + \frac{3}{4}$ c $\frac{5}{6} - \frac{1}{6}$ d $\frac{7}{8} - \frac{3}{4}$

    e $2\frac{3}{5} + 1\frac{4}{5}$ f $8\frac{7}{9} - 3\frac{1}{9}$ g $1\frac{4}{5} - \frac{1}{2}$ h $7\frac{3}{5} - 5\frac{1}{3}$

    i $7\frac{1}{2} - \frac{2}{3}$ j $18\frac{7}{8} - \frac{1}{4}$ k $11\frac{2}{3} - 10\frac{11}{12}$ l $13\frac{1}{4} - 5\frac{1}{2}$.

5. Copy and complete :-

    a $\frac{1}{2} \times \frac{1}{3}$ b $\frac{8}{9} \times \frac{3}{5}$ c $\frac{4}{5} \times \frac{8}{11}$ d $\frac{1}{2} \times \frac{2}{3} \times \frac{3}{4}$

    e $\frac{1}{2} \div 3$ f $\frac{1}{4} \div 2$ g $\frac{5}{6} \div 3$ h $\frac{4}{5} \div 4$.

6. Before her diet, Mrs Barbour weighed $11\frac{1}{2}$ stones.

    She lost $2\frac{3}{4}$ stones on her diet.

    What was her new weight ?

7.
    A hardware shop sells lengths of heavy duty chain.

    1 metre of the chain weighs $2\frac{2}{5}$ kg.

    What will the weight of a $\frac{1}{3}$ metre chain be ?

8. An empty wooden crate weighs $4\frac{7}{8}$ kg.

    It holds 6 large cartons of rice.

    Each carton weighs $1\frac{3}{4}$ kg.

    Calculate the **total** weight of the crate and cartons.

1. Change to a **mixed number** :-

    a $\frac{17}{4}$　　　　b $\frac{49}{9}$　　　　c $\frac{121}{2}$　　　　d $\frac{67}{7}$.

2. Rewrite as an **improper fraction** :-

    a $1\frac{5}{6}$　　　　b $8\frac{2}{7}$　　　　c $5\frac{2}{3}$　　　　d $11\frac{7}{9}$.

3. How many $\frac{1}{3}$ pizza slices can by sold from $4\frac{1}{3}$ pizzas ?

4. Multiply the following fractions and simplify fully (*where possible*) :-

    a $\frac{4}{5} \times \frac{2}{3}$　　　b $\frac{5}{8} \times \frac{7}{10}$　　　c $\frac{3}{5} \times \frac{5}{9}$　　　d $\frac{5}{7} \times \frac{3}{5} \times \frac{1}{2}$.

5. Find and simplify fully (*where possible*) :-

    a $\frac{1}{2} \div 4$　　　b $\frac{5}{6} \div 3$　　　c $\frac{3}{5} \div 6$　　　d $\frac{3}{5} \div 10$.

6. a Calculate the area of a rectangle
       measuring $\frac{1}{4}$ m by $\frac{3}{5}$ m.

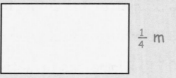

$\frac{1}{4}$ m

$\frac{3}{5}$ m

    b How many $\frac{1}{4}$ metre lengths of wood can
       I cut from a $2\frac{3}{4}$ metre length ?

    c A large box of cereal weighs $\frac{5}{8}$ kg, which is **3** times as much as a small box.
       What is the weight of the small box of cereal ?

7. a A farmer buys $\frac{3}{4}$ of a tonne of animal feed.
       He splits it evenly amongst 3 fields for his cows to feed on.
       What fraction of a tonne is in each field ?

    b A rectangle is 4 metres long.
       It has an area of $\frac{8}{9}$ of a square metre.
       Calculate the width of the rectangle.

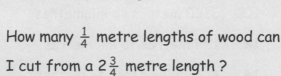

Area = $\frac{8}{9}$ m²

4 m

Chapter 17

Converting Units of Metric Measurement   Revision

Be able to convert between different units of metric measurement.

In Years 4 and 5, you learned to change from one unit to another.

Examples :-

$$3820 \text{ m} = 3820 \div 1000 = 3 \cdot 82 \text{ km}$$

$$0 \cdot 85 \, L = 0 \cdot 85 \times 1000 = 850 \text{ ml}$$

$$0 \cdot 4 \text{ cm} = 0 \cdot 4 \times 10 = 4 \text{ mm}$$

$$20 \text{ g} = 20 \div 1000 = 0 \cdot 02 \text{ kg}$$

Exercise 1

1 cm = 10 mm   1 m = 100 cm

1 km = 1000 m   1 kg = 1000 g

1 litre = 1000 ml

Change :-

1. 1·5 centimetres to millimetres

2. 300 millimetres to centimetres

3. 72·5 centimetres to millimetres

4. 1·9 millimetres to centimetres

5. 0·55 metres to centimetres

6. 45·2 centimetres to metres

7. 3·98 metres to centimetres

8. 2·5 centimetres to metres

9. 0·715 kilometres to metres

10. 3120 metres to kilometres

11. 1·6 kilometres to metres

12. 135 metres to kilometres

13. 3 metres to millimetres

14. 450 millimetres to metres

15. 600 000 millimetres to metres

16. 5 kilometres to centimetres

17. 1 kilometre to millimetres

18. 870 000 centimetres to kilometres

19. 7 000 000 millimetres to kilometres

20. 0·05 kilometres to centimetres

21. 9·5 litres to millilitres

22. 0·04 litres to millilitres

23. 550 millilitres to litres

24. 60 millilitres to litres

25. 425 000 millilitres to litres

26. 0·6 litres to millilitres

27. 5·9 kilograms to grams

28. 350 grams to kilograms

29. 500 grams to kilograms

30. 30 grams to kilograms

31. 3 kilograms to grams

32. 320 320 grams to kilograms.

Metric & Imperial Measurement (Conversion)

Exercise 2 For class discussion

Be able to convert from metric to imperial measurement and vice versa.

1. How much do you already know about Imperial Measurement ?

   Choose one answer each time :-

a	5 cm is round about	(i) 2 feet	or	(ii) 2 inches ?
b	8 km is round about	(i) 5 miles	or	(ii) 5 feet ?
c	1 ounce is round about	(i) 28 grams	or	(ii) 28 kilograms ?
d	30 cm is round about	(i) 12 feet	or	(ii) 1 foot ?
e	1 pints is round about	(i) 1 litre	or	(ii) half a litre ?
f	1 gallon is round about	(i) 4·5 litres	or	(ii) 4·5 millilitres ?
g	2·5 cm is round about	(i) 5 inches	or	(ii) 1 inch ?
h	1 kilogram is round about	(i) 2·2 ounces	or	(ii) 2·2 pounds ?
i	1 litre is round about	(i) 1·75 gallons	or	(ii) 1·75 pints ?

Exact and Approximate Conversions

For discussion.

Use the table shown opposite to discuss the best way of converting from metric to old imperial units and backwards.

The table gives quick conversions and more accurate conversions.

You may want to use a computer to find an even more accurate way of converting.

unit	approximate	more accurate
1 centimetre =	a little less than $\frac{1}{2}$ an inch	0·39 inch
1 inch =	about $2\frac{1}{2}$ centimetres	2·54 cm
1 metre =	a little more than 3 feet	3·28 ft
1 foot =	about a $\frac{1}{3}$ or $\frac{3}{10}$ of a metre	0·30 metre
1 kilometre =	about $\frac{5}{8}$ or 0·6 of a mile	0·62 mile
1 mile =	about $\frac{8}{5}$ or just over $1\frac{1}{2}$ km	1·61 km
1 kilogram =	just over 2 pounds (lbs)	2·2 pounds (lbs)
1 pound (lb) =	about $\frac{1}{2}$ a kilogram	0·45 kg
1 ounce (oz) =	about 25-30 grams	28·3 grams
1 gram =	about $\frac{1}{25}$ of an ounce (oz)	0·04 ounce (oz)
1 litre =	about $\frac{1}{5}$ gallon or $1\frac{3}{4}$ pints	0·22 gal or 1·76 pt
1 gallon =	about $4\frac{1}{2}$ litres	4·55 litres
1 pint =	just over $\frac{1}{2}$ of a litre	0·57 litre

1. Look at the table for converting inches to cm and cm to inches. **Copy** and **complete** :-

   a $\boxed{6 \text{ inches} = 6 \times 2\frac{1}{2} \text{ cm} = ... \text{ cm}}$ b $\boxed{40 \text{ cm is about } 40 \times \frac{1}{2} \text{ inch} = ... \text{ inches.}}$

2. Use the "**approximate**" conversion table to change the following (*roughly*).

a 10 inches to cm	b 60 cm to inches	c 5 metres to feet
d 25 metres to feet	e 30 feet to metres	f 16 km to miles
g 200 km to miles	h 20 miles to km	i 60 miles to km
j 6 kilograms to pounds	k 30 pounds to kilograms	l 6 ounces to grams
m 200 grams to ounces	n 20 litres to gallons	o 10 gallons to litres
p 12 litres to pints	q 15 pints to litres	r 20 litres to pints.

3. If you have a calculator, redo Qu **2**, this time using the more **accurate** conversions.

4. a   I put 40 litres of petrol in my car. Approximately, how many gallons is this ?

   b   A recipe said to use 8 ounces of flour. Approximately, how many grams is this ?

   c   A plastic container holds 8 litres. Approximately, how many pints does it hold ?

   d   A sweetie shop sold 4 ounces of sherbet to a customer. How many grams is this ?

   e   My trouser waist measurement is 36" (*inches*). How many centimetres is this ?

5. This graph has been drawn to show the conversion from **inches** to **centimetres**.

   Can you see that **4 inches = 10 cm** (*approx*) ?

   a   Use the graph to convert to cm :-

   (i)   3 inches   (ii)   2·5 inches.

   b   Use the graph to convert to inches :-

   (i)   5 cm   (ii)   12 cm.

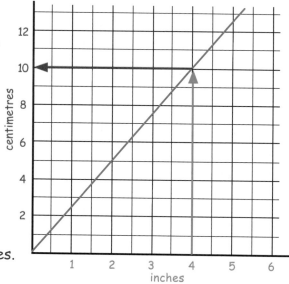

6. a   Copy the graph on to squared paper and extend it to 10 inches along the bottom and 25 cm up the side.

   b   Use it to convert 7 inches to centimetres.

   c   Use it to convert 20 cm back to inches.

7. Make up your own conversion graphs using the approximate conversions on page 145.
   (*for example :- miles to kilometres, ounces to grams, pints to litres .....*)

Be able to interpret which calculation to use in problems involving measure.

This is one of these exercises where you have to decide whether to .....

add, subtract, multiply or divide.

All working **MUST** be shown.

*Refer to page 145 for conversion rates

Exercise 4 *Use the approximate conversions here, or the more accurate ones if using a calculator.*

1. This double-glazed window is 12 feet wide and 6 feet high.

   a   Change these dimensions to **metres**, approximately.

   b   Work out the approximate cost of the glass at £20 per square metre.

6 ft

12 ft

2.

   20 cm

   10 cm

   A wooden frame has to be fitted around this photograph.

   The frame is to cost 50 pence per inch.

   Convert to **inches** and work out the cost of the frame.

3. My brother Kevin is twice my height.

   He is 180 centimetres tall.

   What's my height, **in inches** ?

4.

   A recipe asks for 5 ounces of flour

   How many **grams** of flour will I need ?

5. I have a 12 pound jar of bonbons.

   How many 2 kilogram cartons of bonbons can I fill from this ?

6.

   A butcher bought in 20 kilograms of mince and packed it equally into plastic containers.

   How many 1 pound cartons could they provide ?

7. At the weekend, I cycled 15 miles.

   My dad cycled 6 kilometres further than me.

   How far did we cycle **altogether**, in kilometres ?

8. Tony put up 2 shelves. One was 70 cm long, the other 25 inches.

    How much longer was one shelf than the other, **in inches** ?

9.  A sheet of paper is 10·5 inches long.

    A strip 200 mm is cut off.

    What is the length of the remaining piece of paper, in **inches** ?

10. Hazel bought a 1 litre bottle of juice.

    She filled a half pint tumbler for her grandfather.

    How much juice was left in the bottle ?
    (*Express your answer as a decimal fraction of a litre*).

11. Paul dissolved weedkiller with 5 litres of water.

    Tim used 8 pints to dissolve his.

    How many **litres** of water were used in total ?

12. Billy runs 80 metres of a race before pulling up with a muscle problem.

    Joe manages to run 90 yards before he stops too.

    Who ran further and by how many yards ? (*1 metre is approx 1·1 yards*)

13. To fill her tank with petrol, Daisy put in 53 litres.

    Jess had to put in 12 gallons to fill her car's tank.

    Change Jess' gallons to litres to find who bought more petrol.

14. Colleen and Tanya weigh their suitcases before flying.

    Colleen's weighs 47 pounds. Tanya's weighs 21 kg.

    How much heavier is Colleen's case (*in pounds*) ?

15.  Which speed is faster :-
    155 km/hr or 100 mph ?

16. This truck can hold 6 identical boxes.

    The empty truck weighs 612 kg,

    The fully loaded truck weighs 732 kg.

    Calculate the weight of one of the boxes.
    (*Answer in pounds*).

1 cm ≈ 0·4 inches	1 cm ≈ 0·03 feet	1 km ≈ 0·62 mile	1 metre ≈ 3·3 feet	1 millimetre ≈ 0·04 inch
1 inch ≈ 2·54 cm	1 foot ≈ 30·5 cm	1 mile ≈ 1·61 km	1 foot ≈ 0·3 metre	1 inch ≈ 25·4 mm
1 gram ≈ 0·04 ounce	1 kg ≈ 2·2 pounds	1 litre ≈ 1·76 pints		1 litre ≈ 0·22 gallon
1 ounce ≈ 28·3 grams	1 pound ≈ 0·45 kg	1 pint ≈ 0·6 litre		1 gallon ≈ 4·5 litres

1. Use the above approximate conversions to change :-

    a 12 cm into inches   b 50 cm into feet

    c 200 km into miles   d 6 metres into feet

    e 400 mm into inches   f 1000 grams into ounces

    g 30 kg into pounds   h 50 litres into gallons.

2. Change :-

    a 100 inches into cm   b 6 feet into cm

    c 2000 miles into km   d 30 feet into metres

    e 5 ounces into grams   f 2000 pounds into kg

    g 4 pints into litres   h 12 gallons into litres.

3. This snake can grow to 8 feet in length. How many metres is this ?

4. How many 11 pound bags of potatoes can be
    filled from a sack containing 20 kg ?

5.   A railway sign indicates a 50 miles per hour speed limit.

    Another one shows an 80 kilometre per hour limit.

    Which one allows the faster speed ?

SPEED
LIMIT
50

6. I used to buy 30 pints of milk per month.

    Now I buy 20 litres.

    How much more do I buy now, in litres ?

7. At Ye Olde Sweet Shop, I asked for 2 ounces of soor plooms,
    3 ounces of sherbet lemons and 5 ounces of sports mixtures.

    If all the sweets cost 2 pence per gram how much did I have to pay ?

Chapter 18

Similar Figures

Two figures are said to be CONGRUENT in Maths if they are **exactly the same**.

(*One figure should be able to be lifted and placed on top of the other exactly*).

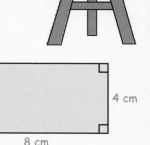

Be able to calculate the missing side in a similar shape.

These 2 rectangles are **congruent**.

8 cm

4 cm

4 cm

8 cm

Two figures are said to be SIMILAR if :–

- they are basically the **same shape** but
- one is an **enlargement** (or **reduction**) of the other.

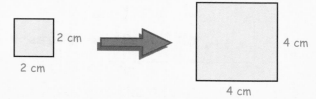

2 cm

2 cm

4 cm

4 cm

Since the above 2 squares are the same basic shape, but the 2nd shape is "2 times" as big as the first, they are said to be SIMILAR.

A rectangle, measuring 8 cm by 2 cm is **not** similar to either of these shapes.

Can you explain why ?

Exercise 1

1.   Look at the following 10 shapes. Match up CONGRUENT pairs :–

2. Look at this rectangle.

Which **two** of the 4 shapes below is mathematically
SIMILAR to this shape - P, Q, R or S ?

| P | | Q | | R | S |

3. You need a ruler here !!

a   Measure the **length** of both the small and large rectangle below.

$w = ?$

$l = ?$

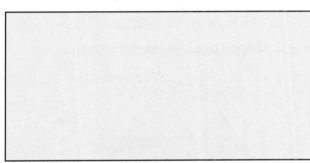

$W = ?$

$L = ?$

b   Now divide the big length (*L*) by the small length (*l*) and
    write down the value of $L \div l$.

c   Measure the width of the small and large rectangles.

d   Write down the value of $W \div w = ?$

e   The answers to **b** and **d** should be the same. Are they ?

This number is called the **SCALE FACTOR** (*or the magnification factor*).

4. These are sketches of figures.

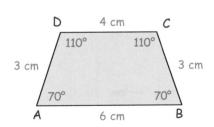

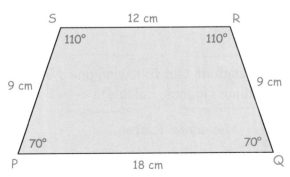

a   Compare the 2 sides AB and PQ and divide to find the **scale factor**.

=> $PQ \div AB = 18 \div 6 = \ldots .$

4. b Do the same for the other pairs of sides :-

(i) Find PS ÷ AD   (ii) Find QR ÷ BC   (iii) Find SR ÷ DC.

c You should have obtained the same answer in all 4 cases.
(*This proves that the 2 shapes are similar*).

5. These 2 shapes are similar.

a Calculate the **scale factor**.
(*Found by dividing 12 ÷ 6*).

b Use this scale factor to calculate
the size of the line SR. (*multiply*)

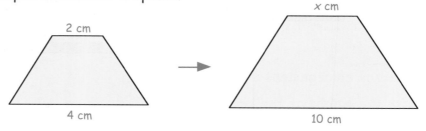

6. These 2 shapes are **similar** trapezia.

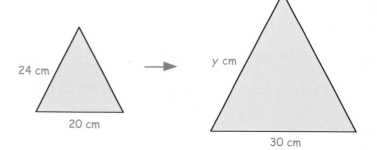

a Calculate the scale factor for the enlargement.

b Use this to calculate the length of the side marked *x*.

7. These 2 triangles are similar.

a Calculate the **scale factor**.

b Calculate the value of *y*.

8. In each of the following pairs of
similar figures, calculate :-

(i) the **scale factor**

(ii) the length of the side marked *x*.

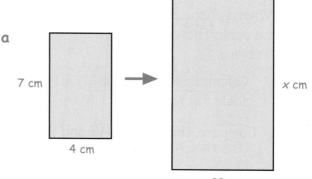

8. b

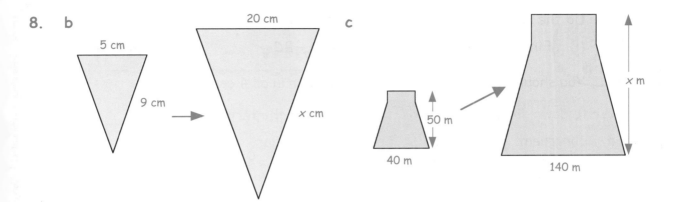

c

9. The 2 picture **frames** are mathematically **SIMILAR**.

16 cm

20 cm

h cm

90 cm

   a   Calculate the **enlargement scale factor**.

   b   Calculate the **height** of the larger frame.

10. A large print is made from a picture slide.

   a   Calculate the **enlargement scale factor**.

   b   Calculate the **length** of the print.

? mm

150 mm

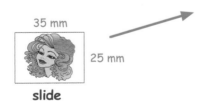

35 mm

25 mm

slide

print

11. When a shape becomes **SMALLER** the scale factor is a decimal (*less than 1*).

   a   Calculate the **REDUCTION** scale factor.
      (*It is not 40 ÷ 10 = ...*)

   b   Use this to calculate the height of the smaller figure.

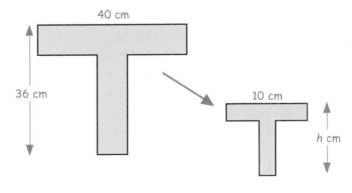

40 cm

36 cm

10 cm

h cm

Revisit - Review - Revise

1. Write down, in your own words, the meaning of the terms :-

    a   congruent   b   similar.

2. Which 2 of these shapes are **congruent** ?

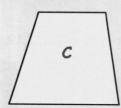
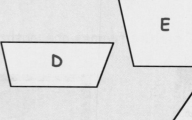

3. Below is a list of pairs of shapes along with their dimensions (sizes).

    A   a square with side 8 cm and a square with side 35 cm.

    B   a rectangle 4 cm by 3 cm and a square with side 4 cm.

    C   a rectangle 6 cm by 5 cm and a rectangle 12 cm by 10 cm.

    D   a circle with diameter 8 cm and a circle with radius 4 cm.

    Which of the above pairs of shapes are :-

    a   congruent   b   similar   c   neither ?

4. The 2 shapes here are **similar**.

    a   Calculate the enlargement scale factor.

    b   Calculate the value of x.

5. A torch is shone on a pink piece of cardboard
    and a grey shadow is cast on a wall.

    a   If the 2 shapes are **similar**,
         calculate the enlargement
         scale factor.

    b   Calculate the width (w)
         of the shadow.

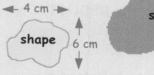
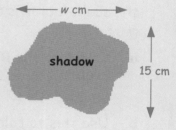

Chapter 19

Bar Graphs and Line Graphs

Be able to interpret and draw a bar graph and a line graph.

Exercise 1

1. The bar graph shows the number of people who donated blood in the transfusion van one week last winter.

   a   How many people gave blood on :–

   (i)   Monday   (ii)   Tuesday

   (iii)   Friday   (iv)   Thursday ?

   b   How many people gave blood in total ?

   c   The transfusion van's heating system broke down one day and the staff were sent home.

   Which day was that ? Give a reason for your answer.

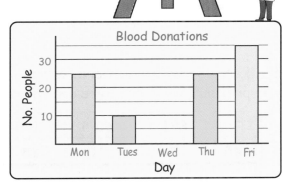

2. This bar graph shows the number of football tops sold in a shop in Oldham, during the World Cup.

   a   How many Spanish tops were sold ?

   b   What was the least popular strip sold ?

   c   Which two strips sold the same number and how many of each was that ?

   d   State an obvious reason for the high sales of English tops in this sports shop ?

   e   How many more England than German tops were sold ?

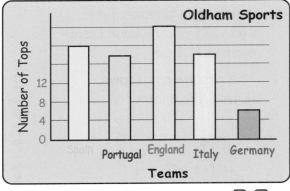

3. Year 6 were asked what they preferred to eat with rice, from a menu.

   a   How many of Year 6 preferred :-

   (i)   Chilli Beef   (ii)   Prawns

   (iii)   Pork   (iv)   Chicken ?

   b   What was the most liked food with rice ?

   c   How many more chose prawns than pork ?

   d   How many less chose stir fry than chicken ?

   e   How many were asked altogether ?

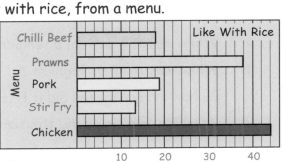

This is called a Horizontal Bar Graph

4. The owner of a small shop asked 30 customers what kind of tinned soup they liked.

The results are shown in the table :-

pea/ham	tomato	chicken	lentil	oxtail	minestrone
3	9	4	7	1	6

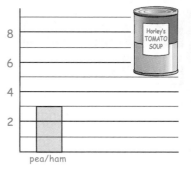

Draw and label a neat bar graph to show this information.

5. Kerry's Electrical Store carried out a survey into which TV channel their customers preferred to view. Here are the results of that survey :-

ITV 1	BBC 1	Ch 4	Ch 5	Sky 1	Sky Sports	Sky Movies
45	30	10	25	50	60	5

Decide on a suitable scale and draw/label a neat bar graph to show these findings.

6. A patient's temperature was taken every hour from 6 am until 1 pm.

The results are shown in this line graph.

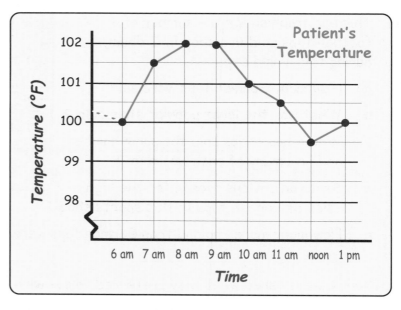

a When was the patient's temperature at its lowest ?

b When was it at its highest ?

c By how many degrees did it rise between 6 am and 8 am ?

d At which two times did the temperature begin to rise ?

e At 9 am, his temperature began to fall.

   For how long did this last and by how many degrees did it fall ?

f What was his estimated temperature at 11.30 am ?

7. Two tent companies .....

   - The Tent Store (in red) and
   - Tents-for-U (in **green**)

   compare their sales.

   The comparative line graph gives
   the sales in hundreds of units.

   a State the sales of The Tent Store in :-

      (i) April   (ii) July   (iii) October.

   b State the sales of Tents-for-U in :-

      (i) March (ii) June   (iii) September.

   c Whose sales were lower in :-

      (i) May   (ii) August   (iii) November ?

   The Tent Store made a £30 profit on each tent.

   Tents-for-U made a £25 profit on each tent.

   d (i) Who made more profit in May ?

      (ii) How much more did that company make in May ?

Sales of Tents

(Line graph: Sales (100's) vertical axis from 2 to 14; Month horizontal axis from Feb to Nov)

8. The temperature in a classroom (°C) was recorded every day at noon for a week.

   The results are shown in the table :-

Mon	Tue	Wed	Thu	Fri
10	8	9	10·5	4·5

   Construct a line graph to show this information.

9. Construct a line graph for the following data which shows the number of ice creams sold from Napoli's ice cream van from February till November 2012.

Month	Feb	Mar	Apr	May	Jun	Jul	Aug	Sep	Oct	Nov
Sales	100	200	600	1000	1200	1000	900	500	100	50

   Make your vertical scale go up in 200's.

10. This table shows 6 months of car sales from two different car dealers, Arnold Clunk and Reg Barney.

    Construct a comparative line graph to show this information.

	Jul	Aug	Sep	Oct	Nov	Dec
Clunk's	100	250	300	250	400	200
Barney's	300	200	350	450	100	150

Interpreting and Drawing Pie Charts

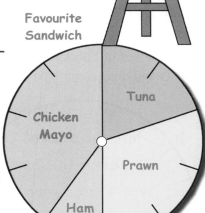

Favourite
Sandwich

Be able to
interpret and
construct a
pie chart.

1. The pie chart shows the results of a survey into
   favourite sandwiches bought from a snack bar.

   a   Write down the fraction (/10) of people who chose :-

   (i)   Prawn   (ii)   Tuna

   (iii) Ham   (iv)   Chicken Mayo.

   b   List the sandwiches in order, from **most** popular
       to **least** popular.

   c   If 300 people were asked, how many of them liked :-

   (i)   Tuna   (ii)   Ham

   (iii) Prawn   (iv)   Chicken Mayo ?

2. This pie chart, showing the sale of sausages in a supermarket
   one Saturday, has been divided into 20 equal parts.

   Supermarket Sausage Sales

   a   What **percentage** does each part stand for ?

   b   What percentage represents :-

   (i)   Beef   (ii)   Pork

   (iii) Other   (iv)   Vegetarian ?

   4000 sausages were sold altogether that day.

   c   How many of the sausages sold were :-

   (i)   Pork   (ii)   Vegetarian

   (iii) Beef   (iv)   Other ?

3. 24 cooks were asked to name their favourite pie filling.

   Favourite
   Pie Filling

   a   What fraction of them voted for mince pie ? ($\frac{90}{360}$ simplified)

   b   What fraction of them voted for :-

   (i)   Rhubarb   (ii)   Steak

   (iii) Cherry   (iv)   Apple ?

   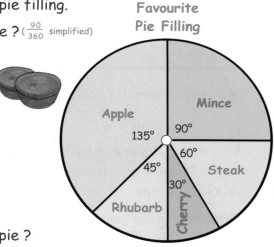

   c   Of the 24 cooks, how many voted for :-

   (i)   Mince   (ii)   Rhubarb

   (iii) Steak   (iv)   Cherry ?

   d   How many did that leave voting for apple pie ?

4. To make her home-made Macaroni Bake, Jenny uses only four ingredients as follows :-

- 40% macaroni pasta
- 30% tomato soup
- 20% diced ham
- 10% cheese

Draw a pie chart to show this information.

5. On a Mediterranean cruise, it was discovered that :-

- 35% of those on the ship were aged 20 - 65
- 40% were senior citizens
- 20% were under 20 years old

a   If the remainder on board were crew members what percentage was that ?

b   Copy (or trace) the blank pie chart and complete it showing the above information.

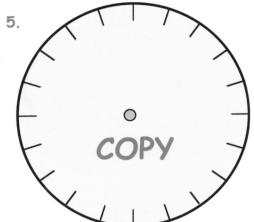

6. The information given below shows the most popular answers to the question :-

"If you were given money to renovate one room in your house, which room would you choose" ?

- 45% said "kitchen"
- 25% said "bathroom"
- of the others, half said "bedroom" and half said "living room".

Draw a pie chart to illustrate this, using a "pie" like this one.

7. There were 60 000 people at Emirates Stadium,

- 30 000 were supporting Arsenal
- 15 000 were Wolves supporters
- 12 000 were neutral supporters
- the remainder were football officials and stewards.

a   Copy the blank pie chart and complete it to show the above information.

b   What is a "neutral" supporter ?

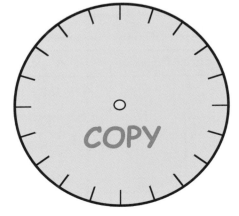

Be able to use a protractor to draw a pie chart.

The table of data shows the number of different vehicles parked in a car/bus park.

When drawing a pie chart, it is sometimes easier to add columns to the table for calculations.

Type of Vehicle	Number
Car	36
Taxi	24
Bus	20
Motorcycle	10

Type of Vehicle	Number	Fraction	Angle
Car	36	$\frac{36}{90}$	$\frac{36}{90} \times 360 = 144°$
Taxi	24	$\frac{24}{90}$	$\frac{24}{90} \times 360 = 96°$
Bus	20	$\frac{20}{90}$	$\frac{20}{90} \times 360 = 80°$
Motorcycle	10	$\frac{10}{90}$	$\frac{10}{90} \times 360 = 40°$
TOTAL	90	1	360°

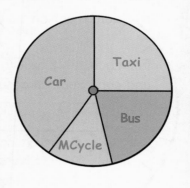

- **Step 1** Add up the Numbers column to get a total (in this case 90).
- **Step 2** Express each "Number" as a fraction of this total. (e.g. $\frac{36}{90}$).
- **Step 3** Find that fraction of 360° each time   (e.g. $\frac{36}{90} \times 360 = 144°$).
- **Step 4** Draw the pie chart using a protractor.

Exercise 3

(A calculator would help in this exercise.)

1. a   Copy and complete the table showing a group of 180 people's favourite vegetable.

   b   Construct a pie chart from the table, using a pair of compasses, a ruler and a protractor.

Vegetable	Number	Fraction	Angle
Lettuce	90	$\frac{90}{180}$	$\frac{90}{180} \times 360 = 180°$
Carrot	60	$\frac{60}{180}$	$\frac{60}{180} \times 360 = ...°$
Turnip	20	$\frac{...}{180}$	$\frac{...}{180} \times 360 = ...°$
Cabbage	10	$\frac{...}{180}$	$\frac{...}{180} \times 360 = ...°$
TOTAL	180	1	360°

2. a   Copy and complete this table which shows the number of grades a class obtained in their maths test.

   b   Construct a pie chart showing this information.

Grades	Number	Fraction	Angle
A	25	$\frac{25}{90}$	$\frac{25}{90} \times 360 = 100°$
B	30	$\frac{30}{90}$	$\frac{30}{90} \times 360 = ...°$
C	20	$\frac{...}{90}$	$\frac{...}{90} \times 360 = ...°$
D	15	$\frac{...}{90}$	$\frac{...}{90} \times 360 = ...°$
TOTAL	90	1	360°

3. a Copy and complete the table showing motorists' favourite colour of car.

Car Colour	Number	Fraction	Angle
Red	7	$\frac{7}{30}$	$\frac{7}{30}$ × 360 = ...°
Silver	4		× 360 = ...°
Blue	6		× 360 = ...°
Black	13		× 360 = ...°
TOTAL	**30**		**360°**

b Construct an accurate pie chart showing this information.

4. For each table below, copy it (adding new columns to show your working) and construct an accurate pie chart to show the information.

a

Favourite TV Soap	Number
Corma Street	60
Westenders	30
Nummerdale	20
Next Door	10
TOTAL	....

b

Women's Ages	Number
60 - 64	380
65 - 69	260
70 - 74	60
75 - 79	20
TOTAL	....

5. Here are the results of a survey asking people's favourite holiday resort.

Torquay	Brighton	York	Blackpool	York	Blackpool	Brighton	Torquay
Blackpool	York	Brighton	Blackpool	Brighton	Blackpool	York	Blackpool
Brighton	Blackpool	Southport	Torquay	Brighton	Southport	Blackpool	Blackpool
York	Brighton	Southport	Blackpool	Blackpool	Torquay	Southport	York
Brighton	Blackpool	Blackpool	Blackpool	Brighton	Blackpool	Brighton	Torquay

a Copy and complete the table below :-

Hotel	Tally Mark	Number	Fraction	Angle
Blackpool				
Torquay				
York				
Brighton				
Southport				

b Using a pair of compasses, a ruler and a protractor, construct an accurate pie chart for this information.

The Mean and The Range

Be able to calculate the mean and the range from a set of data.

The **Range** is a mathematical tool used to measure how **widely spread** out a set of numbers are. Calculate it as follows :-

$$\text{Range} = \text{Highest Score} - \text{Lowest Score}$$

Example :-   The set of numbers 4, 2, 5, 7, 7, 12, 17, 8, 6, 9,

$$\Rightarrow \text{Range} = 17 - 2 = 15.$$

The **Mean** (or **average**) of a set of scores is found by :-

• adding all the scores together

• then dividing by how many scores there are.

$$\text{Mean} = \frac{\text{Total of all the scores}}{\text{Number of scores}}$$

Example :-   Find the **mean** of the set of ages :-   10, 8, 1 and 9.

$$\text{Mean} = \frac{10 + 8 + 1 + 9}{4} = \frac{28}{4} = 7$$

Exercise 4   *(A calculator would help here, though all calculations can be done without using one.)*

Ask your teacher.

1.   Calculate the **range** and the **mean** of :-

a   7, 12, 9, 4

b   10, 27, 15, 19, 24

c   £7, £6, £13, £27, £26, £5

d   11 cm, 24 cm, 38 cm, 30 cm, 16 cm , 37 cm

e   9·1, 7·2, 6·7, 9·6, 9·9, 6·8, 10·4, 4·3, 7·1

f   4·87, 9·76, 8·93, 15·86, 4·58.

2.   George spends his 4 month summer break from art school cleaning the floors and windows in his local gallery.

For this, he gets paid a total of £1304.

What does that **average** out at per month ?

3.   Ten branches of Mason's Stores place bubble gum machines outside each shop.

They find that they contain the following number of bubble gums :-

50,   52,   54,   52,   55,   51,   53,   50,   54,   54.

a   Calculate the **range and the mean** number of bubble gums.

b   The Bubble Gum Company claim that each of their machines should contain an average of 55 bubble gums.

Should Mason's complain to this company ?   (*Explain*).

4. The journey times (in minutes) of a selection of trains travelling from Bramley Park to Blythe Central are shown below :-

| 5 | 8 | 9 | 8 | 3 | 7 | 10 | 4 | 7 | 5 | 9 | 5 | 7 | 5 | 8 | 20 | 2 | 8 | 7 | 3 |

a What is the **range** of these times ?

b Calculate the **mean** time for the journeys.

c One train took much longer than the mean time - which one ? - suggest a reason.

5. Competitive golfers use the mean when calculating their average number score.

The winner of the latest competition scored a total of 270 for his 4 rounds. Monty finished in second place, 6 shots behind.

a What was Monty's total score ?

b What was Monty's average score per round ?

c If his average score per round had been 67, would he have won ? (*Explain*).

6. In an ice-skating competition, the marks given by the judges of eight countries were as follows :-

| 6·6 | 6·6 | 6·2 | 6·5 | 6·1 | 6·9 | 6·4 | 6·7 |

a What was the **range** and the **mean** mark ?

b How many marks above the **mean** was the highest mark awarded ?

7. The weight of fish in each tin of *Algi's* sardines is always the same, but the actual number of sardines in each tin varies.

Here are the number of sardines which were found in tins bought by sardine lovers :-

| 8 | 5 | 10 | 5 | 9 | 6 | 8 | 8 | 6 | 8 | 16 | 6 | 9 |

a Calculate the **mean** number of sardines per box and also state the **range**.

b Relative to the mean, comment on the large number of sardines in one of the tins.

8. Anders spent 6 days in his native Norway, eating his favourite dish in various Fish and Chip shops each day and recording how much he paid in £'s.

When he came to England, he bought the same dish in 4 different Fish and Chip shops.

The prices are shown in the table :-

Anders' Fish & Chips					
Norway £9·50	£10·80	£8·60	£9·80	£8·30	£7·72
England	£4·50	£4·75	£4·80	£4·95	

a Calculate the **mean** cost for fish & chips in each country.

b How much **cheaper**, on average, is fish & chips in England than in Norway ?

Revisit - Review - Revise

1. A survey was carried out in a sweet shop, where children were asked to name their favourite Hiribo jelly sweet

   a How many chose Jelly Frogs ?

   b How many **more** chose Jelly Worms than Jelly Gummy Bears ?

   c How many **less** chose Jelly Fried Eggs than Jelly Babies ?

   d How many were asked **altogether** ?

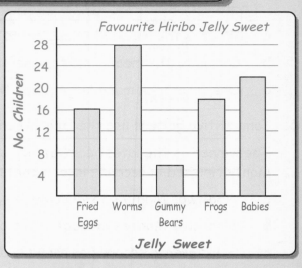

2.

   The line graph shows the number of bikinis sold by two swimwear firms over a period of 10 months.

   Swimsport's sales are shown in **red**. Paddlepro's sales are in **green**.

   a In which month did sales peak for both companies ? Why then ?

   b Who sold more bikinis in May - how many more ?

   c Which firm had the biggest fall in sales between two months - which 2 months was that ?

   d Overall, who sold more bikinis over the 10 month period ?

   e Suggest a reason for an increase in sales by both companies later in the year.

3. In a garden centre survey, 240 people were asked which method they preferred to get rid of weeds in their garden.

   The results are shown in the pie chart.

   a What **angle** represents "Watering Can" ?

   b How many people preferred :-

      (i) to use a spray   (ii) to burn the weeds ?

   c How many preferred to put weedkiller down using a watering can ?

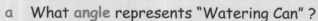

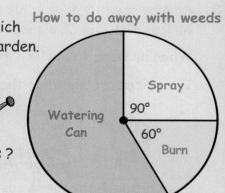

How to do away with weeds

4. The table shows the eye colour of children in a Year 6 class.

Eye colour	Number	Fraction	Angle
Brown	10	$\frac{10}{30}$	$\frac{10}{30} \times 360 = \dots°$
Blue	12		$\times 360 = \dots°$
Green	7		$\times 360 = \dots°$
Grey	1		$\times 360 = \dots°$
TOTAL	?		360°

Ask your teacher.

a   How many children are in the class ?

b   Copy and complete the table.

c   Construct a neat accurate **pie chart** to show the information.

5. a   Calculate the **mean** weight in grams.

> 60 g, 30 g, 150 g, 80 g, 100 g, 110 g, 40 g, 70 g.

b   Now calculate the **range** of weights.

6.

mean number - 17 per box

The contents of ten boxes of marbles are examined.

The boxes have the following number of marbles :-

> 16, 18, 14, 17, 15, 16, 15, 15, 18, 16.

a   Why is the manufacturer's claim wrong ?

b   An eleventh box is examined.

How many marbles would need to be in that box in order for the manufacturer's claim to **then** be considered to be correct ?

7.

The **mean** age of 5 boys is 15 years old.

Four of the them are aged 13, 14, 16 and 19.

What is the age of the fifth one ?

Chapter 20

3-D Shape & Volume

2D and 3D   Revision

Exercise 1

1.   Name all the 2-D and 3-D shapes below :-

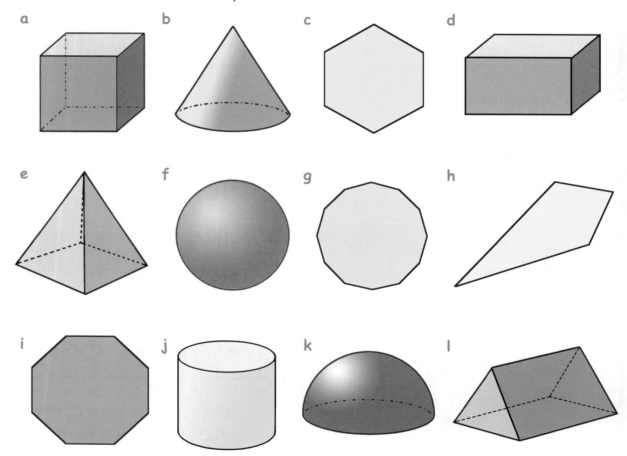

a   b   c   d

e   f   g   h

i   j   k   l

2.   a   Which of the shapes in Question 1 are **two dimensional** ?

b   Which one of these **two dimensional** shapes is an irregular polygon ?

c   Explain why this is an irregular polygon.

3.   List all the **two dimensional** shapes you need to build a :-

a   cube   b   pyramid   c   cylinder   d   triangular prism.

4.   For each of the shapes in Question 3, write down how many :-

a   vertices it has   b   edges it has.

5. How many sides are there in a :-

    a   pentagon   b   octagon   c   quadrilateral   d   nonagon ?

6. Which 3-dimensional shapes will you get from each net below ?

a

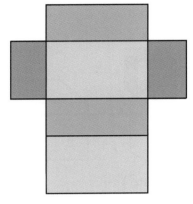

b

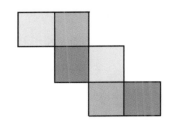

c

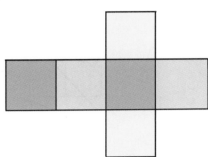

d

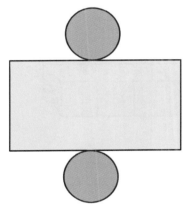

e

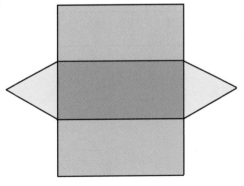

f

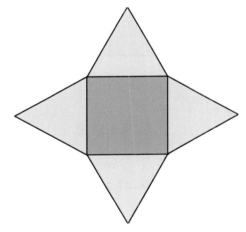

g

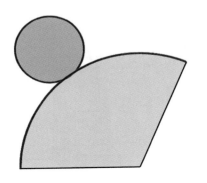

h

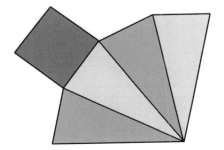

Be able to find the volume of a shape by counting cubes.

The volume of a shape is simply the "amount of space" it takes up.

One unit of volume we use is the "cubic centimetre".

The small cube shown measures 1 cm by 1 cm by 1 cm.

It has a volume of 1 cubic centimetre.

or for short :-   1 cm³ .

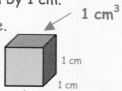

1 cm³

1 cm
1 cm
1 cm

Exercise 2

1. State the volume of each of the following shapes, (in cm³) :-

a 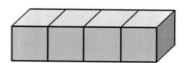   b 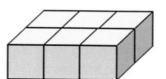   c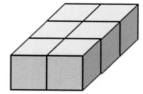

d    e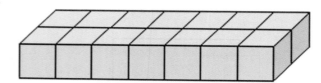

f 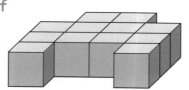   g 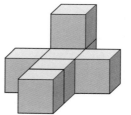   h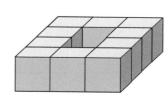

i 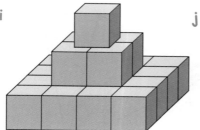   j   k

2. a How many cubes are on the top layer of this shape ?

    b How many layers does it have ?

    c What is its total volume ?

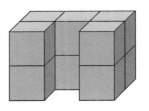

3.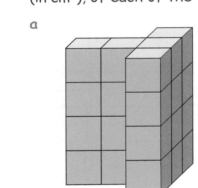

    a How many cubes are on the top layer of this shape ?

    b How many layers does it have ?

    c What is its total volume ?

4. What is the total volume of this shape ?

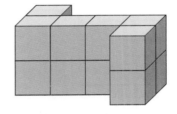

5. By working out the volume of the top layer first, calculate the total volume, (in cm³), of each of the following shapes :–

    a   b   c

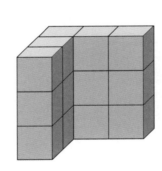

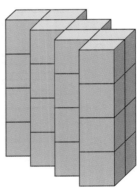

    d   e   f

hollow

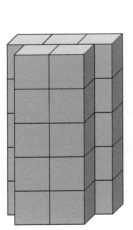

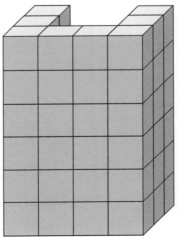

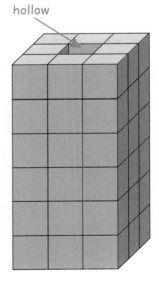

6. These shapes are cuboids made up using 1 cm cubes.

Find the number of cubes in 1 layer and use this to calculate the **volume** of each cuboid.

a

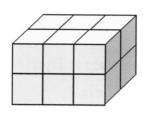

b

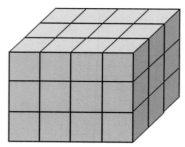

7. Calculate the **volume** of each cuboid :–

a

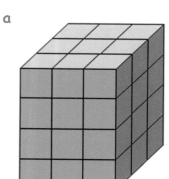

b

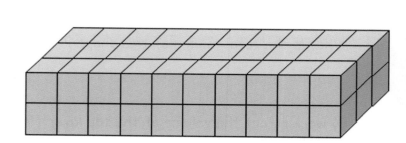

c

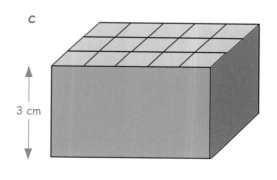

3 cm

d

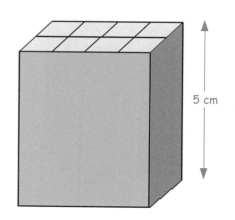

5 cm

e

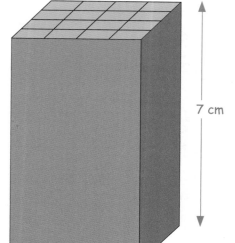

7 cm

f

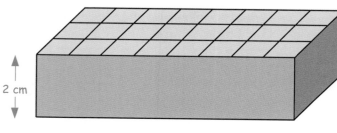

2 cm

Volume of a Cuboid – (a formula)

Be able to find the volume of a cuboid using a formula.

The top layer of this cuboid shown is made up of

$(6 \times 4) = 24$ cm^3.

There are also 5 layers. This means

Volume $= (6 \times 4) \times 5 = 120$ cm^3.

To find the volume of a cuboid, you can do so by simply multiplying :-

Length x Breadth x Height.

Formula :-

Volume = Length x Breadth x Height,

or simply $V = L \times B \times H$

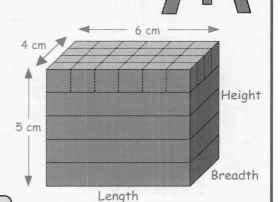

Note - if all the sides are given in cm, the volume is measured in cm^3.

Exercise 3

1. Copy and complete for this cuboid :–

$V = L \times B \times H$
$V = 7 \times 5 \times 4$
$V = \dots\dots\dots$ cm^3

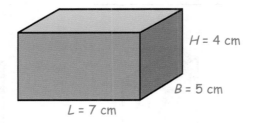

$H = 4$ cm
$B = 5$ cm
$L = 7$ cm

2.

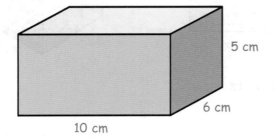

5 cm
6 cm
10 cm

Use the formula $V = L \times B \times H$ to calculate the **volume** of this cuboid. (*Show your working*).

3. Use the formula to calculate the **volume** of this cuboid.

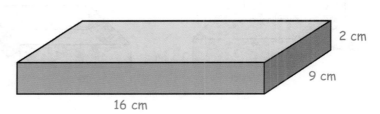

2 cm
9 cm
16 cm

4. Calculate the volume of each of the following cuboids. (*Show your working*).

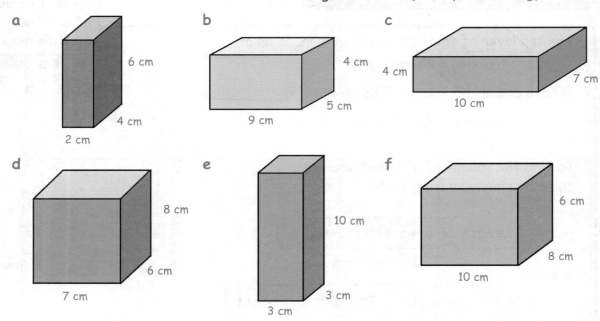

a   6 cm   4 cm   2 cm

b   4 cm   5 cm   9 cm

c   4 cm   7 cm   10 cm

d   8 cm   6 cm   7 cm

e   10 cm   3 cm   3 cm

f   6 cm   8 cm   10 cm

5. Calculate the volume of each shape :-

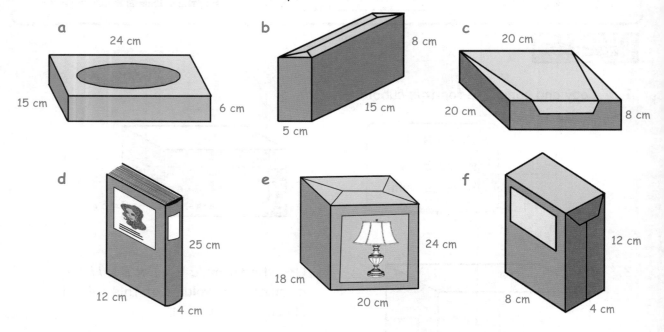

a   24 cm   15 cm   6 cm

b   8 cm   15 cm   5 cm

c   20 cm   20 cm   8 cm

d   25 cm   12 cm   4 cm

e   24 cm   18 cm   20 cm

f   12 cm   8 cm   4 cm

6. Calculate the volume of each of these objects :-

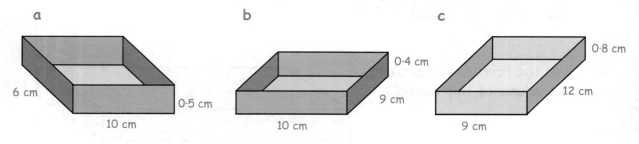

a   6 cm   0·5 cm   10 cm

b   0·4 cm   9 cm   10 cm

c   0·8 cm   12 cm   9 cm

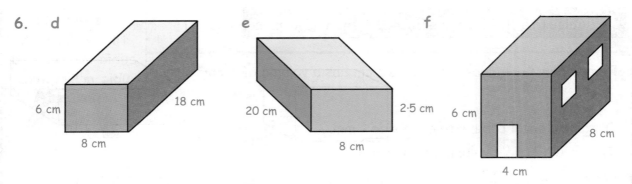

6.   d   e   f

18 cm   6 cm   8 cm

20 cm   2·5 cm   8 cm

6 cm   8 cm   4 cm

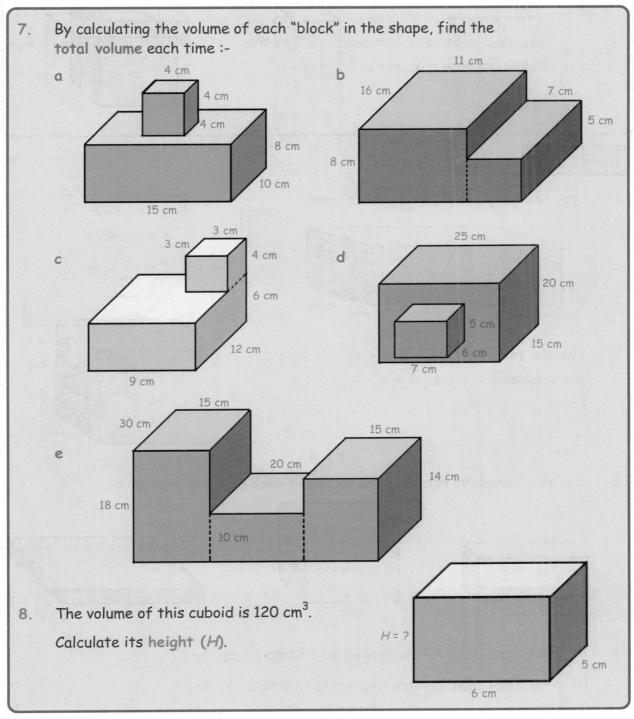

7.   By calculating the volume of each "block" in the shape, find the total volume each time :-

a   4 cm   4 cm   4 cm   8 cm   10 cm   15 cm

b   11 cm   16 cm   7 cm   5 cm   8 cm

c   3 cm   3 cm   4 cm   6 cm   12 cm   9 cm

d   25 cm   20 cm   5 cm   15 cm   6 cm   7 cm

e   15 cm   30 cm   20 cm   15 cm   14 cm   18 cm   10 cm

8.   The volume of this cuboid is 120 cm³.

Calculate its **height** (*H*).

$H = ?$ 5 cm   6 cm

Volume - Cubic Metres and Cubic Millimetres

Remember :- A cube with sides 1 cm has a volume of 1 cm³.

Imagine a small cube with each side 1 mm.

This would have a volume of $\boxed{1 \text{ mm}^3}$.

(*1 cubic millimetre*).

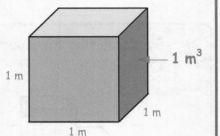

Imagine a large cube with each side 1 metre.

This would have a volume of $\boxed{1 \text{ m}^3}$.

(*1 cubic metre*).

Exercise 4

1. Copy and complete for this cuboid, in mm³ :-

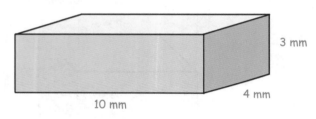

$$V = L \times B \times H$$
$$V = 10 \times 4 \times 3$$
$$V = \text{..........} \text{ mm}^3$$

2. Use the formula $V = L \times B \times H$ to calculate the volume of this cuboid in m³ :-

    (*Show your working*).

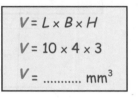

3. Use the formula to calculate the volume of each of these shapes :-

    a   b   c

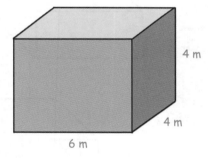

4. a   How many cubic millimetres would fit into a 1 cm³ box ?

    b   How many cubic centimetres would fit into a 1 m³ box ?

Revisit - Review - Revise

1. Write down the volume of each shape shown, in cubic centimetres :-

   a

   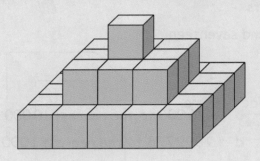

   b

   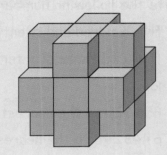

2. Calculate the volume of each cuboid :-

   a

   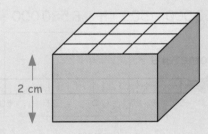

   2 cm

   b

   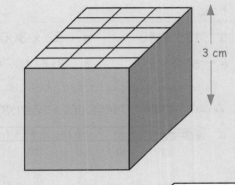

   3 cm

   c

   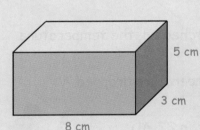

   5 cm
   3 cm
   8 cm

   d

   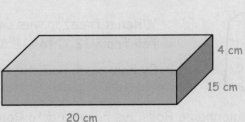

   4 cm
   15 cm
   20 cm

   e

   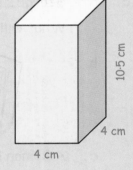

   10·5 cm
   4 cm
   4 cm

3. The volume of this cuboid is 120 mm³.

   Calculate its **height**.

   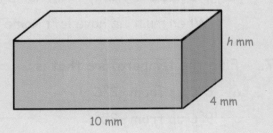

   h mm
   4 mm
   10 mm

4. How many cubic centimetres would fit into a box 20 cm by 20 cm by 15 cm ?

Chapter 21

1. Write in words :-   a   4007   b   56 807   c   891 898.

2. Write the following numbers using digits :-

    a   five hundred and twenty thousand and seventeen

    b   four and three quarter million.

3. Round :-

    a   856 329 to the nearest 1000   b   476 000 to the nearest 10 000

    c   6 443 298 to the nearest 100 000   d   9 399 778 to the nearest 1 000 000.

4. Find :-

    a   135 × 40   b   52 × 300   c   215 × 600   d   312 × 5000

    e   630 ÷ 70   f   21 600 ÷ 400   g   5 150 000 ÷ 500   h   8 580 000 ÷ 6000.

5. What temperatures are shown on these 2 thermometers ?

    a 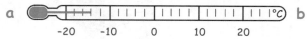 b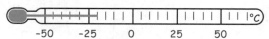

6. a   George's bank balance was **£220**. He signed a cheque for £350.

    What will George's new balance be ?

    b   When a freezer was switched on, the temperature
    fell from 12°C to -11°C

    By how much had the temperature dropped ?

    c   A Roman Legionnaire Bossipus returned to Rome in 22 AD.

    He had been away from Rome for 35 years.

    When must he have left Rome ?

7. Find the temperature that is :-

    a   6°C up from –2°C   b   8°C down from 3°C

    c   9°C up from –25°C   d   4°C down from –15°C.

8. Find :-

    a   6 + (-13)   b   -2 + (-5)   c   -11 + 11   d   -8 + (-8)

    e   12 + (-3)   f   -9 + (-9)   g   -7 + 12   h   -50 + (-50).

9. Make an **accurate** drawing of each of the following figures using a ruler, compasses and a protractor. (*Clearly show all your construction lines*).

a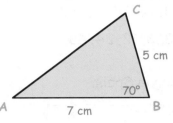

b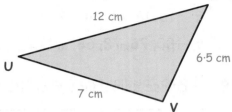

c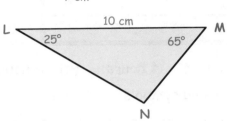

d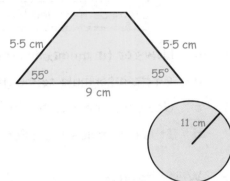

10. The **radius** of a circle is 11 centimetres.

   Write down the length of its **diameter**.

11. a   Use a pair of compasses to draw a circle with a **radius** of 4·5 cm.

   b   Draw in a diameter and radius and label all parts of your diagram.

12. Use short or long division where appropriate :-

   a $9\overline{)567}$ b $11\overline{)902}$ c $17\overline{)3927}$ d $24\overline{)3240}$.

13. Work out the answer to $1479 \div 12$, giving your answer :-

   a   with a remainder   b   as a fraction   c   as a decimal   d   to nearest whole no.

14. Set down and work out :-

   a $10 - 2 \times 3$ b $20 + 10 \div 2$ c $200 \div 10 - 3 \times 6$

   d $\frac{1}{2}$ of $10 - 8$ e $25 - \frac{1}{4}$ of $(50 - 30)$ f $16 + \frac{1}{3}$ of $18 - 12$.

15. Work out the value of these expressions when $p = 6$, $q = 4$ and $r = 2$:-

   a $3p - q$ b $8r + p$ c $p^2 - q^2$ d pqr

   e $(p - q)^2$ f $3r^2$ g $\sqrt{p - r}$ h $\dfrac{3p - 2q}{r}$.

16. To change a number of kilograms into pounds (weight) :-

   > Multiply the kilograms by eleven, then divide your answer by five.

   a   Write a formula for changing kilograms (K) into pounds (P). $P = ... \times K \div ...$

   b   Change 25 kilograms to pounds.

17. Describe each pattern of numbers carefully and write down the next three numbers each time :-

    a   15, 18, 21, 24, 27, ...

    b   3, 14, 25, 36, 47, ...

    c   80, 76, 72, 68, ...

    d   3, 6, 12, 24, 48, ...

18. A cruise ship sailed from Portsmouth to Santander in Spain.

No. of Hours (H)	1	2	3	4	5
Distance travelled (D)	25	50	75	?	?

    a   How far (in miles) did the ship travel in   (i)   4 hours   (ii)   5 hours ?

    b   Write a formula connecting D and H using symbols.

    c   Use your formula to find how far the ship had travelled in 12 hours.

    d   It is 600 miles from Portsmouth to Santander. How long did the ship take ?

19. Write down :-

    a   the first ten non-zero multiples of :-   (i)   4   (ii)   6.

    b   the lowest common multiple (l.c.m.) of 4 and 6.

20. Write down the lowest common multiple (l.c.m.) of :-

    a   8 and 10   b   6 and 15   c   3, 6 and 8.

21. Write down :-

    a   the factors of 12 and of 15

    b   the highest common factor (h.c.f.) of 12 and 15.

22. Write down the highest common factor (h.c.f.) of :-

    a   16 and 24   b   30 and 50   c   18, 27 and 45.

23. Write down all the prime numbers between :-

    a   40 and 60   b   70 and 100   c   120 and 130.

24. Write down why each of these numbers is definitely not a prime number :-

    a   253 406   b   1 852 365   c   25 365 460.

25. Write each of the following numbers as the product of prime factors :-

    (For example, 18 = 2 x 3 x 3 and 40 = 2 x 2 x 2 x 5).

    a   16   b   30   c   50   d   210.

26. Write down 2 equivalent fractions for :–   a $\frac{1}{3}$ b $\frac{5}{6}$.

27. Find and **simplify** where possible :–

    a $\frac{3}{5} + \frac{1}{5}$ b $\frac{7}{8} - \frac{1}{4}$ c $\frac{1}{3} + \frac{1}{6}$ d $\frac{3}{4} - \frac{1}{5}$.

28. Change to **improper** fractions :–   a $3\frac{1}{5}$ b $4\frac{2}{7}$.

29. Change to **mixed numbers** :–   a $\frac{5}{2}$ b $\frac{23}{5}$.

30. Find each of the following, leaving your answer as a **mixed number** :–

    a $6\frac{1}{3} + \frac{5}{6}$ b $8\frac{3}{4} - 3\frac{1}{2}$ c $10\frac{1}{2} - 7\frac{1}{3}$ d $8\frac{3}{5} + 3\frac{2}{3}$

    e $9\frac{5}{6} - 2\frac{1}{4}$ f $5\frac{1}{5} - 1\frac{1}{3}$ g $10 - 6\frac{4}{5}$ h $4\frac{1}{6} - 3\frac{2}{5}$.

31. Copy the set of axes shown opposite.

    a Plot the point A(-1, 3) and write down the coordinates of the new point A' when A is translated 4 right and 2 down.

    b Plot L(3, 3), M(5, -1) and N(3, -2).

    c What kind of triangle is ΔLMN ?

    d Reflect ΔLMN over the blue dotted line, showing its final position on your diagram, (ΔL'M'N').

    e Write down the coordinates of the three points L', M' and N'.

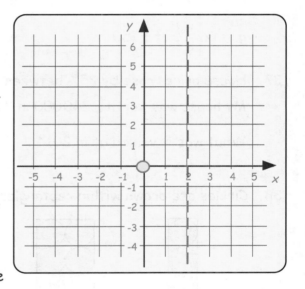

32.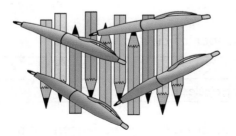

    a Write down the ratio of :-

       pens : pencils

    b Simplify this ratio as far as possible.

33. Express each of the following ratios in its simplest form :–

    a 8 : 12   b 40 : 70   c 21 : 14   d 18 : 34

    e 45 : 75   f 24 : 40   g 100 : 125   h 37 : 41.

34. In a charity cycle ride, the ratio of male riders to female riders was **2 : 5**.

   a If there were 60 males, how many of the riders were female ?

   b There were in fact 200 females.

   How many riders were there altogether ?

35. Write each percentage as a fraction in its simplest form :-

   a 30%   b 5%   c $66\frac{2}{3}$ %   d 150%.

36. Do the following by using their fractional equivalents instead of the percentages :-

   a 10% of £110   b 20% of £40   c 40% of £60

   d 5% of £240   e 75% of £18   f $33\frac{1}{3}$ % of £150

   g $66\frac{2}{3}$ % of £150   h 15% of £60   i 90% of £90.

37. House prices rose by **25%** between 2004 and 2014.

   My house was worth £240 000 in 2004.

   What was it valued at in 2014 ?

38. Circles are drawn within rectangles as shown below :-.

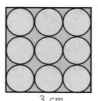
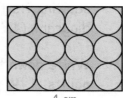

   1 cm   2 cm   3 cm   4 cm
   3 circles   6 circles   9 circles   12 circles

   a Draw pattern number 5 and count the number of circles.

   b Copy and complete this table :-

Length (L) cm	1	2	3	4	5
No. of circles (C)	3	...	...	...	...

   c Write a formula connecting the number of circles C to the length L cm.

   d Use the formula to find how many circles are needed for a rectangle 10 centimetres long.

   e If one of the rectangles has 54 circles, what must its length be ?

39. Shown below are two tables of values connecting pairs of letters.

Write down a formula (*using symbols*) connecting the 2nd letter to the 1st letter.

a

d	1	2	3	4	5	6
H	7	9	11	13	15	17

H = ... × d + ...

b

y	1	2	3	4	5	6
T	30	35	40	45	50	55

T = ... × y + ...

40. For each of these calculate the **area** in cm², mm² or m². (*Show all working*).

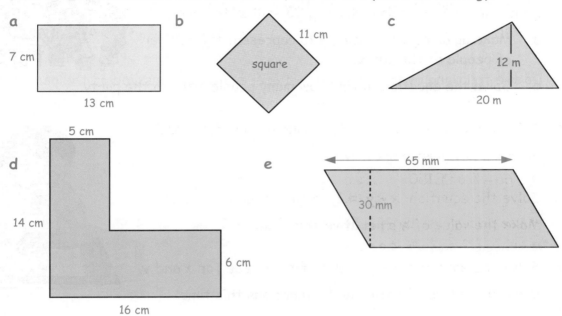

a 7 cm 13 cm

b square 11 cm

c 12 m 20 m

d 5 cm 14 cm 16 cm 6 cm

e 65 mm 30 mm

41. Write down the answers to :-

   a   0·73 × 10   b   10 × 9·247   c   100 × 0·509   d   0·036 × 1000

   e   47·2 ÷ 10   f   7 ÷ 100   g   3040 ÷ 1000   h   16·5 ÷ 1000.

42. Set down and find :-

   a   2·34 × 8   b   9 × 5·67   c   8·64 ÷ 6   d   13·36 ÷ 4.

43. How much change from a £10 note will I receive if I buy a bottle of water for £1·35 and 2 candy bars at 86p each ?

44. I bought 3 skateboards for my nephews costing £137·25 altogether.

What was the cost of each skateboard ?

45. Change each of these fractions to a decimal. Round to 2 decimal places if necessary.

   a $\frac{1}{4}$ b $\frac{4}{5}$ c $\frac{3}{8}$ d $\frac{2}{7}$.

46. Solve these equations to find the value of x :-

    a $x + 5 = 19$ b $x - 3 = 8$ c $12 + x = 32$

    d $25 - x = 19$ e $3x = 21$ f $4x = 18$

    g $2x + 3 = 15$ h $5x - 1 = 29$ i $3x + 11 = 11$

    j $10x - 10 = 10$ k $\frac{1}{2}x = 30$ l $\frac{1}{3}x = 6$.

47. There were x people at a party.

    At midnight, 8 went home leaving 23 still at the party.

    a   Make up an equation using x to represent the number of people at the party.

    b   Solve the equation to find how many people went to the party.

48. Solve the equation $x - y = 6$, to find a value for x and y.

    Both x and y must be **positive**.

49. Solve the equation $x + y = 2$, to find a value for x and y.

    Make the value of x a **negative** this time.

50. Solve the equation $x + y = 9$, to find a value for x and y.

    Make the values of both x and y **fractions** this time.

51. If you add the **complement** of 60° to the **supplement** of 70°, what angle do you get ?

52. Copy and complete each diagram below, filling in **all** missing angles :-

    a   b   c   d

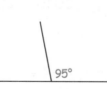
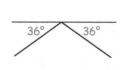
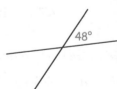

    e   f   g   h

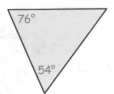
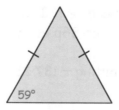
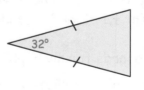
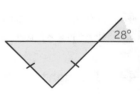

53. Calculate the size of the angle marked *,
    at the centre of this regular octagon.

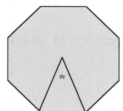

54. Find and simplify fully (*where possible*) :–

     a $\frac{3}{4} \times \frac{3}{5}$ b $\frac{2}{5} \times \frac{3}{4} \times \frac{5}{6}$ c $\frac{1}{3} \div 2$ d $\frac{6}{7} \div 3$.

55. How many $\frac{1}{2}$ litre flasks can I fill from $8\frac{1}{2}$ litres of water ?

1 cm ≈ 0·4 inches	1 cm ≈ 0·03 feet	1 km ≈ 0·62 mile	1 metre ≈ 3·3 feet	1 millimetre ≈ 0·04 inch
1 inch ≈ 2·54 cm	1 foot ≈ 30·5 cm	1 mile ≈ 1·61 km	1 foot ≈ 0·3 metre	1 inch ≈ 25·4 mm
1 gram ≈ 0·04 ounce	1 kg ≈ 2·2 pounds	1 litre ≈ 1·76 pints	1 litre ≈ 0·22 gallon	
1 ounce ≈ 28·3 grams	1 pound ≈ 0·45 kg	1 pint ≈ 0·6 litre	1 gallon ≈ 4·5 litres	

Use the table of conversions above to answer Questions 56, 57 and 58.

56. Change :–

     a   8 kilometres into miles   b   50 mm into inches   c   20 metres into feet

     d   100 grams into ounces   e   60 litres into gallons   f   30 kg into pounds.

57. Change :–

     a   5 feet into centimetres   b   20 inches into cm   c   300 pounds into kg

     d   6 ounces into grams   e   9 pints into litres   f   7 miles into km.

58.

Galleon Ride

At the fairground, children have to be over 40 inches tall to be allowed on the Galleon Ride.

Tracy is 103 centimetres tall.

Will she be allowed on the ride ?

59. a   Are these two shapes congruent ?

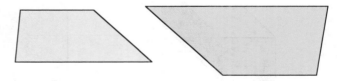

     b   Are the two shapes similar ?

60.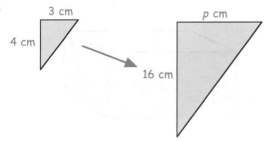

3 cm

4 cm

p cm

16 cm

The 2 triangles here are similar.

     a   Calculate the enlargement scale factor.

     b   Calculate the value of *p*.

61. This table shows how many men, women, boys and girls were at a birthday party.

present	number	fraction	angle
Men	3	$\frac{3}{12}$	$\frac{3}{12}$ × 360 = ...°
Women	6		× 360 = ...°
Girls	2		× 360 = ...°
Boys	1		× 360 = ...°
TOTAL	**?**		**360°**

a How many were at the party altogether ?

b Copy and complete the table.

c Construct a neat accurate **pie chart** to show the information.

62. a Calculate the **mean** price in pence of a 2 litre carton of milk.

70p, 60p, 160p, 80p, 100p, 120p, 50p, 80p.

b Now calculate the **range** of prices.

63. Calculate the volume of each cuboid :–

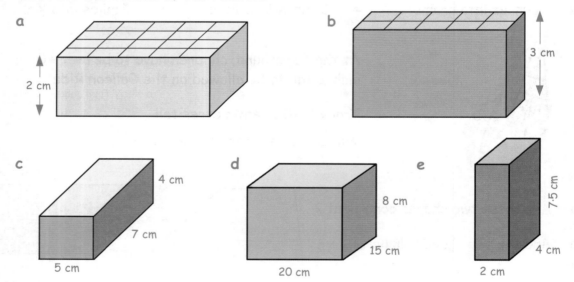

a 2 cm

b 3 cm

c 4 cm, 7 cm, 5 cm

d 8 cm, 15 cm, 20 cm

e 7·5 cm, 4 cm, 2 cm

64. The volume of this cuboid is **60 mm**^{3}.
Calculate its **height**.

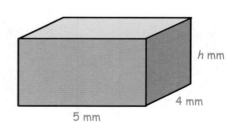

h mm

4 mm

5 mm

Ch 0 - Revision - Page 1

a nineteen thousand and seventy
b one hundred and eight thousand, nine hundred and forty.
260 705 km
a 17 500   b 800 000
a 24 700 b 800 000 700 000
a (i) 8000   (ii) 27 000
b (i) 40 000   (ii) 310 000
c (i) 700 000   (ii) 500 000
27 000 + 6000 = 33 000
a CXL   b CDLV
c DCCLXXIX   d DCCCLXXX
a 141   b 385
c 457   d 940
a 800   b 2300   c 80 000
d 52 000 e 675 939 f 401 000
a 41 233 b 473 029 c 327 849
£132 000
a ∠YZX acute   b ∠PAG right
c ∠ITF obtuse   d ∠NQZ reflex
a 60° b 130°
a   b

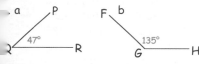

270°
a 492   b 2848
c 14 378   d 34 236
a 1560   b 28 454
c 132 678
a 20 500   b 12 700
c 5803   d 370
a 624   b 3256
c 543   d 7200
a (i) $86\frac{1}{2}$ (ii) $255\frac{5}{6}$
b (i) 63·75   (ii) 374·8
−8°C
a 3, −1, ..., −9 b −1, 9, ..., 29
a −5°C b −1°C c −14°C d −23°C
a 13 cm²
a 160 cm²   b 121 cm²
c 21 m²
a (0) 4 8 12 16 20 24
b (0) 12 24 36 48 60 72
a 1 3 5 15
b 1 2 4 5 8 10 20 40
a 1 2 3 6
b 1 2 3 5 6 10 15 30
a 11 13 17 19   b 83 89

---

30. a 36   b 144   c 27   d 8000
31. 95° obtuse   297° reflex
    180° straight   89° acute
    90° right
32. a 45°   b 135°
33. a 115° b 23° c all four 22·5°
    d 55° e both 32°
    f

34. a 9 thousandths b 9 tenths
35. a 9·2   b 0·92   c 3·883
36. a 454·63   b 80·01
    c 23·916   d 1
37. a $\frac{3}{5}$ b $1\frac{1}{4}$
38. a 39   b 49
39. a 6·8   b 1·0
40. a 200·7 b 5·5 c 21·45 d 0·93
41. 1 cuboid, 5 cubes, 2 cones, 1 sphere, 2 cylinders, 2 triangular prisms
42. a 7   b 15   c 10
43. a cone b pentagonal pyramid
44.

45. a $\frac{5}{8}$ b $\frac{2}{5}$ c $\frac{1}{3}$ d $\frac{1}{3}$
46. $\frac{1}{4}$ $\frac{9}{32}$ $\frac{5}{16}$ $\frac{3}{8}$ $\frac{1}{2}$
47. a $\frac{22}{5}$ a $\frac{101}{10}$
48. a $6\frac{1}{3}$ b $6\frac{3}{4}$
49. A′(2, 5)
50. a/b on diagram   c rhombus
    d P′(6, 0), Q′(4, 4), R′(6, 8), S′(8, 4)
51. a $\frac{27}{100}$ b $\frac{3}{5}$ c $\frac{9}{25}$ d $\frac{1}{25}$
52. a 25% b 90% c 92% d 15%
53. a 35 kg b £7 c 65 g d 4 cm
54. a £30   b £90
55. a 84 cm³   b 20 cm³
56. a 103 mm   b 9·85 cm
    c 850 m   d 16·05 km
    e 11005 ml   f 13·2 kg
57. a 0·768 secs b 0·109 secs
58. a 12   b 9   c 5
    d 9   e 12   f 8
59. a −   b +   c ×
    d ÷   e ÷   f −

---

60. a 3   b 9   c 11   d 18
    e 7   f 12   g 1·5   h 32
    i 99   j 30   k 100   l 7
61. a $\frac{2}{3}$ b $\frac{1}{2}$ c $\frac{4}{5}$ d $\frac{5}{8}$
    e $\frac{9}{10}$ f $\frac{2}{5}$ g $\frac{3}{10}$ h $\frac{7}{8}$
62. a $5\frac{3}{5}$ b $6\frac{1}{2}$ c $5\frac{1}{2}$ d 7
    e $6\frac{2}{5}$ f $3\frac{1}{4}$ g $14\frac{2}{5}$ h $8\frac{1}{2}$
63. a $2\frac{2}{3}$ b $4\frac{1}{2}$ c $6\frac{4}{5}$ d $5\frac{1}{4}$
64. a 0250   b 1935
65. a 9.55 pm   b 3.10 am
66. a 2 mins 40 secs b 6 mins 40 secs
67. a 135 mins   b 105 mins
68. a 1 hr 15 mins   b 2050
69. a (i) 200 ft   (ii) 800 ft
       (iii) 1300 ft (iv) 700 ft
    b 60 - 70 minutes
70. a (i) $\frac{2}{5}$ (ii) $\frac{3}{10}$
      (iii) $\frac{1}{5}$ (iv) $\frac{1}{10}$
    b (i) 100 (ii) 75 (iii) 75.

Ch 1 - Whole Numbers - Page 9

Ch 1 - Exercise 1 - Page 9

1. a 3 million   b 9000
   c 800 000   d 50 000
2. a 800 000   b 8000
   c 8 million   d 80 000
3. a nine thousand and six
   b sixty four thousand, two hundred and five
   c eighty nine thousand, eight hundred and ninety eight
   d six hundred and seventy five thousand, and twenty
   e three million five hundred and one thousand
   f four million, six hundred and three
   g seven million, seven hundred and eighty nine thousand, nine hundred and eighty seven
   h nine million, nine hundred and ninety nine thousand, nine hundred and ninety nine
4. a 5629   b 20012
   c 780 301   d 6 240 007
   e 4 407 003   f 9 090 009
5. a 65 420 65 204 64 205 62 405 54 206 52 540 52 450
   b 7 568 000 6 875 000 6 587 000 5 768 000 5 678 000

6. a 820   b 1800
   c 13200   d 105300
   e 130000   f 120200
   g 910000   h 900000
   i 6250000   j 500000

7. A 6700   B 21000   C 32000
   D 31800   E 33100   F 90000
   G 106000   H 109000   I 118000
   J 340000   K 390000   L 3500000
   M 4250000   N 5700000
   O 6050000   P 315000
   Q 329000   R 341000
   S 1900000   T 2500000
   U 4100000

8. a 5600   b 72350
   c 720000   d 400000
   e 1500000   f 9600000

9. a 7000000   b 4500000
   c 8250000   d 9750000

10. a £49500000
   b four million, nine hundred and fifty thousand pounds

Ch 1 - Exercise 2 - Page 11

1. a 70   b 80   c 130
   d 6240   e 75510   f 372990
   g 1285640   h 5298790

2. a 100   b 200   c 8300
   d 9500   e 25600   f 562800
   g 2475400   h 9886000

3. a 1000   b 5000
   c 46000   d 73000
   e 541000   f 387000
   g 3865000   h 4845000

4. a 10000   b 60000
   c 80000   d 100000
   e 110000   f 220000
   g 1630000   h 6280000

5. a 100000   b 100000
   c 400000   d 800000
   e 800000   f 2600000
   g 7900000   h 1900000

6. a 1000000   b 1000000
   c 2000000   d 4000000
   e 6000000   f 6000000
   g 8000000   h 10000000

Ch 1 - Exercise 3 - Page 12

1. a 112   b 265   c 534   d 272
   e 544   f 2232   g 1824   h 4734
   i 10670   j 18438
   k 37200   l 61033

2. a 259   b 384   c 468   d 712
   e 1134   f 1228   g 2144   h 1998
   i 12725   j 19170
   k 16803   l 21749
   m 57468   n 8348

---

   o 14848   p 42800
3. answers checked by dividing
4. 1470
5. 1910
6. 4232 grams
7. 3834
8. £14322
9. 10080 minutes
10. 25623 bananas
11. 13152
12. 15112 pence = £151·12
13. 16702 m²
14. 6000

Ch 1 - Exercise 4 - Page 14

1. a 432   b 1575
   c 30668   d 20976
   e 39933   f 68800
   g 269979   h 463650
2. 960   3. 1728 apples
4. 680   5. 350 mins
6. 2000   7. 9880
8. a £21692   b £14820
9. 45960
10. £435512
11. 569250 pins

Ch 1 - Exercise 5 - Page 16

1. a 340   b 1260   c 1140
   d 1650   e 8920   f 14280
   g 12200   h 13600   i 69000
   j 169600   k 48000   l 1170000

2. a 13080   b 24680
   c 10450   d 193080
   e 68600   f 98480
   g 585630   h 65520
   i 274140   j 246900

3. a 43200   b 105600
   c 228000   d 125300
   e 151600   f 183000
   g 292500   h 325600
   i 738900   j 1464000
   k 4236000   l 1808000
   m 2202000   n 952000
   o 14301000   p 47880000

4. a 1200   b 7200
   c 28000   d 45000
   e 350000   f 48000
   g 180000   h 450000
   i 2100000   j 5400000
   k 28000000   l 48000000

5. a 70   b 70
   c 700   d 60
   e 60   f 3000
   g 7000   h 51000
   i 7000   j 520
   k 3100   l 630

---

6. a 760000   b 125
   c £1390   d 72000

Ch 2 - Negative Numbers - Page 19

Ch 2 - Exercise 1 - Page 19

1. a -3°C   b -12°C   c -8°C   d -80°
2. Black means you have money in bank
   Red means you are overdrawn and
   owe bank money
   An OVERDRAFT occurs when mone
   is withdrawn from a bank account
   and the available balance goes below
   zero.
3. a She has £375 of her own in bank
   b He is £400 overdrawn
   c £33
   d -£5, - needs £5 to clear
   e -£50
4. a (i) +1966   (ii) +312
     (iii) -21   (iv) -729
   b 56   c 82   d 35 AD   e 9 BC
   f 13 BC
5. 75
6. Various
7. a (i) +100   (ii) -100
     (iii) 0   (iv) +150
     (v) -200   (vi) +250
     (vii) -25   (viii) -175
     (ix) +275
   b (i) 100 m   (ii) 25 m
     (iii) 50 m   (iv) 75 m
     (v) 50 m   (vi) 250 m
     (vii) 200 m   (viii) 125 m
     (ix) 300 m   (x) 450 m
8. 600 m
9. -225 m
10. a 14°C   b 23°C   c 32°C   d 12°C
   e 0°C   f 5°C   g -16°C   h 7°C
   i -3°C   j -42°C   k -20°C   l -60°C
   m -7°C   n -5°C
11. a 4° up   b 14° down
   c 40° down   d 25° up
   e 17° down   f 7° up
   g 17° down   h 22° down
   i 41° up   j 70° down
12. 19°C
13. a 15°C   b -5°C   c -25°C   d -75°C

Ch 2 - Exercise 2 - Page 23

1. a 17   b 16   c 29   d 4
   e 6   f 0   g -6   h -7
   i -16   j 7   k 0   l 11
   m -3   n -9   o -13   p -15
   q -20   r -30   s -8   t -34
   u -30   v -70   w -25   x -8

a 23   b 1   c 0   d 1
e 7   f -9   g -6   h -6
i -1   j -1   k 8   l 4
6 – (–2) = 6 + 2 = 8

Ch 3 – 2-D Shapes – *Page 25*

Ch 3 – Exercise 1 – *Page 26*

1. Check Drawings

Ch 3 – Exercise 2 – *Page 28*

1. Check Drawings

Ch 3 – Exercise 3 – *Page 30*

1. Check Drawings
   The 2 shorter sides are not long
   enough to meet to form a triangle

Ch 3 – Exercise 4 – *Page 32*

1. Check Drawings

Ch 3 – Exercise 5 – *Page 34*

a-d

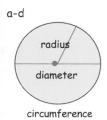

7 cm
50 mm
a 6 cm b 3 cm
a see sketch   b 12 cm
48 cm by 16 cm
a 4 cm b 2 cm
a 7 cm b 3·5 cm c 8·5 cm
9/10/11 see pupils designs

Ch 4 – Whole Numbers 2 – *Page 37*

Ch 4 – Exercise 1 – *Page 37*

a 89   b 446   c 843   d 966
e 762   f 1579   g 719   h 837
a 64 r1   b 452 r3
c 479 r6   d 876 r2
681
£587
944
363
a 16   b 7
a 166   b 4
337

Ch 4 – Exercise 2 – *Page 38*

1. a 14   b 59   c 293   d 764
   e 21   f 79   g 354   h 783
2. a 25   b 54   c 42   d 21
3. a 4   b 22   c 34   d 41
   e 52   f 34   g 6   h 122
   i 112   j 211   k 313   l 152
   m 115   n 25   o 112   p 123
4. 23
5. 31
6. 53
7. 21
8. 23
9. 215
10. 203
11. 23
12. 15

Ch 4 – Exercise 3 – *Page 40*

1. a 4 r 2   b 22 r 4   c 34 r 1   d 41 r 4
   e 52 r 10 f 34 r 15 g 6 r 3   h 122 r1
2. a $4\frac{1}{2}$ b $13\frac{1}{2}$ c $34\frac{1}{3}$ d $34\frac{3}{8}$
   e $52\frac{1}{17}$ f $35\frac{1}{2}$ g $111\frac{3}{4}$ h $200\frac{6}{7}$
3. a 5·5   b 41·5   c 27·5   d 41·2
   e 51·5   f 42·25   g 251·5   h 284·2
4. a 34   b 84   c 24   d 26
   e 32   f 30   g 102   h 113
   i 101   j 315   k 50   l 113
5. a 108 r 18   b $108\frac{1}{4}$
   c 108·25   d 108
6. a 28   b £245·50
   c £209   d £174·25
   e $202\frac{1}{2}$ litres   f 31
   g £14·25

Ch 4 – Exercise 4 – *Page 42*

1. 55
2. 12 875 miles
3. 7650
4. 115 weeks (+ 4 days)
5. £1993
6. 1148 km
7. 427, with 8 left over
8. 5590 ft
9. 86 400 secs
10. 148
11. a £31·48   b £5·73
12. £270·25
13. £2·75, £2·85 - box of 6 cheaper
14. £63·20 online £71·40 supermarket
    £8·20 saved
15. £3·28
16. £1·95

17. £36·99
18. £224·20
19. £1·30
20. 7 apples & 3 pears

Ch 4 – Exercise 5 – *Page 45*

1. a add 140 then take 1 (285)
   b take 60 then take 8 (222)
   c add 4000 then take 100 (300)
   d take 530 from 780 the add
     7 – 4 (253)
   e add 23 to 45 & add 3 zeros
2. a 97   b 119   c 104   d 126
   e 145   f 316   g 328   h 540
   i 1310   j 330   k 720   l 440
   m 68 000   n 45 000
   o 99 995   p 1 110 000
   q 6 000 000   r 5 100 000
3. a 264 000   b £2 350 000
4. a 9 × 800 add 9 × 30 (7470)
   b 14 × £6 - 14 × 1p (£83·86)
   c 18 × £2 take 18 × 2p (£35·82)
   d 300 ÷ 3, 120 ÷ 3 & add (140)
   e 500 ÷ 5, 105 ÷ 5 & add (130)
   f 174 ÷ 2 ÷ 3 (29)
5. a 520   b 12 900
   c 405 000   d 728 000
   e £25·87   f £47·88
   g £41·30   h 39·90
   i 180   j 630
   k 3400   l 120 000
   m 21 000   n 2700
   o 190   p 14 000
6. a £14 985   b £610

Ch 4 – Exercise 6 – *Page 47*

1. a 249   b 204 kg
   c £156 300   d 3842 m
   e 39·6   f 845·73
   g 38 760   h 87 600
   i 65 000   j 80 000
   k 1 400 000   l 8 000 000
2. a 12 135   b 587 676
   c 340 460   d 923
3. a 93 000   b 200 000
   c 800 000   d 40
4. 880 000
5. a 60   b 140   c 80
   d 240   e 700   f 654 900

Ch 4 – Exercise 7 – *Page 48*

1. a 49   b 14   c 50
   d 45   e 95   f 50
2. a 20   b 4   c 2
   d 4   e 14   f 6
   g 30   h 15   i 1

3. a 30   b 15   c 180
   d 2   e 0   f 2
4. a (3 + 7) x 2 = 20   b 16 – (7 x 2) = 2
   c (20 + 18) ÷ 2 = 19
   d (40 + 20) ÷ (4 x 5) = 3
   e (15 + 30) ÷ (12 – 3) = 5
   f (5 + 8) x (6 – 2)) + 5 = 57
5. a 100   b 20   c 240
   d 50   e 60   f 79
   g 100   h 3   i 4

Ch 5 - Algebra 1 - *Page 50*

Ch 5 - Exercise 1 - *Page 50*

1. a 9   b 2   c 24   d 1
   e 14   f 2   g 9   h 27
   i 0   j 18   k 12   l 5·4
2. a 20   b 28   c 16   d 32
   e 64   f 160   g 1280   h 2
3. a 16   b 4   c 41
   d –5   e 40   f 4
4. a 11   b 24   c 18
   d 21   e 90   f 31
   g 2   h 2   i 5
5. a 9   b 25   c 1   d 2
   e 49   f 18   g 6   h 1
   i 3   j 4   k 5   l 49
6. a 18   b 3   c 16
   d 18   e 19   f 33
   g 88   h 0   i 16
7. a 1   b 2   c 4
   d 2   e 2   f 1
   g 1   h 3   i 0
8. a 7   b 90   c 100
   d 250   e 60

Ch 5 - Exercise 2 - *Page 52*

1. a $W = x + y$ b 5   c 2·5
2. a $L = m – n$ b 2·25   c 12·75
3. a $S = D ÷ T$ b 60   c 330 m
4. a $C = 5k + 10$ b £40
5. a $F = 1·8 x C + 32$ b 50°F
6. a $T = 10 x g + h$ b 215
7. a $P = 2a + 2b + c$ b 26   c 16
8. a $L = x + y$ b $P = 6x + 2y$ c 38
9. a $P = 2m + 4n$ b 32   c 5

Ch 5 - Exercise 3 - *Page 54*

1. the 3 times table starting at 6
2. a the times 4 table starting at 4
   b the times 6 table starting at 6
   c the times 5 table starting at 15
   d the times 10 table starting at 30
   e the times 9 table starting at 18
   f times 8 table starting 56 –> down
3. 24, 28, 32
4. 2b 36, 42, 48   2c 40, 45, 50

2d 80, 90, 100   2e 54, 63, 72
2f 16, 8, 0
5. begin at 8 and go up 3 each time
6. a begin at 5 and go up 2 each time
   b begin at 4 and go up 3 each time
   c begin at 8 and go up 4 each time
   d begin at 7 and go up 10 each time
   e begin at 83 and go up 5 each time
   f begin at 2 go up 0·5 each time
   g begin at 14 and go up 1 each time
   h begin at 52 go down 4 each time
7. a 15, 17, 19   b 19, 22, 25
   c 28, 32, 36   d 57, 67, 77
   e 108, 113, 118   f 4·5, 5·0, 5·5
   g 21, 22, 23   h 36, 32, 28
8. a

   b 3, 6, 9, 12, 15, 18, 21
   c start with 3 matches and add 3
   d 30
9. a 24   b 6, 12, 18, 24, 30, 36
   c start with 6 cherries and add 6
   d 54

Ch 6 - Multiples/Factors - *Page 58*

Ch 6 - Exercise 1 - *Page 58*

1. a 4, 8, 12, 16, 20, 24, 28, 32, 36, 40
   b 3, 6, 9, 12, 15, 18, 21, 24
   c 5, 10, 15, 20, 25, 30, 35, 40, 45
   d 10, 20, 30, 40, 50, 60, 70
2. a 9, 12, 15, 18, 21, 24
   b 30, 36, 42, 48, 54, 60
   c 24, 32, 40, 48, 56, 64, 72
   d 54, 63, 72, 81, 90, 99
3. a 2, 4, 6, 8, 10, 12, 14, 16, 18, 20
   b Even numbers
   c 1, 3, 5, 7, 9, 11, 13, 15, 17, 19
   d Odd Numbers
4. a The even numbers from 44 to 56
   b multiples of 5 from 35 to 60
   c multiples of 10 from 120 to 160
   d multiples of 6 from 60 to 90
   e multiples of 9 from 81 to 117
   f multiples of 20 from 60 to 140
   g multiples of 15 from 15 to 75
   h multiples of 50 from 600 to 800
   i multiples of 13 from 39 to 91
   j multiples of 250 from 500 to 1500
5. a 3, 6, 9, 12, 15, 18, 21, ...33, 36
   b 4, 8, 12, 16, 20, 24, ...44, 48
   c 12, 24, 36   d 12
6. a 4, 8, 12, 16, 20, 24, ...36, 40
   b 6, 12, 18, 24, 30, 36, ...54, 60
   c 12, 24, 36,   d 12
7. a 10   b 6   c 36

   d 12   e 18   f 20
   g 30   h 56   i 30
   j 72   k 36   l 44
8. a 30   b 24   c 40
   d 10   e 42
   f 18   g 120
9. 20 days
10. 120 seconds or 2 minutes

Ch 6 - Exercise 2 - *Page 60*

1. 1, 2, 5, 10
2. 1, 2, 4, 7, 14, 28
3. 1, 2, 3, 6, 9, 18
4. 1, 2, 4, 5, 10, 20
5. a 1, 2, 4, 8
   b 1, 2, 3, 4, 6, 8, 12, 24
   c 1, 3, 9, 27
   d 1, 2, 11, 22
   e 1, 2, 3, 5, 6, 10, 15, 30
   f 1, 31
   g 1, 2, 4, 8, 16, 32
   h 1, 2, 5, 10, 25, 50
   i 1, 67
   j 1, 2, 4, 5, 8, 10, 20, 40
   k 1, 3, 5, 9, 15, 45
   l 1, 2, 3, 4, 5, 6, 10, 12, 15, 20, 30, 60
6. a 1, 3, 9 (3)   b 1, 7, 49 (3
   c 1, 2, 3, 4, 6, 9, 12, 18, 36 (9)
   d 1, 2, 4 (3)   e 1, 5, 25 (3
   f 1, 2, 4, 8, 16, 32, 64 (7)
   g 1, 2, 4, 8, 16 (5)
   h 1, 2, 4, 5, 10, 20, 25, 50, 100 (9)
7. a yes   b square no's
   c factors match up in pairs except
      for the middle one which only
      matches up with itself.
8. 1 row of 36,   2 rows of 18,
   3 rows of 12, 4 rows of 9,
   6 rows of 6 + reverse
9. a 1, 2, 3, 4, 6, 12
   b 1, 2, 3, 6, 9, 18
   c 1, 2, 3, 6   d 6
10. a 1, 3, 5, 15
    b 1, 2, 4, 5, 10, 20
    c 1, 5   d 5
11. a 3   b 4   c 10
    d 4   e 12   f 20
    g 17   h 6
12. a 1   b 1
    c 1   d 1
13. a 4   b 5
    c 7   d 8
14. 1, 2, 3, 4, 5, 6, 8, 9, 10, 12,
    15, 18, 20, 24, 30, 36, 40,
    45, 60, 72, 90, 120, 180, 360
15. 1000 itself

1, 2, 5, 10.
It has more than 2 factors
It has exactly 2 factors
a 1, 5 - Yes
b 1, 2, 4, 8, 16 - No
c 1, 3, 5, 15 - No
d 1, 17 - Yes
e 1, 23 - Yes
f 1, 3, 9, 27 - No
g 1, 29 - Yes
h 1, 5, 7, 35 - No
i 1, 2, 4, 11, 22, 44 - No
j 1, 47 - Yes
k 1, 3, 17, 51 - No
l 1, 2, 31, 62 - No
2, 3, 5, 7, 11, 13, 17, 19, 23, 29, 31,
37, 41, 43, 47, 53, 59, 61, 67, 71, 73,
79, 83, 89, 97
a - e

f 101, 103, 107, 109, 113, 127, 131,
   137, 139, 149, 151, 157, 163, 167,
   173, 179, 181, 191, 193, 197, 199

Ch 6 - Exercise 4 - *Page 63*

$2 \times 2 \times 3 \times 5$
a $3 \times 3 \times 5$
b $2 \times 2 \times 3 \times 3$
c $3 \times 3 \times 11$
a $2 \times 2 \times 2 \times 2$
b $2 \times 3 \times 3$
c $2 \times 2 \times 5$
d $3 \times 3 \times 3$
e $2 \times 3 \times 5$
f $2 \times 3 \times 3 \times 3$
g $3 \times 3 \times 5$
h $2 \times 2 \times 2 \times 2 \times 3$
i $2 \times 2 \times 17$
j $2 \times 7 \times 7$
k $2 \times 2 \times 5 \times 5$
l $2 \times 3 \times 3 \times 3 \times 3$

Ch 7 - Fractions 1 - *Page 65*

Ch 7 - Exercise 1 - *Page 65*

a $\frac{2}{4}$ $\frac{3}{6}$ ..   b $\frac{2}{6}$ $\frac{3}{9}$ ..
c $\frac{6}{8}$ $\frac{9}{12}$ ..   d $\frac{4}{6}$ $\frac{6}{9}$

e $\frac{2}{20}$ $\frac{3}{30}$ f $\frac{4}{10}$ $\frac{6}{15}$
g $\frac{10}{14}$ $\frac{15}{21}$ ..   h $\frac{2}{200}$ $\frac{3}{300}$ ..
i $\frac{18}{40}$ $\frac{27}{60}$ ..   j $\frac{14}{22}$ $\frac{21}{33}$ ..
k $\frac{16}{38}$ $\frac{24}{57}$ ..   l $\frac{34}{42}$ $\frac{51}{63}$ ..
m $\frac{68}{70}$ $\frac{102}{105}$ ..   n $\frac{6}{622}$ $\frac{9}{933}$ ..
o $\frac{214}{230}$ $\frac{321}{345}$ ..   p $\frac{22}{16}$ $\frac{33}{24}$ ..

2. a $\frac{3}{4}$ b $\frac{8}{9}$ c $\frac{4}{5}$ d $\frac{1}{2}$
   e $\frac{3}{4}$ f $\frac{1}{2}$ g $\frac{3}{4}$ h $\frac{13}{17}$
   i $\frac{9}{10}$ j $\frac{5}{6}$ k $\frac{13}{131}$ l $\frac{4}{5}$
   m $\frac{1}{20}$ n $\frac{1}{15}$ o $\frac{12}{101}$ p $\frac{1}{3}$

Ch 7 - Exercise 2 - *Page 66*

1. a $5\frac{1}{2}$ b $5\frac{2}{3}$
2. a $4\frac{1}{4}$ b $4\frac{3}{5}$ c $8\frac{1}{2}$ d $3\frac{2}{5}$
   e $12\frac{2}{3}$ f $8\frac{1}{2}$ g $2\frac{1}{2}$ h $18\frac{1}{3}$
   i $4\frac{1}{3}$ j $3\frac{1}{8}$ k 3   l $2\frac{3}{4}$
3. a $\frac{14}{3}$ b $\frac{73}{9}$
3. a $\frac{5}{2}$ b $\frac{21}{5}$ c $\frac{23}{3}$ d $\frac{52}{5}$
   e $\frac{108}{7}$ f $\frac{80}{9}$ g $\frac{79}{10}$ h $\frac{419}{20}$

Ch 7 - Exercise 3 - *Page 67*

1. a >   b <   c <   d =
2. a <   b <   c >
   d >   e =   f <
3. a $\frac{2}{5}, \frac{1}{2}, \frac{2}{3}$ b $\frac{2}{3}, \frac{3}{4}, \frac{4}{5}$
   c $\frac{27}{12}, \frac{21}{8}, \frac{8}{3}, \frac{7}{2}$ d $\frac{3}{5}, \frac{3}{4}, \frac{17}{20}, \frac{9}{10}$
4. No - Fractions add to over 1 whole.

Ch 7 - Exercise 4 - *Page 68*

1. a $\frac{17}{21}$ b $\frac{2}{15}$ c $\frac{1}{8}$ d $1\frac{1}{12}$
2. a $\frac{13}{15}$ b $\frac{1}{4}$ c $1\frac{7}{24}$ d $1\frac{3}{10}$
   e $\frac{1}{2}$ f $\frac{1}{12}$ g $1\frac{1}{10}$ h $\frac{5}{18}$
3 a $1\frac{1}{12}$ b 0   c $\frac{23}{30}$
4. a $10\frac{5}{6}$ b $2\frac{5}{12}$ c $2\frac{5}{8}$ d $11\frac{1}{10}$
   e $1\frac{1}{6}$ f $21\frac{7}{24}$ g $29\frac{9}{20}$ h $1\frac{2}{5}$
   i $17\frac{1}{9}$ j $25\frac{11}{20}$ k $3\frac{1}{2}$ l $\frac{1}{12}$
   m $1\frac{7}{12}$ n $2\frac{1}{6}$ o $1\frac{7}{20}$ p $1\frac{1}{6}$
5. a $2\frac{2}{3}$ b $1\frac{3}{5}$ c $2\frac{3}{8}$ d $2\frac{2}{5}$
6. a $2\frac{4}{5}$ b $2\frac{3}{7}$ c $4\frac{1}{6}$ d $1\frac{2}{5}$
   e $\frac{3}{10}$ f $5\frac{5}{8}$ g $5\frac{2}{7}$ h $4\frac{2}{3}$
7. $2\frac{5}{8}$ metres
8. a $3\frac{9}{10}$ b $1\frac{31}{40}$ c $5\frac{9}{20}$

9. a $2\frac{7}{10}$ b $1\frac{3}{4}$ c $1\frac{5}{8}$ d $4\frac{23}{30}$
   e $2\frac{5}{6}$ f $4\frac{9}{14}$ g $4\frac{19}{30}$ h $2\frac{23}{30}$
10. a $1\frac{1}{4}$ b $\frac{1}{8}$ c $1\frac{7}{8}$
11. $2\frac{3}{4}$ hours

Ch 8 - Coordinates - *Page 72*

Ch 8 - Exercise 1 - *Page 73*

1. B(5, 3), C(3, -2), D(-4, -1), E(0, 3),
    F(-1, -3), G(-3, 0), H(5, -3), I(0, -2)
2. a J(4, 4), K(-3, 3), L(-4, -2), M(-1, -2),
       N(3, -1), O(0, 0), P6, -3), Q(0, -3),
       R(0, 2), S(-2, 0), T(-2, -1)
    b S   c Q, R   d (i) J   (ii) S & T
    e (i) K   (ii) T and N
    f S and T or R and Q
    g J(4, 4)
3. a See diagram
4. a a kite   b parallelogram
    c isos triangle   d rhombus
    e pentagon   f hexagon
5. a see diagram
    b S(-3, -3)   c $(1, -\frac{1}{2})$
6. a diagram   b (-3, -1)   c (1, -1)
7. a -3   b (-1,-2), (-3,-4) etc.
8. a diagram   b (-5, -1)   c (0, 1)
9. a 0   b (5, 0), (4, 0) etc c square
10. a K(-4, -7) L(-7, -3)   b (-1·5, -3)

Ch 8 - Exercise 2 - *Page 75*

1. a/ diagram
    c (0, 2) (1, -1) (-6, 1)
       (-5, -1) (-4, 1) (-6, 5)
    d A'(-2, 1) B'(-3, -2) C'(4, 0)
       D'(3, -2) E'(2, 0) F'(4, 4)
    e A''(2, -1) B''(3, 2) C''(-4, 0)
       D''(-3, 2) E''(-2, 0) F''(-4, -4)
2. a diagram
    b G'(-1, -5) H'(-6, 4) I'(3, 0) J'(5, 3)
    c yes
3. a diagram
    b A'(2, -1), B'(5, -1), C'(5, -3), D'(2, -3)
    c A''(-2,-1)B''(-5,-1)C''(-5,-3)D''(-2, -3)
4. a A(1, 2), B(5, 2), C(5, 4)
    b A'(1, -2), B'(5, -2), C'(5, -4)
    c A''(-1, -2), B''(-5, -2), C''(-5, -4)
5. a diagram   b trapezium
    c/d E'(2, -1), F'(3, -6),
         G'(5, -6), H'(6, -1)
6. a diagram
    b P'(0, 1), Q'(1, 6), R'(4, 7), S'(5, 2)
    c P''(0, -1), Q''(-1, -6),
       R''(-4, -7), S''(-5, -2)
7. a/b diagram
    c/d I'(-1,2) J'(-3,2) K'(-3,4) L'(-1,4)

8. a/b/c diagram
    d P'(3, 0) Q'(4, −1) R'(3, −2) S'(−2, −1)
9. a/b diagram
    c M'(−1, 3) N'(−1, −2) P'(1, 3)
10. E'(−2, −2) F'(−2, 2) G'(2, 2) H'(2, −2)
11. D(8, −1)   12. T(3, 6)
13.

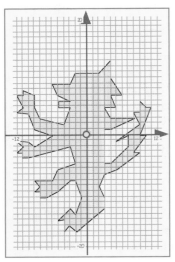

15.

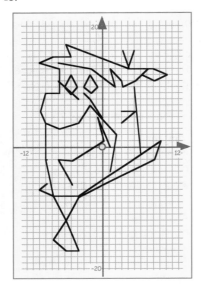

Ch 9 - Exercise 1 - Page 80

1. a 2:3   b 3:2
2. a 3:1   b 1:3
3. a 9:19 b 19:9
4. a 29:23 b 23:29
5. a 7:3   b 3:7
6. a 2:15 b 15:2 c 2:17 d 17:15
7. a 9:8   b 5:2   c 2:9   d 8:5
    e 1:5   f 2:8   g 5:20
8. a 43:27 b 27:43 c 43:140
9. a 20:3 b 3:23

10. a 50:61   b 50:11

Ch 9 - Exercise 2 - Page 82

1. 5:3
2. 6:7
3. a 2:3   b 5:6   c 1:2   d 3:8
    e 1:1   f 6:1   g 2:1   h 3:2
    i 2:1   j 5:7   k 2:3   l 5:8
    m 9:4   n 7:5   o 27:2 p 1:9
    q 1:100 r 50:1 s 1:3   t 9:4
    u 1:100 v 1:4000000
4. a 2:1   b 4:3   c 7:2   d 4:3
5. a 200:4   b 50:1
6. a 15:5   b 3:1
7. a 4:1   b 1:4
8. a 20:16   b 5:4
9. a 80000:16000   b 5:1
10. a 44:55   b 4:5
11. a 48:176   b 3:11
12. a 72:60   b 6:5
13. a 1:10   b 1:1000 c 1:3
    d 1:20   e 1:12   f 1:8
    g 1:4   h 7:366 i 1:24

Ch 9 - Exercise 3 - Page 84

1. 21
2. 32 litres
3. a (i) 18   (ii) 48
    b (i) 8   (ii) 54
4. a 4   b 10   c 16   d 30
5. 160
6. 170
7. a 14   b 10
8. a 52   b (i) 7 (ii) 35
9. a £50 b £100 c £3500
10. a 56   b 105
11. a 21   b 56
12. 378
13. a OMG b Med   c Mild
    d Light e Very Strong
14. a 8   b 25   c 14
    d 12   e 24

Ch 9 - Exercise 4 - Page 87

1. £1·05
2. a 7p   b £12   c £9
    d 60p   e 20p   f £21
3. 20 tonnes
4. 6 km per hour
5   €1·10 per £
6. 2 kg
7. 1·5 per sec
8. 8 metres per second
9. Slow Fit - £48
    Tyres R us - £44 - cheaper

Ch 9 - Exercise 5 - Page 88

1. £56·40
2. £8·10
3. $75
4. a 5·4 m³   b 625 times
5. a £4·80   b £20·40
6. a 500   b 3500
    c 30000   d 1800000
7. a no   b no
    c no   d yes
8. a 300   b 50 mins
9. a 50 mins b 54 lines
10. a £45   b 35 mins
    c 28 kg   d £4·00

Ch 10 - Percentages - Page 92

Ch 10 - Exercise 1 - Page 92

1. Copy and Learn
2. a £12   b £24   c £48
    d £4   e £2   f £180
    g £5   h £10   i £35
    j £4·2   k £152   l £210
    m £31   n £62   o £1·50
    p £27   q £18   r £9
    s £7   t £14   u £21
    v £360   w £1300 x £6
3. a 10% + half your answer
    b 10% halved and halved again
    c Find 10%, half this and half again
      Then add the final 2 values.
4.   a £12   b 24 km
    c 35 km   d 10p   e 36 ml
    f 200 mm g 10 cm h 90 litres
5. 168 pupils
6. 75 trees
7. 204 g
8. 38 cats
9. a £55   b (i) 17 kg (ii) 68 kg
    c £270   d (i) 90   (ii) 40%
    e 24
10. £20

Ch 10 - Exercise 2 - Page 94

1. a £195   b 374·4 km c £14·14
    d 340·2 ml e 27 kg   f 158·4 mm
    g £47·40 h 16·8 cm i 7200 km
    j 1·26 cm k 19 km   l £57500
    m £808   n 187·5 km o £7·50
2. a 336   b 688   c 1872
    d £5·40   e 80·04 kg
3. a (i) 9·1 kg   (ii) 60·9 kg
    b 2 hr 42 min
4. a (i) £18 (ii) £138 b £16·02
5. a 11040 ml   b £2183

£61·60 - £59·25 - Shop B better
a £9600   b £16 800
a £896   b 4730
c £67·20 d £4200
69 mph
. a £31·08 b £344·50 c 42 psi
. a £102·30 b £11 872
. a £10 000 b £10 000

Ch 11 - Exercise 1 - *page 98*

a

b Tables   1 2 3 4 5 6
   Children 3 6 9 12 15 18
c 3
d No. of children = 3 × no. of tables
e C = 3 × T
f C = 60
a

b Stars   1 2 3 4 5 6
   Circles   5 10 15 20 25 30
c 5
d No. of circles = 5 × no. of stars
e C = 5 × S
f C = 200
. a Glasses 1 2 3 4 5 6
    Strawb 6 12 18 24 30 36 b 42
  b No. of strawbs = 6 × no. of glasses
  c S = 6 × G
  d S = 60
. a Footballs 1 2 3 4 5 6
    Cost   7 14 21 28 35 42
  b Cost = 7 × No. of footballs
  c C = 7 × F
  d £210
. a Bushes 1 2 3 4 5 6
    Roses   8 16 24 32 40 48
  b No. of Roses = 8 × no. of Bushes
  c R = 8 × B
  d R = 400
. a Pots   1 2 3 4 5 6
    Marig   10 20 30 40 50 60
  b No. of Marig = 10 × no. of Pots
  c M = 10 × P
  d M = 150
7. a 20
   b P = 20 × B
   c P = 360
8. a P = 30 × N   b P = 18 × T
   c H = 24 × D   d p = 100 × N
   e C = 1·25 × M   f C = 3·5 × T

1. a

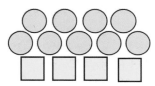

   b Squares 1 2 3 4 5 6
      Circles   3 5 7 9 11 13
   c 2
   d C = 2 × S + 1
   e C = 21
2. a

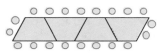

   b Tables   1 2 3 4 5 6
      Children 8 12 16 20 24 28
   c 4
   d C = 4 × T + 4
   e C = 84
3. a (i) £20   (ii) £26
   b £3
   c C = 3 × D + 5
   d £47
4. a 50 kg
   b 1450 kg
   c W = 50 × P + 1200
   d W = 1700 kg
5. a

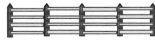

   b Posts   2 3 4 5 6 7
      Supports 4 8 12 16 20 24
   c 4
   d S = 4 × P – 4
   e S = 76
6. a

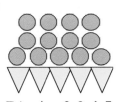

   b Triangles 2 3 4 5 6 7
      Circles   4 7 10 13 16 19
   c 3
   d C = 3 × T – 2
   e C = 148
   f (i) T = 8   (ii) T = 12
      (iii) T = 20   (iv) T = 30
7. a W = 3 × T + 7
   b F = 5 × K – 3
   c B = 10 × F + 5
   d G = 0·5 × C + 7
   e C = 4 × T + 8
   f T = 6 × P + 24

g C = 9 × D – 2
h D = 0·8 × T + 0·5
i W = 60 × B + 180
j S = 250 × Y – 150

Ch 12 - Exercise 1 - *page 107*

1. a See diagram
   b See diagram
   c 20 cm²
   d 10 cm²
2. ab See diagram
   c 24 cm²
   d 12 cm²
3. a/b See diagram
   c 25 cm²
   d 12·5 cm²
4. a (i) (ii) see diagram
      (iii) 40 cm²   (iv) 20 cm²
   b (i) (ii) see diagram
      (iii) 50 cm²   (iv) 25 cm²
   c (i) (ii) see diagram
      (iii) 90 cm²   (iv) 45 cm²
   d (i) (ii) see diagram
      (iii) 48 cm²   (iv) 24 cm²
   e (i) (ii) see diagram
      (iii) 88 cm²   (iv) 44 cm²
   f (i) (ii) see diagram
      (iii) 66 cm²   (iv) 33 cm²
   g (i) (ii) see diagram
      (iii) 28 cm²   (iv) 14 cm²
5. a 18 cm²
   b 9 cm²
   c A = $\frac{1}{2}$ area of the surrounding
      rectangle

Ch 12 - Exercise 2 - *page 109*

1. a 20 cm²   b 18 cm²
   c 60 cm²   d 42 cm²
   e 500 mm²   f 4080 mm²
2. 675 cm²
3. 2500 cm²
4. a 275 mm²   b 170 cm²
   c 26 m²
5. (432 + 360) cm² = 792 cm²

Ch 12 - Exercise 3 - *page 111*

1. a (i) 28 cm   (ii) 40 cm²
   b (i) 36 cm   (ii) 40 cm²
   c (i) 36 cm   (ii) 81 cm²
   d (i) 40 cm   (ii) 60 cm²
   e (i) 18 cm   (ii) 18 cm²

f (i) 54 cm   (ii) 170 cm²
g (i) 36 cm   (ii) 54 cm²
h (i) 56 cm   (ii) 84 cm²
i (i) 2 cm   (ii) $\frac{1}{4}$ cm²

2. a 121 cm²   b 24000 mm²
   c 5 m²   d 72$\frac{1}{2}$ cm²

3. a 160 m²   b 10   c £160
4. a 14·8 m   b £35
5. £375

Ch 12 - Exercise 4 - page 113

1. a 99 cm²   b 65 cm²   c 72 cm²
   d 60 cm²   e 22 cm²   f 52 cm²
   g 92 cm²   h 27 cm²   i 36 cm²
2. 5400 mm²
3. 100 m²
4. 15 m²
5. 1200 cm²
6. 240 cm²
7. 12 m²
8. a USRP and TSQP
   b 810 cm² and 432 cm²
9. 13 cm

Ch 12 - Exercise 5 - page 115

1. a ABCDEF all 36 cm²
   b A - 26 cm   B - 30 cm
     C - 40 cm   D - 74 cm
     E - 31·4 cm   F - 24 cm
   c *"Though the areas of shapes are*
     the same, it does not mean that
     their perimeters are the same".
2. a P, Q, R, S and T are all 32 cm
   b P - 64 cm²   Q - 48 cm²
     R - 15 cm²   S - 60 cm²
     T - 45 cm²
   c No
3. No.

Ch 13 - Decimals - page 117

Ch 13 - Exercise 1 - page 117

1. a 25   b 39·7   c 62·85
   d 480·06   e 620   f 576
   g 796·5   h 2308·4   i 1800
   j 770   k 5439   l 17308
   m 1213·4   n 22034·2   o 59008
   p 200999
2. a 0·52   b 0·727   c 2·468
   d 11·853   e 0·035   f 0·141
   g 1·165   h 47·217   i 0·009
   j 0·035   k 0·765   l 18·432
   m 0·005   n 0·003   o 12·006
   p 318·444

3. a 15 cm   b 1·725 km   c 5·9 kg

Ch 13 - Exercise 2 - page 118

1. a 15·6   b 19·78   c 78·5
   d 373·94   e 486·24   f 1353·06
   g 1703·4   h 1522·56
2. a 52·2   b 77·2   c 43·75
   d 116·82   e 242·96   f 25·14
   g 817·6   h 2442·84
3. a 261·6   b £290·94   c 202·3 g
   d 0·08   e 921·6 g   f 77·16 km

Ch 13 - Exercise 3 - page 119

1. a 5·49   b 13·73   c 12·69
   d 15·83   e 0·07   f 0·16
   g 15·94   h 5·64
2. a 4·9   b 7·4   c 3·02
   d 6·39   e 0·34   f 13·51
   g 8·7   h 0·02
3. a 48·2 g   b £6·58
   c £2·49   d 12·14 sq m
   e (i) 5·57 (ii) 12·84   (iii) 8·09
     (iv) 28·79 (v) 9·57   (vi) 0·17

Ch 13 - Exercise 4 - page 120

1. £17·75
2. a €42·35   b €2·85
3. £52·32
4. £299·70
5. £33·75
6. PC palace cheaper (£19·50/card)
   Games store (£19·99/card)
7. 85p
8. £45·13
9. £5·85
10. £248·97
11. Box of 8 cheaper (£1·51 each)
    box of 6 (£1·54 each)
12. 4·621 kg
13. £30·54
14. 5·85 km

Ch 13 - Exercise 5 - page 122

1. a 0·6   b 0·25
   c 0·625   d 0·437
2. a 0·375   b 0·8   c 0·714
   d 0·167   e 0·583   f 0·182
3. a 0·667, 0·714, 0·778, 0·833
     $\frac{2}{3}$, $\frac{5}{7}$, $\frac{7}{9}$, $\frac{5}{6}$
   b 0·69, 0·67, 0·62, 0·58
     $\frac{7}{12}$, $\frac{31}{50}$, $\frac{2}{3}$, $\frac{69}{100}$
4. a 3·667   b 2·833
   c 3·875   d 2·143
5. 3·333 litres

Ch 14 - Algebra 3 - page 124

Ch 14 - Exercise 1 - page 124

1. a $x = 4$ b $x = 3$ c $x = 16$
   d $y = 10$ e $y = 9$ f $y = 22$
   g $p = 20$ h $p = 60$ i $p = 0$
   j $k = 18$ k $h = 15$ l $g = 80$
   m $q = 4$ n $w = 3$ o $z = 9$
   p $f = 40$ q $x = 68$ r $y = 246$
2. a $x = 2$ b $m = 5$ c $p = 6$
   d $q = 4$ e $t = 6$ f $a = 10$
   g $b = 12$ h $d = 6$ i $x = 12$
   j $p = 11$ k $p = 14$ l $m = 9$
   m $x = 11$ n $t = 8$ o $p = 3$
   p $b = 2·5$ q $c = 4·5$ r $n = 9·5$
   s $x = 5·25$ t $x = 3·4$ u $x = 4·8$

Ch 14 - Exercise 2 - page 125

1. a $x = 3$ b $x = 4$ c $x = 5$
2. a $x = 1$ b $x = 5$ c $x = 4$
   d $x = 8$ e $x = 5$ f $x = 9$
   g $x = 9$ h $x = 2$ i $x = 9$
   j $x = 10$ k $x = 3$ l $x = 7$
   m $x = 7$ n $x = 3$ o $x = 0$
   p $x = 5$ q $x = 3·5$ r $x = 2·5$
3. a $x + 8$
   b (i) $x + 8 = 21$ (ii) $x = 13$
4. a $x + 8 = 17$ b Bob - £9
5. a $x - 7 = 14$ b $x = 21$
6. a (i) $x + 14 = 31$ (ii) $x = 17$
   b (i) $2·3 + x = 3·1$ (ii) $x = 0·8$
   c (i) $p + 20 = 34$ (ii) $p = 14$
7. a $A = 4 \times x$
   b (i) $4 \times x = 24$ (ii) $x = 6$ cm
8. a $x = 14$ b $x = 27$ c $x = 80$
   d $x = 50$ e $x = 50$ f $x = 16$
   g $x = 66$ h $x = 100$ i $x = 7$
   j $x = 10$ k $x = 18$ l $x = 48$

Ch 14 - Exercise 3 - page 127

1. a $y = 3$ b $y = 4$ c $y = 2$
2. various answers
3. various answers
4. various answers
5. various answers
6. various answers
7. various answers
8. You get a straight line

9. All straight lines

a   b

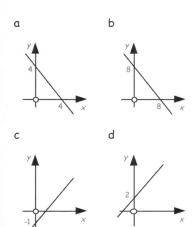

c   d

n 15 - Exercise 1 - *page 130*

  a obtuse   b straight   c acute
  d reflex   e right
  Check diagrams
  a 20°   b 86°
  c 70°   d 175°
  a 62°   b 78°   c 30°
  d 47°   e 36°   f 12°
  Check diagram

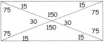

h 15 - Exercise 2 - *page 131*

  a 130°   b 155°   c 90°
  d 150°   e 142°   f 90°
  g 90°   h 62°   i 114°
  j 131°   k 89°   l 40°
  Various

Ch 15 - Exercise 3 - *page 132*

  a 122°   b 35°   c 53°
  d 25·5°   e 90°   f 139°
  g 58°   h 88°   i 101·5°
  a 58°, 58°   b 145°, 145°
  c 127°, 127°   d 154·5°, 154·5°
  e 90°, 90°   f 41°, 41°
  g 122°, 122°   h 92°, 92°
  i 78·5°, 78·5°
  Various

Ch 15 - Exercise 4 - *page 133*

1. a 35°, 80°, 65°   b sum = 180
2. various answers
3. a 95°   b 85°
4. a 50°   b 42°   c 46°
   d 33°   e 100°   f 36°
   g 139°   h 133°

5. a 40°   b 75°
6. Isosceles triangle
7. a 38°   b 104°
8. a   b   c   d

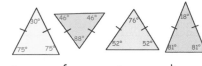

   e   f   g   h

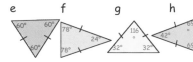

9. a 50°   b 25°
10. a   b   c   d

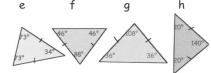

   e   f   g   h

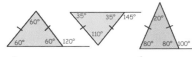

11. a 55°   b 55°   c 70°
12. a   b   c

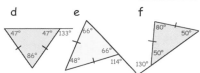

   d   e   f

13. various answers
14. a 61°   b 61°   c 58°
15.

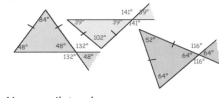

16. a equilateral
   b 60°
17. a 72°   b 54°   c 108°
   d 540°
18. a 60°   b 60°   c 120°
   d 720°
19. a 135°   b 1080°
20. a 140°, 1260°
   b 144°, 1440°

Ch 15 - Exercise 5 - *page 138*

1. a 50°   b 45°   c 130°
   d 55°   e 60°   f 156°
   g 130°   h 57°   i 60°
   j 36°, 144°, 144°
   k 130°, 50°, 50°

l 37°   m 50°   n 76°, 28°
o 67°, 46°   p 48°, 84°   q 70, 65°
r 55°, 55°, 70°
s 75°, 30°, 105°
t 41°, 41°, 98°, 139°, 139°
u 69°, 69°, 69°, 42°, 111°, 111°

Ch 16 - Exercise 1 - *page 140*

1. a $\frac{3}{5}$ b $\frac{5}{18}$ c $\frac{5}{8}$
2. a $\frac{8}{15}$ b $\frac{7}{12}$ c $\frac{4}{15}$
   d $\frac{10}{21}$ e $\frac{1}{2}$ f $\frac{1}{2}$
   g $\frac{11}{24}$ h $\frac{1}{5}$ i $\frac{2}{5}$
   j $\frac{1}{3}$ k $\frac{1}{5}$ l $\frac{1}{10}$
3. $\frac{5}{16}$ m²

Ch 16 - Exercise 2 - *page 141*

1. $\frac{1}{8}$
2. $\frac{1}{16}$
3. a $\frac{1}{20}$ b $\frac{3}{8}$ c $\frac{2}{3}$
4. a $\frac{1}{8}$ b $\frac{1}{16}$ c $\frac{1}{15}$
   d $\frac{1}{3}$ e $\frac{3}{20}$ f $\frac{5}{24}$
   g $\frac{11}{60}$ h $\frac{47}{150}$
5. $\frac{1}{12}$

Ch 16 - Exercise 3 - *page 142*

1. a $5\frac{2}{3}$ b $4\frac{4}{5}$ c $5\frac{1}{4}$ d $11\frac{1}{4}$
2. a $\frac{11}{4}$ b $\frac{29}{6}$ c $\frac{72}{11}$ d $\frac{95}{6}$
3. 20
4. a $\frac{5}{7}$ b $\frac{5}{4}$ c $\frac{2}{3}$ d $\frac{1}{8}$
   e $\frac{1}{6}$ f $5\frac{2}{3}$ g $1\frac{3}{10}$ h $2\frac{4}{15}$
   i $6\frac{5}{6}$ j $3\frac{5}{8}$ k $\frac{3}{4}$ l $7\frac{3}{4}$
5. a $\frac{1}{6}$ b $\frac{8}{15}$ c $\frac{32}{55}$ d $\frac{1}{4}$
   e $\frac{1}{6}$ f $\frac{1}{8}$ g $\frac{3}{20}$ h $\frac{1}{5}$
6. $8\frac{3}{4}$
7. $\frac{4}{5}$ kg
8. $15\frac{3}{8}$ kg

Ch 17 - Exercise 1 - *page 144*

1. 15 mm   2. 30 cm   3. 725 mm
4. 0·19 cm   5. 55 cm   6. 0·452 m
7. 398 cm   8. 0·025 m   9. 715 m

10. 3·12 km   11. 1600 m   12. 0·135 km
13. 3000 mm   14. 0·45 m   15. 600 m
16. 500 000 cm 17. 1 000 000 18. 8·7 km
19. 7 km   20. 5000 cm   21. 9500 ml
22. 40 ml   23. 0·55 L   24. 0·06 L
25. 425 L   26. 600 ml   27. 5900 g
28. 0·35 kg   29. 0·5 kg   30. 0·03 kg
31. 3000 g   32. 320·32 kg

Ch 17 - Exercise 2 - page 145

Class discussion

1 a 2 inches b 5 mile   c 28 g
   d 1 ft   e 1 litre   f 4·5 litres
   g 1 inch   h 2·2 lbs   i 1·75 pints

Ch 17 - Exercise 3 - page 146

1. a 15 cm   b 20 inches
2. a 25 cm   b 30 in   c 15 ft
    d 75 ft   e 10 m   f 10 miles
    g 125 miles h 32 km   i 96 km
    j 12 lbs   k 15 kg   l 150 g
    m 8 oz   n 4 gal   o 45 L
    p 21 pints   q 7·5 L   r 35 pints
3. a 25·4 cm   b 152·4 in   c 16·4 ft
    d 82 ft   e 9 m   f 9·92 miles
    g 124 miles h 32·2 km   i 96·6 km
    j 13·2 lbs   k 13·5 kg   l 169·8 g
    m 8 oz   n 4·4 gal   o 45·5 L
    p 21·12 pints q 8·55 pints
    r 35·2 pints
4. a 8 gallons b 200 g   c 14 pints
    d 100 g   e 90 cm
5. a (i) approx 7·5 cm
       (ii) approx 6·2 cm
    b (i) approx 2 in
       (ii) approx 4·75 in
6. a Check graph
    b 17·5 cm c 8 in
7. a Check graph

Ch 17 - Exercise 4 - page 147

(Calculator answers in brackets)

1. a 4 m by 2 m
    b £160
2. £15 (£11·70)
3. 45 in (35·1 in)
4. 125 g (141·5 g)
5. 3 cartons (2·7 cartons)
6. 40 (44)
7. 54 km (54·3 km)
8. 10 in (2·3 in)
9. 0·5 in (2·7 in)
10. 0·75 L
11. about 9 litres
12. Joe by 2 yards
13. Jess by 1 L (Jess by 1·6 L)

14. 5 lbs (0·8 lbs)
15. 100 mph is faster -
    160 km/hr (161 km/hr)
16. 40 lbs (44 lbs)

Ch 18 - Similar Shapes - page 150

Ch 18 - Exercise 1 - page 150

1. A - H, B - F, C - I, D - G, E - J
2. Q and S
3. a small 4 cm - large 8 cm
    b 2
    c small 2 cm - large 4 cm
    d 2
    e yes
4. a SF = 3   b all - 3   c similar
5. a SF = 2   b 16 cm
6. a SF = 2·5 b 5 cm
7. a SF = 1·5 b 36 cm
8. a SF = 5, 35 cm
    b SF = 4, 36 cm
    c SF = 3·5, 175 cm
9. a SF = 4·5 b 72 cm
10. a SF = 6   b 210 mm
11. a SF = 0·25 ($\frac{1}{4}$)
    b 9 cm

Ch 19 - Statistics - page 155

Ch 19 - Exercise 1 - page 155

1. a (i)   25   (ii) 10
       (iii) 35   (iv) 25
    b 95   c Wed - no people
2. a 20
    b Gemany
    c Portugal & Italy 18
    d Shop is in England
    e 18
3. a (i)   18   (ii) 38
       (iii) 19   (iv) 44
    b Chicken
    c 19
    d 31
    e 132
4.

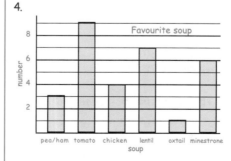

5.

6. a noon   b 8 and 9 am
    c 2°   d 6 am and noon
    e 3 hrs, 2·5°
    f 100°
7. a (i) 800 (ii) 1200 (iii) 200
    b (i) 1000 (ii) 800   (iii) 300
    c (i) Tent store
       (ii) Tents-for-U
       (iii) same
    d (i) Tents store   (ii) £2500
8.

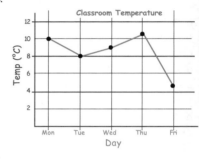

9.

10.

Ch 19 - Exercise 2 - page 158

1. a (i) $\frac{3}{10}$ (ii) $\frac{2}{10}$ (iii) $\frac{1}{10}$ (iv) $\frac{4}{10}$
    b Chicken Mayo, Prawn, Tuna, Ham
    c (i) 60   (ii) 30
       (iii) 90   (iv) 120

2. a 5%

b (i) 45% (ii) 25%
(iii) 10% (iv) 20%
c (i) 1000 (ii) 800
(iii) 1800 (iv) 400
a $\frac{1}{4}$

b (i) $\frac{1}{8}$ (ii) $\frac{1}{6}$ (iii) $\frac{1}{12}$ (iv) $\frac{3}{8}$
c (i) 6 (ii) 3 (iii) 4 (iv) 2
d 9

5. a 5%   b

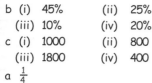

7. a

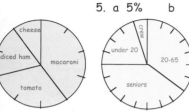

b supports neither team

19 - Exercise 3 - *page 160*

a 180°, 120°, 40°, 20°   b

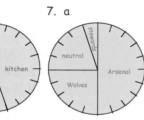

a 100°, 120°, 80°, 60°   b

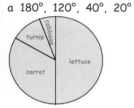

a 84°, 48°, 72°, 156°   b

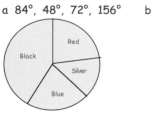

a 180°,90°,60°,30°   b 190°,130°,30°,10°

---

5. a Blackpool 15 (135°)
Torquay 5 (45°)
York 6 (54°)
Brighton 10 (90°)
Southport 4 (36°)
b

Ch 19 - Exercise 4 - *page 162*

1. a range = 8,   mean = 8
   b range = 17,   mean = 19
   c range = £22, mean = £14
   d range = 27 , mean = 26 cm
   e range = 6·1,   mean = 7·9
   f range =11·28, mean = 8·8
2. £326 per month
3. a range = 5,   mean = 52·5
   b yes average is less than 55
4. a range = 18,
   b mean = 7
   c 20 min - delayed, broke down ....
5. a 276
   b 69
   c Yes (268) he would have won by 2
6. a range = 0·8,   mean = 6·5
   b 0·4
7. a range = 11,   mean =8
   b 16 -it has twice the average
8. a Norway mean = £9·12
      England mean = £4·75
   b £4·37 cheaper

Ch 20 - 3D and Volume - *page 166*

Ch 20 - Exercise 1 - *page 166*

1. a cube   b   cone
   c hexagon d   cuboid
   e pyramid (square based)
   f sphere   g   dodecagon
   h kite   i   octagon
   j cylinder k   hemi-sphere
   l triangular prism
2. a c, g, h and i
   b h
   c angles/sides not all equal
3. a 6 squares
   b 4 triangles and a square
   c two circles and a rectangle
   d 3 rectangles and two triangles

---

4. cube   a 8   b 12
   pyramid   a 5   b 8
   cylinder a 0   b 2
   prism   a 6   b 9
5. a 5   b 8
   c 4   d 9
6. a cuboid   b cube   c cube
   d cylinder e tri prism
   f pyramid g cone   h pyramid

Ch 20 - Exercise 2 - *page 168*

1. a 4 cm³   b 6 cm³   c 6 cm³
   d 12 cm³ e 14 cm³ f 12 cm³
   g 7 cm³   h 10 cm³ i 21 cm³
   j 7 cm³   k 16 cm³
2. a 5   b 2   c 10 cm³
3. a 10   b 3   c 30 cm³
4. 12 cm³
5. a 20 cm³ b 15 cm³ c 28 cm³
   d 25 cm³ e 48 cm³ f 48 cm³
6. a 12 cm³ b 36 cm³
7. a 36 cm³ b 60 cm³ c 45 cm³
   d 40 cm³ e 112 cm³ f 48 cm³

Ch 20 - Exercise 3 - *page 171*

1. 140 cm³
2. 300 cm³
3. 288 cm³
4. a 48 cm³   b 180 cm³ c 280 cm³
   d 336 cm³ e 90 cm³   f 480 cm³
5. a 2160 cm³ b 600 cm³ c 3200 cm³
   d 1200 cm³ e 8640 cm³ f 384 cm³
6. a 30 cm³   b 36 cm³   c 86·4 cm³
   d 864 cm³ e 400 cm³ f 192 cm³
7. a 1264 cm³ b 1968 cm³ c 684 cm³
   d 7710 cm³ e 20400 cm³
8. 4 cm

Ch 20 - Exercise 4 - *page 174*

1. 120 mm³
2. 96 m³
3. a 36 mm³   b 130 m³
   c 600000 cm³ or 0·6 m³
4. a 1000   b 1000000

Ch 21 - Revision Yr 6 - *page 176*

1. a four thousand and seven
   b fifty six thousand eight hundred
     and seven
   c eight hundred and ninety one
     thousand eight hundred and
     ninety nine

2. a 520 017   b 4750 000
3. a 856 000   b 480 000
   c 6 400 000   f 9 000 000
4. a 5400   b 15600
   c 129 000   d 1560 000
   e 9   f 54
   g 10 300   h 1430
5 a -14°C   b -20°C
6. a -£130   b 23°
   c 13 BC
7. 4°C   b -5°C   c -16°C d -19°C
8. a -7   b -7   c 0   d -16
   e 9   f -18   g 5   h -100
9. See drawings
10. 22 cm
11. a see drawing

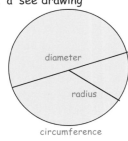

12. a 63   b 82   c 231   d 135
13. a 123 r 3   b 123$\frac{1}{4}$
    c 123·25   d 123
14. a 4   b 25   c 2
    d -3   e 20   f 10
15. a 14   b 22   c 20   d 48
    e 4   f 12   g 2   h 5
16. a $P = 11 \times k \div 5$ b 55 lbs
17. a start at 15 - go up by 3 each time
       30, 33, 36
    b start at 3 - go up by 11 each time
       58, 69, 80
    c start at 80 - go down by 4 each time
       64, 60, 56
    d start at 3 - and double each time
       96, 192, 384
18. a (i) 100 miles   (ii) 125 miles
    b $D = 25 \times H$ c 300 ml   d 24 hrs
19. a 4, 8, 12, 16, 20, 24, 28, 32, 36, 40
       6, 12, 18, 24, 30, 36, 42, 48, 54, 60
    b 12
20. a 40   b 30   c 24
21. a 1, 2, 3, 4, 6, 12   1, 3, 5, 15
    b 3
22. a 8   b 10   c 9
23. a 41, 43, 47, 53, 59
    b 71, 73, 79, 83, 89, 97,
    c 127
24. a even b ÷ 5   c ÷ 10
25. a 2 × 2 × 2 × 2   b 2 × 3 × 5
    c 2 × 5 × 5   d 2 × 3 × 5 × 7
26. a $\frac{2}{6}$, $\frac{3}{9}$ b $\frac{10}{12}$, $\frac{15}{18}$

27. a $\frac{4}{5}$ b $\frac{5}{8}$ c $\frac{1}{2}$ d $\frac{11}{20}$
28. a $\frac{16}{5}$ b $\frac{30}{7}$
29. a $2\frac{1}{2}$ b $4\frac{3}{5}$
30. a $7\frac{1}{6}$ b $5\frac{1}{4}$ c $3\frac{1}{6}$ d $12\frac{4}{15}$
    d $7\frac{7}{12}$ e $3\frac{13}{15}$ f $3\frac{1}{5}$ g $\frac{23}{30}$
31. a A(-1, 3) --> A'(3, 1)
    b   c right angled
    d

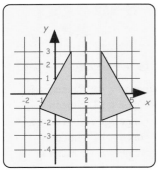

    e L'(1, 3), M'(-1, -1), N'(1, -2)
32 a 4:10   b 2:5
33. a 2:3   b 4:7   c 3:2   d 3:4
    e 3:5   f 3:5   g 4:5   h 37:41
34. a 150   b 80
35. a $\frac{3}{10}$ b $\frac{1}{20}$ c $\frac{2}{3}$ d $\frac{3}{2}$
36. a £11   b £8   c £24
    d £12   e £13·50 f £50
    g £100 h £9   i £81
37. £300 000
38. a

    b 3, 6, 9, 12, 15
    c $C = 3 \times L$ d 30   e 18 cm
39. a $H = 2d + 5$ b $T = 5y + 25$
40. a 91 cm²   b 121 m²
    c 120 cm²   d 136 cm²
    e 1950 mm²
41. a 7·3   b 92·47   c 50·9   d 36
    e 4·72   f 0·07   g 3·04   h 0·0165
42. a 18·72 b 51·03   c 1·44   d 3·34
43. £6·93
44. £45·75
45. a 0·25   b 0·8   c 0·38   d 0·29
46. a 14   b 11   c 20
    d 6   e 7   f 4·5
    g 6   h 6   i 0
    j 2   k 60   l 18
47. a $x - 8 = 23$ b $x = 31$
48. various, $x = 10$, $y = 4$
49. various, $x = -2$, $y = 4$
50. various, $x = 3\frac{1}{2}$, $y = 5\frac{1}{2}$
51. 30° + 110° = 140°

52. a 49°   b 85°
    c 108°   d 48°, 132°, 132°

a   b

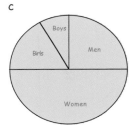

c   d

53. 45°
54. a $\frac{9}{20}$ b $\frac{1}{4}$ c $\frac{1}{6}$ d $\frac{2}{7}$
55. 17
56. a 4·96 cm   b 2 inches
    c 66 feet   d 4 ounces
    e 13·2 gallons   f 66 pounds
57. a 152·5 cm   b 50·8 cm
    c 135 kg   d 169·8 g
    e 5·4 litres   f 11·27 miles
58. 40" = 101·6 cm - Tracy is 103 cm OK
59. a no   b yes
60. a 4   b 12 cm
61. a 12   b 90°, 180°, 60°, 30°
    c

62. a 90p   b 110p
63. a 40 cm³   b 30 cm³
    c 140 cm³   d 2400 cm³
    e 60 cm³
64 3 mm